# CHARLES BEARD AND THE CONSTITUTION

## A CRITICAL ANALYSIS OF
## "AN ECONOMIC INTERPRETATION
## OF THE CONSTITUTION"

# Charles Beard and the Constitution

## A CRITICAL ANALYSIS OF

## "AN ECONOMIC INTERPRETATION

## OF THE CONSTITUTION"

BY ROBERT E. BROWN

PRINCETON, NEW JERSEY

PRINCETON UNIVERSITY PRESS

1956

ROBERT E. BROWN is associate professor of history at
Michigan State University. He is also the author of
*Middle-Class Democracy and the Revolution in Massa-
chusetts, 1691-1780* (Cornell University Press), which
won second prize in the 1954 Albert J. Beveridge competition of the American Historical Association, and in
1954-55 he held the first Thomas Jefferson Fellowship
at the University of Virginia.

Printed in the United States of America

# PREFACE

A work such as this naturally owes its being to the contributions of many minds over a period of years. Many of my ideas have been hammered out, and not a few pounded flat, by the exchange of views with my colleagues and friends from time to time. To these people I can only offer thanks, for their number is legion. As a body, my students, both undergraduate and graduate, deserve much for their contributions to my thinking. More than they realized, they served as the anvil on which many of the ideas presented here were fashioned, and they have been long-suffering recipients of the "Brown" in contrast with the "Beard" interpretation of the Constitution. The readers and critics of the manuscript have made numerous pertinent suggestions which have forced me to clarify my thinking and to keep my generalizations in harmony with my facts. And my wife, B. Katherine Brown, has rendered invaluable assistance not only through such routine functions as those of typist and proofreader, but also through research and a critical reading of the manuscript.

I am indebted to the Alumni Board of Trustees of the University of Virginia for the grant of a Thomas Jefferson Fellowship and for permission to take time from a research project on Virginia in order to do the necessary revision on this manuscript. And finally, my thanks go to the Macmillan Company for permission to use the material from Charles A. Beard's *An Economic Interpretation of the Constitution of the United States* (copyright, 1913 and 1935).

ROBERT E. BROWN

*Michigan State University*
*East Lansing, Michigan*
*July 1, 1955*

# CONTENTS

Preface                                                                    v

Charles Beard and the Constitution                                         3

Beard's Preface                                                           24

    I. "Historical Interpretation in the United States"    26

    II. "A Survey of Economic Interests in 1787"           33

    III. "The Movement for the Constitution"               56

    IV. "Property Safeguards in the Election of
        Delegates"                        61

    V. "The Economic Interests of the Members of
        the Convention"                   73

    VI. "The Constitution as an Economic Document"          92

    VII. "The Political Doctrines of the Members
        of the Convention"               112

    VIII. "The Process of Ratification"                    138

    IX. "The Popular Vote on the Constitution"             157

    X. "The Economics of the Vote on the
        Constitution"                   171

    XI. "The Economic Conflict over Ratification as
        Viewed by Contemporaries"       182

"Conclusions"                                                            194

Index                                                                    201

# CHARLES BEARD AND THE CONSTITUTION

## A CRITICAL ANALYSIS OF
## "AN ECONOMIC INTERPRETATION
## OF THE CONSTITUTION"

# CHARLES BEARD
# AND THE CONSTITUTION

In 1913 there appeared a book which caused more than a ripple of interest in both academic and nonacademic circles. From the moment of its debut, *An Economic Interpretation of the Constitution of the United States* by Charles A. Beard was a subject of heated controversy. Few books in American history have aroused such bitter partisanship; few have elicited the extremes of both commendation and condemnation that were heaped on this single volume.[1]

The thesis of *An Economic Interpretation of the Constitution,* best stated in Beard's "Conclusions," is a double-edged one:

1. Instead of being a document drawn up by patriotic men for the protection of life, liberty, and the pursuit of happiness, the Constitution was the work of consolidated economic groups —personal property interests including money, public securities, manufacturers, and trade and shipping—groups that were personally interested in the outcome of their labors. These groups, according to Beard, originated the move for and dominated the Philadelphia Convention which wrote the Constitution. In the Constitution, essentially an economic document, they incorporated their philosophy that private property came before government and was not subject to control by popular majorities. The same groups also dominated the state conventions which finally ratified the Constitution. In ratification the cleavage was between substantial property interests that favored the Constitution and small farmers and debtors who opposed it. And the men who framed the Constitution benefited directly from the government which they set up.

[1] For an excellent brief summary of the book and its influence from 1913 to 1935, see Maurice Blinkoff, *The Influence of Charles A. Beard upon American Historiography,* in the University of Buffalo *Studies,* Monographs in History, XII (May, 1936), No. 4, Ch. II.

2. Instead of being a document embodying democratic principles, the Constitution was put over in an undemocratic society by undemocratic methods for the express purpose of checking democratic majorities. There was no popular vote on the calling of the Convention, property qualifications for voting and officeholding excluded the propertyless masses from participation, about three-fourths of the adult men failed to vote on the Constitution, it was ratified by probably not more than one-sixth of the adult men, and in five states there is doubt as to whether a majority of the voters actually approved of ratification.[2]

In his Preface the author explained that his work was "frankly fragmentary," designed to open new fields for research rather than to present a completed study. His explanation for publishing a fragmentary work was that he was unable to give much time to uninterrupted study and therefore could not expect to do a thorough job within a reasonable time. So he published the book with the hope that other historical scholars would turn away from barren political history and would devote their time to the real economic forces which shaped politics. As will be noted later, this explanation eventually assumed some importance.

Such a novel, and earthy, interpretation of a document long held in reverence by the American people naturally aroused a great deal of interest and not a little animosity. The book was reviewed widely in current scholarly and popular outlets, the reviews showing in some detail both the friendly and the hostile attitudes toward the book at the time.

On the friendly side, several reviewers pointed out the novelty of the thesis and its anticipated value in the field of historical scholarship. One said that as "a pioneer work in a new field," the book had "first-rate importance," the only criticism being that Beard used Portland when he clearly intended Portsmouth.[3] William E. Dodd, whose work Beard

[2] Charles A. Beard, *An Economic Interpretation of the Constitution of the United States* (New York, 1913), pp. 324-25.
[3] *The Nation*, xcvii (July 31, 1913), 104-05. Blinkoff cited some of these reviews but did not analyze them in any detail.

had praised in a footnote, forgot to mention what the thesis was, praised Chapter V on the economic holdings of the Founding Fathers, believed that future studies would show why a majority of the people at the time were hostile to both the Fathers and their Constitution, and declared that Beard had "certainly succeeded beyond the promises of his preface."[4] Instead of being arid as Beard claimed, said a third reviewer, the book, based on a great mass of original data, was replete with human interest and full of information of importance to every student of American history or political science.[5] A sociologist predicted that believers of the old interpretation would get a "rude awakening" from this "interesting and instructive volume." He also believed that to a limited extent at least, Beard's thesis was "unassailable," and that Beard had been fair and impartial in his account.[6]

The *New York Times* was especially friendly, a position it was to reverse when Beard resigned from Columbia University in 1917. After reviewing Beard's thesis of the Fathers' work in the interest of the upper classes while the propertyless masses were ignored, the *Times* said that this was a timely book because of attacks then being made on the Constitution. The Fathers had placed the dollar above the man, but now reformers were placing the man above the dollar, went on the *Times*, as it referred to Beard's "laborious researches and luminous exposition."[7] A week later the *Times* placed *An Economic Interpretation* on its list of the 100 best books of the year, a list based on the opinion of experts; the newspaper believed that the book had a vital theme and would not be quickly superseded.[8]

One reviewer insisted some five times that Beard was talking about "personality" rather than "personalty," considered Chapter V on the personal and financial interests of the framers

---

[4] *American Historical Review*, xix (October, 1913), 162-63.

[5] *Annals of the American Academy of Political and Social Science*, xlix (September, 1913), 250-51.

[6] Arnold B. Hall of the University of Wisconsin, *American Journal of Sociology*, xix (November, 1913), 405-08.

[7] *New York Times*, November 23, 1913, vii, 637:1.

[8] *Ibid.*, November 30, 1913, vi, 655:2, 678:1.

as the most direct contribution, praised Beard for his presentation "of facts that must be taken into account by anyone desiring to understand the making of our constitution"—then forgot to say what the thesis of the book was.[9] And finally, a reviewer expressed "fruitful enthusiasm" over the exaltation of economic over political history, then called the book a distinct contribution and a "suggestive and stimulating essay."[10]

Sometimes the critics combined praise and blame in about equal proportions, although most of them seemed to be definitely on one side or the other. Pointing out that the value of the work lay in the careful gathering of evidence, obviously a reference to Chapter V, one reviewer charged Beard with using only those facts which bolstered his own thesis and neglecting other relevant facts and interpretations. Conceding that Beard had made plain the economic interests at the time and their great importance, he also accused Beard of failure to show what other forces were operative and how important they were compared with the economic.[11]

On the other hand, hostile critics were not in the least backward in pointing out what they considered wrong with *An Economic Interpretation.* The book was branded as a "half truth" which stressed some economic motives but left out others equally important. This critic was one of the few who went beyond content and ideology to criticize Beard's historical method—his contradictions and insufficient evidence.[12] Another characterized the author as "more like the holder of a brief than an impartial seeker for truth."[13]

Two reviewers predicted sudden death and oblivion for this drastic new interpretation of the Constitution—predictions that could hardly have been further from reality. The *Educational Review* declared that "a good deal of labor without, we fear, any very important result" had gone into the book, as the reviewer expressed the belief that the myth of "the Economic

[9] *Washington Historical Quarterly,* v (January, 1914), 63.
[10] *American Economic Review,* iv (March, 1914), 117-19.
[11] *Journal of Political Economy,* xxii (May, 1914), 492-95.
[12] *South Atlantic Quarterly,* xii (July, 1913), 269-73.
[13] *The Dial,* lv (August 1, 1913), 87.

Man" had been exploded.[14] John H. Latané, in the *American Political Science Review*, declared that it would "require more convincing evidence than Dr. Beard has so far presented to upset the traditional view" that the Fathers were great patriots. Latané also touched on the problem of historical method, pointing out that six men who favored a strong central government held only $21,046 in public securities, whereas five men who opposed a strong central government held $87,979.[15]

One of the most vitriolic critics of *An Economic Interpretation* was ex-President William Howard Taft. Taft spoke before some 1,100 members of the Pennsylvania Society at the Waldorf-Astoria in New York, at a meeting presided over by J. P. Morgan partner Henry P. Davidson and attended by Supreme Court justices, senators, governors, ambassadors, and other notables. Taft, whose dieting had reduced him to a wispy 270 pounds, was in fine fettle to draw and quarter the Progressive Party in general and Charles A. Beard in particular. Dripping satire with every word, he credited "these God-forgetting Progressive days" with inspiring an associate professor at Columbia, a "sapient investigator," to make a "muckraking investigation" designed to establish the reactionary nature of the Constitution. There was no doubt that the ex-President linked *An Economic Interpretation* with the Progressive movement and that his own sympathies were on the side of the creditors rather than the debtors, whether in 1913 or 1787.[16]

A few more reviews will suffice to show the opposition to Beard's work. The *New York Times* carried two critical letters, one of which pointed out that, unlike 1913, there were no great "interests" in 1787; there were no large fortunes; little manufacturing or industrialization existed; and most men were farmers. Both writers claimed to have read Elliot's *Debates* on the Constitution and both contended that Beard had not used the evidence in these *Debates*.[17] A well-known scholar of

[14] *Educational Review*, XLVI (September, 1913), 207.
[15] *American Political Science Review*, VII (November, 1913), 697-700.
[16] *New York Times*, December 14, 1913, IV, 5:1.
[17] *Ibid.*, December 14, 1913, VII, 744:1; December 21, 1913, VI, 758:1.

the Constitution, Edward S. Corwin, declared that had Beard "been less bent on demonstrating the Socialist theory of economic determinism and class struggle as an interpretation of history, his own performance would have been less open to criticism."[18] Orin G. Libby, who had done work on the Constitution and with whom Beard sometimes disagreed in *An Economic Interpretation*, credited Beard with showing the influence of personal wealth. But Libby also criticized Beard for placing great stress on the suffrage without actually going into the problem, for stressing personal property over other kinds, and for failure to account for the lack of revolution when the people had an opportunity to do something in 1801 and 1829.[19]

Most of the reviews and other expressions of the time emphasized content and ideology, and many of them obviously reflected the views of their authors toward the Progressive movement, which was then in full flower. Occasionally some critic went beyond content and viewpoint to the basic problem, historical method, but these few critics did not carry their criticisms beyond this initial stage, and in the course of time they seem to have been forgotten.

In the years between 1914 and the early 1930's, *An Economic Interpretation of the Constitution* continued to be a subject of much controversy. This period has been covered sufficiently by Blinkoff and thus needs little additional comment. Those who praised the work as authoritative and scholarly included William E. Dodd, Edward Channing, Max Farrand, Walter Lippmann, Harold U. Faulkner, Albert Jay Nock, Samuel Eliot Morison and Henry Steele Commager, John Chamberlain, and E. W. Spaulding. Taft, Corwin, Albert Bushnell Hart, President Nicholas Murray Butler of Columbia University, and others continued to blast the work as inspired either by Marx or, by inference, the Devil. The author recently heard a member of the Columbia University faculty tell the story cited in a

[18] *History Teachers Magazine*, v (February, 1914), 65-68.
[19] *Mississippi Valley Historical Review*, i (June, 1914), 113-17.

footnote by Blinkoff. When Butler was asked, "Have you read Beard's last book?" he replied, "I hope so."[20]

Blinkoff also did the extremely valuable research in discovering the extent to which writers of textbooks and other works on American history had adopted the Beard thesis on the Constitution between 1913 and 1935. He concluded that Beard's influence was very slight in elementary school texts, with only 3 of 47 new texts and none of 32 revisions adopting the Beardian interpretation. Among high school texts, only 6 of 40 new books and 4 of 32 revisions emphasized the thesis. But of the college texts, 37 out of 42 new books and 14 out of 19 revisions presented Beard's interpretation. In addition, many general historical writings also incorporated Beard's findings.[21] Thus by 1935, in spite of all the adverse criticism, *An Economic Interpretation* had made its greatest impact at the top rung of the educational ladder, where critical evaluation of texts was theoretically at its best.

Beard's impact at the college level is perhaps best demonstrated by his election as president of the American Historical Association, from which position he precipitated a hot war of words over *An Economic Interpretation*. In his presidential address, "Written History as an Act of Faith," at the annual meeting of the Association in Urbana, December 28, 1933, Beard expounded his concept of the nature of history and the role of the historian. In the process he discarded the old concept made famous by the German historian Leopold von Ranke that the historian could write history objectively as it actually happened. In its place he substituted the concept of a subjective history centered in the historian and having as its guiding star the present and the future rather than the past.

Beard naturally made the distinction between the history that had actually taken place, history as actuality, and what we can know of history, that is, written history. The latter he defined as "thought about past actuality." This thought was conditioned and limited by historical records and knowledge,

[20] Blinkoff, *The Influence of Charles A. Beard*, pp. 18-21.
[21] *Ibid.*, pp. 21-38.

and the latter, in turn, were "authenticated by criticism and ordered with the help of the scientific method." But in this scheme, according to Beard, the historian himself was the important factor. He was the one who selected and organized historical materials, but he was not an objective, impartial machine. He was the product of his age, said Beard, and every student of history knew that historians were influenced by their biases, prejudices, beliefs, affections, and experiences, especially social and economic. Hence the historian writes history subjectively as he sees it through this screen of influences, not objectively as it actually happened. History as "thought about past actuality" is always colored by these subjective factors within the historian himself—it inevitably reflects the thought of the author in his time and cultural setting. Instead of being scientific, the historian is more or less a guesser, and the history he writes is something of an "act of faith."

The historian, said Beard, has three choices as to interpretation of history and three elements in his frame of reference. He can believe that history is chaotic, that it moves in cycles, or that it moves in some direction toward a better order of things. His frame of reference includes things deemed necessary for mankind, things deemed possible, and things deemed desirable. The frame can be large or small, informed or uninformed, illuminated or unilluminated. But whatever it is, the supreme issue before the historian is that he decide what he thinks history is doing and what his own frame of reference is in relation to this history. The historian's influence and chances for immortality will in the end depend on his analysis of the present and the correctness of his forecast for the future. Beard's own guess was that the world, i.e. history, was moving toward a collectivist democracy rather than toward capitalistic or proletarian dictatorship.

In his modified relativistic history, however, Beard insisted that the scientific method and spirit must be retained as the only method capable of obtaining accurate knowledge of historical facts, personalities, situations, and movements. The scientific method was valuable not only in history but also in safeguarding democracy from the tyranny of authority, bureaucracy, and brute power. We should not abandon tireless inquiry into objective realities, especially economic realities and relations. But more fundamental than any aspect of historical method is the fact that any selection and arrangement of the facts is controlled "inexorably" by the frame of reference in the mind of the historian.[22]

While there was no direct reference to *An Economic Interpretation* in Beard's presidential address, the connection was made apparent in a paper, "The Writing of American History in America from 1884 to 1934," delivered by Professor Theodore Clark Smith at the 1934 meeting of the American Historical Association. Smith showed the development from the literary historians to the scientific historians, with its accompanying philosophy of objective history. But the scientific school, Smith reported regretfully, was being displaced by informal and popular historians, who cast aside the whole ideal of impersonality and impartiality—partisans, sophisticates, ironists, debunkers.

In particular, Smith singled out Beard and *An Economic Interpretation of the Constitution* in his attack on the newer historians. The economic interpretation of history, definitely doctrinaire and discarding impartiality as "incompatible with a specific theory of human activity," Smith continued, had its origins in Marxian theories, but, because it was so illuminating, many writers who were not socialistic employed it with zest. Beard, the first and ablest of this school, he said, emphasized the class conflict as an interpretation of the Constitution with "skill and plausibility." Then Smith went on to summarize the arguments which Beard had presented in his presidential address the year before. The real test of history according to Beard was the largeness of the philosophy which underlay it, said Smith, and to Beard the only valid history was that which traced the forward movement of society toward a collectivist democracy. That, or some similar act of faith, is all that makes history worth while: to discover causation is pure illusion; to

[22] Charles A. Beard, "Written History as an Act of Faith," *American Historical Review*, XXXIX (January, 1934), 219-29.

offer any other interpretation than one based on a bold philosophy is to leave history to be the prey of prejudice.

Smith was concerned about the ease with which a growing number of writers discarded impartiality because it was uninteresting, contrary to social belief, uninstructive, or inferior to a bold social philosophy. He pointed out that in some countries history under these precise ideals had become so functional that it was systematically used to educate people in soviet or fascist thinking. Given the agitation for "patriotic" history by various groups in this country, a similar fate might well befall history here in its use as an instrument for developing the "right kind" of citizens.[23]

The attack by Smith soon elicited a reply by Beard in defense of himself and his historical concepts and methods, the latter of which are extremely important from the standpoint of this critical analysis. In an article entitled "That Noble Dream" he accused Smith of dividing the historical profession into two groups, those who had a "noble dream" and produced sound, creditable history and the opposition who were ignoble and produced unsound, discreditable work. Beard then asked whether there was a sharp division in the profession that could not be bridged, and the answer was a qualified no. There were three points at issue he said—ideal, method, and belief in the possibility of achievement—and on two of these there was no conflict. Both schools had the same ideal—the truth. But while the scholar of the new school, who sought knowledge for useful purposes, might have different ends in view, Beard said, false history could not serve those ends. Persons who sought for economic interests behind the scenes were not necessarily hostile to truth. As for the second point, method, the new school could be as patient in their inquiries and as rigorous in their criticism and documentation as the so-called "objective" historians. In intentions and methods, therefore, there was no necessary antagonism between the two schools.

The only difference then, Beard contended, was in achievement—whether or not it was possible to find and state the

[23] Theodore Clark Smith, "The Writing of American History in America from 1884-1934," *ibid.*, xl (April, 1935), 439-49.

objective truth of history. With this, Beard went into a long discourse to show that the "objective" historians really wrote from a point of view which reflected their own social and economic environment. Objective history, therefore, was impossible. The economic interpretation was a partial selection of facts just as was any other interpretation, Beard continued, but the economic historian could be as zealous in the search for truth, as cold and impartial, as any other historian. As for Smith's accusation of Marxian influence, Beard said his economic interpretation rested on documentation older than Marx as well as on Marx himself. He paid tribute to Marx's amazing range of scholarship and penetrating thought, but denied that an economic interpretation had to be used for the purposes Marx adopted.

Beard closed his article with a plea for harmony in the profession. No school should have a monopoly, and all schools —objective, economic, or "new"—should be equally accepted by the Association. Historians must continue to collect documents and write monographs, but they must also consider the philosophical side, the totality of history, and include all conditioning factors such as race, sex, economics, and politics. They should distinguish between particular facts that may be established by scientific method on the one hand and the "objective" truth of history on the other, however, if illusions are to be dispelled. Even more pressing, they should examine the assumptions upon which the selection and organization of historical facts are made, and ask themselves where they are going, what interpretations are open, what are actually chosen, and by what processes the multitude of historical facts can be brought into a meaningful whole. Through the discussion of such questions, the "noble dream" of the search for truth might be brought nearer to realization, not extinguished. But in the final analysis, he said, historians would be human beings, not immortal gods.[24]

These battles of the pen are essential to an understanding of the Introduction which Beard wrote to the 1935 edition of

[24] Charles A. Beard, "That Noble Dream," *ibid.*, XLI (October, 1935), 74-87.

*An Economic Interpretation of the Constitution.* In this Introduction Beard reviewed the history of his book, denying the
charges that it was written functionally as part of the Progressive movement, though he said he was doubtless influenced by
the spirit of the times. He claimed that he had become interested in the Constitution long before the reform era, that he
had "read voluminous writings of the Fathers" and had been
struck by their emphasis on economic factors. In particular, he
was impressed by the philosophy in James Madison's *Federalist*
No. 10, which seemed to furnish a clue to practical activity
connected with the adoption of the Constitution.

Beard appeared to be making greater claims for his book in
1935 than he did in 1913 as far as its foundation on source
materials was concerned. In the 1935 Introduction he made the
statement about having "read voluminous writings of the
Fathers," said that his masters had taught him to go behind
the secondary accounts to the sources, and added that as a
result he had read the letters, papers, and documents pertain-
ing to the Constitution written by the men who helped to draft
it and get it adopted. But as we have already seen, many
reviewers criticized him for failure to use extensive sources,
and we shall have occasion to examine this point in more detail
later.

In addition, Beard made other denials or qualifications of
criticisms or interpretations of his work. He said that his was
*an* interpretation, not *the* interpretation or the only interpretation. The reader was warned ahead of time of the emphasis.
Again he countered the charges of Smith that his work was
partisan and Marxist. He said he had never claimed that all
history could be explained in economic or any other terms, but
he insisted that economic factors were of primary importance.
As for Marxism, his views went further back than Marx,
although he knew about Marx and became more interested in
Marx when he found the latter using ideas expressed by earlier
writers. He also denied that he had accused the members of
the Constitutional Convention of working for their own
pockets, or that the form of government established and the
powers conferred were determined in every detail by the

conflict of economic interests. In fact, he said he had never been able to discover an all-pervading determinism in history.

And finally, what alterations, if any, had twenty-two years of praise and criticism wrought in Beard's thinking if he were to write the book anew? Very few. Aside from the efforts to correct erroneous views about the book, he said he would make only two or three minor changes in fact, none of which materially altered his interpretation in any way. Apparently what had started as a "fragment" designed to direct research into new channels had now become so widely accepted that the author himself was satisfied with the results. If *An Economic Interpretation* was not the *whole* interpretation of the Constitution, it appeared to have met the test as an *economic* interpretation. During the twenty-two-year span Beard had done none of the work outlined in his book as essential for a sound interpretation, and apparently by this time most other writers were willing to accept the fact that Beard had said the last word on the economic origins of the Constitution.[25]

What has happened to *An Economic Interpretation of the Constitution* since 1935, when Blinkoff did his work on Beard and the 1935 edition with its qualifying Introduction appeared? A detailed survey would require too much space and would not serve any useful purpose here. Two pieces of writing that have been done since that date give sufficient information on the importance of the book, and in particular point up the problem to be considered in this critical analysis.

In 1938 the *New Republic* conducted a symposium on "Books That Changed Our Minds," and one of two titles most frequently mentioned was *An Economic Interpretation of the Constitution*.[26] Max Lerner wrote the article on this particular book, an article which sheds a great deal of light on the status of the book after the new edition of 1935 with its modifying Introduction.

[25] Beard, *An Economic Interpretation of the Constitution*, 1935 ed., pp. v-xvii.
[26] Richard Hofstadter, "Charles Beard and the Constitution," *Charles A. Beard: An Appraisal*, ed. Howard K. Beale (Lexington, Ky., 1954), p. 88.

Lerner summarized much that has already been given here but did add a few significant items. He said that Beard wrote in response to new movements afoot for social justice, that he proceeded on the "theory of economic determinism," and that the Fathers resorted to an extralegal *coup*. When Beard resigned from Columbia, said Lerner, the *New York Times* reversed itself, approved the resignation, and said that when Beard's book came out it was pointed out to Beard that it was bad, grossly unscientific, and followed the line of Marxian economic determinism.

As for the Introduction to the 1935 edition, Lerner said that it had "received all too little notice." He then went on to show the modification of Beard's views as expressed in 1935—his denial of socialist leanings and the Marxian influence. But as Lerner insisted, the admission that the impetus for Beard's thinking was primarily American does not prevent its import from being Marxian. Beard had tried to do too much, Lerner continued, in attempting to show that the Founding Fathers were motivated by personal interests. All that was needed was to show that the Fathers were thinking in terms of their class interests, which in turn they identified with the country's interests. It is also important to note Lerner's statement that by 1935 Beard was satisfied with his work and had come to believe that *An Economic Interpretation* had passed the test of time.

Criticisms of Beard's book, according to Lerner, should not blind us to its importance. This lay in the directness with which it cut through the whole tissue of liberal idealism and rhetoric to the economic realities in American history and life. The influence was not to be measured by the number of copies sold, which was not large (though numerous printings have evidenced a continuing interest in the book). Lerner characterized *An Economic Interpretation* as a book which becomes a legend—more often discussed than read, and better known for its title than its analysis. Its thesis has increasingly seeped into our writing of history: it is a "classic" which not only deals with history but has made history.

Of particular importance to this analysis was the praise

which Lerner heaped on Beard's historical method. He spoke
of Beard as a "scientific intruder" on the motives of the Fathers
and likened the "sheer masterful structure" of the work to a
superbly conducted military campaign. The "heart of the book"
was "the amazing Chapter V" on the economic interests of the
Convention delegates—a statement which has often been made
and which will necessitate extended treatment of that chapter.
Lerner characterized Beard's scholarship as "thorough and systematic," and said that what irritated his opponents was that
he used "all the paraphernalia of scientific method," that his
research was a *"tour de force"* which "could put to shame on
the level of sheer scholarship" anyone who challenged him.
Technical flaws were few and unconvincing, and citations,
when not from primary statistical sources, came from the
Fathers themselves, especially Madison's *Federalist* No. 10.
Beard was the only historian since Frederick Jackson Turner,
said Lerner, whose historical method had been widely recognized as taking the shape of a theory or thesis. The book was
a *"tour de force* of historical research" in which Beard "piled
up massive evidence" from the sources, Lerner concluded, and
its very title showed that a "new higher criticism" had come
into existence.[27]

Lerner's writings reflect the esteem accorded to Beard's
historical methods by 1939.

An article by Richard Hofstadter, "Charles Beard and the
Constitution," published in *Charles A. Beard: An Appraisal* in
1954, shows the present status of *An Economic Interpretation
of the Constitution.* Hofstadter stated what seems to be generally accepted—that a large part of the book's thesis "has
been absorbed into the main body of American historical
writing." A book that once shocked informed and critical
minds shocks them no longer. While it has not been divested
of all elements of controversy, "it has entered calmly into history," becoming "less and less a book to argue over, and
increasingly a book that must be studied if we are to locate
our own thinking in the stream of intellectual events."

[27] The article appeared in the *New Republic* of May 10, 1939, and is
reprinted in Lerner, *Ideas Are Weapons* (New York, 1939), pp. 152-69.

As Lerner had done in 1939, Hofstadter placed great emphasis on Beard's historical method. Although the book's content had been debated endlessly, no attention had been paid "to one of the work's greatest achievements," its method, said Hofstadter, for methodologically speaking the book was a "triumph of systematic intelligence." He claimed that historical method in this country had never adequately recognized Beard's techniques. Again following Lerner, he praised the work of Chapter V—"his famous chapter" on the economic holdings of the Fathers—and claimed that had Beard's historical method been adopted, immense contributions to historical understanding would have resulted.

Hostadter also showed the changes which had taken place in Beard's thinking over the years. These included his modifications in the 1935 edition and his views in *The Republic* (1943) and the *Basic History of the United States* (1944). By this time Beard had conceded on many occasions that there were other factors besides the economic in history, although economic forces were still fundamental. In *The Republic* he added the threat-of-a-military-dictatorship to the radical-agrarian-vs.-conservative-capitalistic view of the Constitution, and in the *Basic History* he played down considerably the class motives behind the Constitution. The imminent threat of fascism had brought Beard to view the Constitution in a somewhat different light.[28]

A glance at current popular textbooks on American history and government would seem to justify the view that the thesis of *An Economic Interpretation of the Constitution* has been generally accepted into the writing of American history. There are variations, of course, but on the whole the book and its conclusions seem to have had a much greater impact on the thinking of historians and political scientists than did Beard's own modifications in the 1935 edition and his later writings.[29]

[28] Hofstadter, "Charles Beard and the Constitution," pp. 75-92.

[29] For works which follow the interpretation that early American society was undemocratic, that the Constitution represented a conservative counterrevolution by upper-class propertied interests, and that democracy did not arrive until the time of Andrew Jackson, see John D. Hicks, *A Short History of American Democracy* (Boston, 1949), pp. 48-49, 53-54,

As Lerner said, the Introduction to the 1935 edition was not as well known as it should have been, and one might well add that the "Conclusions" have been much more influential than the Introduction. In addition, and regardless of any minor modifications in the thesis, Beard's historical method seems to be gaining stature as the years go by.

My own interest in the Beard interpretation of the Constitution grew out of a seminar study of Massachusetts during the Confederation period. As a graduate student I naturally started with the almost universally accepted view that colonial society was undemocratic and that the Revolution was a dual revolution for independence from England and for democracy for the lower classes within the colonies. I had also accepted the Beard interpretation that the Constitution represented a conservative counterrevolution on the part of the upper classes to protect their property, and the general view that democracy

---

85, 100, 103-06, 119, 124-26, 128-30, 148, 154-55, 187-88, 224-26; Arthur Cecil Bining, *A History of the United States*, 2 vols. (New York, 1950), I, 185, 187, 194, 198, 219-20, 230-31, 250-52, 276-77, 287, 394-97; Oscar Theodore Barck, Jr., Walter L. Wakefield, and Hugh Talmage Lefler, *The United States: A Survey of National Development* (New York, 1950), pp. 91-92, 152, 167, 186-87, 192-93, 209-10, 215-16, 227, 229, 243, 285, 306-07; Merle Curti, Richard H. Shryock, Thomas C. Cochran, and Fred Harvey Harrington, *An American History*, 2 vols. (New York, 1950), I, 115-17, 144-45, 158-62, 192-96, 202-03, 209, 212, 251, 253, 446-49; Leland D. Baldwin, *The Stream of American History*, 2 vols. (New York, 1952), I, 151-52, 157-58, 184-87, 202, 205, 223-24, 239, 269-73, 276, 289-90, 295-99, 304, 306, 315-45, 440-42; William Anderson, *American Government*, 3rd ed. (New York, 1946), pp. 24, 31, 36, 51, 54, 56-57; Claudius O. Johnson, *Government in the United States*, 3rd ed. (New York, 1944), pp. 3-4, 123-24; Frederic A. Ogg and P. Orman Ray, *Introduction to American Government*, 9th ed. (New York, 1948), pp. 12-13, 15, 25-26, 78; John H. Ferguson and Dean E. McHenry, *Elements of American Government* (New York, 1950), pp. 24, 33, 41, 44. Either these authors cite Beard directly or their account distinctly shows the influence of Beard. The authors who have deviated most from the Beard interpretation are Samuel Eliot Morison and Henry Steele Commager, *The Growth of the American Republic*, 2 vols. (New York, 1950), I, 116, 163-67, 171-75, 179-82, 198-99, 234, 237, 240, 274-81, 296-98, 300, 303, 309, 311, 316, 335, 381-82, 393, 468-71, but even Morison and Commager considered American society as undemocratic until the time of Jackson and looked on the Constitution as something of a conservative reaction.

did not really arrive in this country until the rise of the common man under Andrew Jackson.

My study of the Massachusetts constitution of 1780 brought a rather rude awakening. Imbued with the idea that "the people" were struggling to democratize their society, I was suddenly confronted with what appeared to be a stupid reaction on their part. The people did not abolish the old, undemocratic charter as they should have done early in the Revolution. Then in 1778 by a vote of all adult men regardless of property qualifications, they rejected a constitution which appeared to be more democratic than the old charter. And finally in 1780 they adopted, again by full male suffrage, a constitution which appeared to be even more undemocratic than the colonial charter had been.

The contradiction of a people struggling for more democracy and then voting themselves out of the right to vote directed my attention to an earlier period in Massachusetts history. Instead of such an illogical contradiction existing, perhaps there was something wrong with the old, accepted interpretation. Obviously the Revolution had as one aim independence from England, but perhaps the other aim, democratization of American society, was a misconception. The result was a Ph.D. thesis, "The Road to Revolution in Massachusetts," University of Wisconsin, 1946, and a book, *Middle-Class Democracy and the Revolution in Massachusetts, 1691-1780,* which was recently published.

In my work on Massachusetts the seeming contradiction of the Massachusetts constitution of 1780 was resolved. Instead of a colonial society of upper and lower classes, rich and poor, enfranchised and unenfranchised, I found a predominantly middle-class society in which most men owned property, most men were farmers, and most men could vote. There was little class conflict in the colony, and naturally the Revolution there was not a "dual revolution." Having a democratic society in which property ownership was widespread, and emphasizing time and again that they were trying to keep what they had, it was not surprising that the people of Massachusetts incorporated their ideas in the constitution of 1780. Given the

20

middle-class society which existed before the Revolution, it would have been surprising if they had done otherwise. And since most of the people owned property, naturally they would adopt a government which had as one of its functions the protection of property. After all, they had fought the Revolution with the slogan "life, liberty, and property." In the course of my research I found many references to other colonies indicating that Massachusetts was not unique in its possession of a democratic, middle-class society.

The study on Massachusetts, plus the fact that I gave advanced undergraduate and graduate courses on the Revolution and Constitution, led me to the debates in the Constitutional Convention and the ratifying conventions in the states. Here, it seemed, would be the best source of information on the nature of American society in 1787 and what the Fathers were trying to accomplish in writing the Constitution. Most of the delegates were practical politicians who had firsthand knowledge of the electorate and of economic conditions at the time. They knew from experience whether the country had a class-ridden society or whether it was predominantly agricultural, middle-class, and democratic. They also knew whether the constitution which they were writing would be subjected only to the vote of the upper classes because of property qualifications for voting or whether it had to meet the approval of the masses because most men were voters.

What I found in the debates, added to what I had found about Massachusetts, convinced me that Beard's interpretation of the Constitution had long been in need of a critical analysis. There were economic divisions in society in 1787, but they were not the divisions between personalty on the one hand and debtors and realty on the other hand that Beard emphasized. There were also economic groups behind the Constitution, but again they were not as Beard pictured them. If the men in the Convention, as well as most other witnesses, gave an entirely different account of the social structure and of democracy in 1787, where had Beard gotten his information? This critical analysis is the result of that question.

It was a long road from a seminar on Massachusetts in the Confederation period to a critical analysis of *An Economic Interpretation of the Constitution,* but undoubtedly the road had to be traveled before the destination could be reached. What follows is the fruit of that journey. To borrow a chapter from Beard, it is not intended as a definitive work, but merely as a suggestion for a change of direction in future research on the Constitution. The field is large, and although I have started and shall continue to explore it along the lines laid out here, there is obviously room for many workers in the vineyard. In the interest of better history, both the evidence and the suggested thesis presented here should be subjected to the most critical analysis possible. If they fail to meet the test, they will be discarded as they should be, and historical research will be the better because of it.

In the following pages I have attempted to analyze *An Economic Interpretation of the Constitution of the United States* from the standpoint of historical method. I am not particularly concerned with approval or disapproval of Beard's social philosophy, or with Beard as a man, a friend, a teacher, or a publicist. Much has been made of Beard's historical method, but little has been done by way of testing its validity. Yet this historical method is in reality the very foundation upon which the Beard interpretation of the Constitution must rest.

Questions to be asked and answered are those customarily applied to any historical work. Did the author go to the primary sources for his information or did he rely heavily on other secondary writings? Did he amass sufficient evidence to make his generalizations representative, or is his evidence merely a partial picture? And in particular, were his conclusions justified by the evidence which he presented, or were there unresolved contradictions and inconsistencies which would invalidate his interpretation? In short, did the actual evidence which Beard presented really justify the Beard interpretation of the Constitution? If the answers are favorable, we must accept Beard's thesis as valid, for the historian, like the judge, should base his conclusions on the best available evidence. But if the answers are unfavorable, perhaps the time has come for us to look elsewhere for an explanation of the writing and adoption of the Constitution.

The method used here is simply a chapter-by-chapter analysis of Beard's use of evidence and the conclusions which he drew from his evidence. In the interest of completeness, I have included points both large and small, important and otherwise. If some of the points seem too unimportant to deserve notice, it must be remembered that Beard himself considered them of sufficient significance to include them. If I seem to have gone into too much detail in my discussion of Chapter V, it is only because this has been considered the most important chapter—the heart of the thesis.

The suggestion has been made that a work such as this would have been more relevant forty years ago, but the facts do not buttress such a view. If, as is generally conceded, the Beard thesis has come to be accepted into the main stream of historical writing, there is perhaps even more justification for a critical analysis now than ever. Forty years ago there were many unbelievers; today there are few. If the Beard thesis is even more influential now in the writing and teaching of American history than it has been since it first appeared, a critical analysis is as relevant at this late date as it would have been at any time during the past four decades.

BEFORE we examine the method used in *An Economic Interpretation of the Constitution*, a word needs to be said about the Preface. Beard did not claim that this book on the Constitution was definitive. He called it a fragmentary work designed to suggest new lines of historical research. It was an outline of the work that needed to be done. The reason for publishing such an incomplete work, according to Beard, was lack of time for doing the research which he had outlined. He said he could give only an occasional period to uninterrupted studies and therefore could not expect to do within a reasonable time the work on the Constitution which he had outlined. So he was printing this incomplete study in the hope of encouraging scholars to abandon barren political history and to study the real economic forces which conditioned great political movements.

How far is such an explanation valid? If a scholar is too busy with academic work, such as teaching and administration, to do extensive research and writing, a work which opens new vistas for other scholars and indicates work to be done is certainly justified. And there is little question but that Beard should be given credit for having directed attention toward neglected areas of economic history, although one might question the particular approach which he stimulated. In the interests of historical method and careful scholarship, however, it should be noted that during the six years between 1910 and 1915, when he might well have done some of the essential research for a definitive study, and when he presumably was too busy to do exhaustive research for *An Economic Interpretation*, Beard wrote six books by himself and revised one of these, edited one book, wrote four books in conjunction with other authors, wrote thirteen articles, read and reviewed thirty-five books, wrote two prefaces or introductions for other books, and composed three "letters to the editor."[1] He was

[1] *Charles A. Beard: An Appraisal*, ed. Howard K. Beale (Lexington, Ky., 1954), pp. 265-86.

24

obviously a human dynamo when it came to production, but whether this massive output is a valid excuse for an admittedly fragmentary job on *An Economic Interpretation* each reader will have to decide for himself.

# CHAPTER I

# "HISTORICAL INTERPRETATION
# IN THE UNITED STATES"

BEFORE starting his survey of the origins of the Constitution, Beard wrote a chapter on historical interpretation in which he rejected previous schools of historical writing and then made a strong plea for economic determinism or the economic interpretation of history. These schools were the Bancroft, which emphasized the role of God in American history; the Teutonic, tracing the achievements of the English-speaking peoples to the political genius of the Germanic race; and the scientific or factual, which avoided interpretation by the impartial presentation of the facts. These schools, particularly the second and third, contributed the ideas of scrupulous care in the documentation of materials and a critical spirit in the use of materials. But all three were inadequate: they touched the surface only and did not explain deeper causes or relations.

Having rejected the old interpretations of history, Beard then presented a new hypothesis, the theory of economic determinism. The hypothesis that economic elements were the chief factors in political development had been little used, Beard declared, and until the theory of "economic determinism" had been tried, it could not be found wanting.

In particular, Beard condemned what he called the juristic approach to constitutional history and constitutional law. Here, economic factors had been neglected even more than they had been in other historical studies. The juristic approach was designed, not to provide an understanding of the Constitution, but to inculcate a spirit of reverence for that document. It ignored party conflicts and economic pressures, and dealt only in terms of broad generalities such as justice and liberty. Nowhere in the juristic approach, Beard declared, was there any evidence that the Constitution was designed to protect the rights of any class or secure the property of any group.

An economic interpretation of constitutional history, on the other hand, is based on different conceptions, Beard continued. Law is not abstract principle but a guide to concrete action: it is a part of the social fabric or it has no reality. Instead of abstractions, most law is concerned with property and governs the process by which men acquire and transfer economic goods. The fact that constitutional law deals primarily with organs of government, the suffrage, and administration does not obscure the real function of government. Since government is primarily concerned with making rules to determine property relations, the classes whose rights are to be determined must obtain from the government the rules which will favor their economic interests. Thus constitutional history becomes the process by which various economic groups seek to protect their particular interests by making or altering the fundamental law of the land.

Since this work is primarily concerned with Beard's historical method, the first major criticism of his approach in Chapter I concerns his use of the writings of James Madison, pp. 14-15. Beard stated that *An Economic Interpretation* was based on Madison's political philosophy, a philosophy which is found in all of Madison's serious writings, but particularly in perhaps the best-known of his works, *The Federalist* No. 10. *The Federalist* No. 10, as is well known, was one of a series of eighty-five articles which were published in the New York newspapers during the debates over ratification of the Constitution. Written by Alexander Hamilton, James Madison, and John Jay, and later published in book form, these eighty-five articles offered various reasons as to why the people should adopt the Constitution. Of the eighty-five, Beard chose Madison's No. 10 as presumably the most important and based his interpretation of the Constitution upon it.

The choice of No. 10 immediately raises the question of why this particular *Federalist* number should be considered more important than the other eighty-four. After *Federalist* No. 1, which outlined the purpose and scope of the articles, the remainder were divided as follows: on the utility of the Union (2-14), on the insufficiency of the Confederation to preserve the Union (15-22), on the necessity of a government at least as energetic as the one set up by the Constitution (23-38), and on the conformity of the Constitution to republican principles (39-84). Two other topics were to be included—analogy of the Constitution to the state government and additional security which its adoption would afford to republican government, liberty, and property—but by the time the authors reached No. 85, they decided that these topics had already been sufficiently covered. The entire series included practically every argument, economic and political, that could be thought of at the time in support of the Constitution.[1] Why, then, did Beard choose No. 10?

Many of *The Federalist* numbers emphasized economic factors in government, but only Madison's No. 10 presented the particular kind of economic interpretation which Beard presented in his book. Both 9 and 10 showed the utility of the Union as a safeguard against domestic faction and insurrection. In 10 Madison argued that there were two methods for curing factions—remove the causes or control the effects. But to remove the causes meant either the destruction of liberty or giving every citizen the same opinions, passions, and interests. It would be unwise, however, to destroy liberty just to end factions, and men would have different opinions, passions, and interests as long as their reason was fallible and they were at liberty to exercise their reason.

There was another reason why men would never have the same interests, opinions, and passions, and it was in the exposition of this that Madison explained his famous philosophy of government. The natural diversity of abilities or faculties among men, in which rights of property originated, Madison continued, presented an insuperable obstacle to a uniformity of interests. And the first object of government was to protect this diversity of abilities or faculties. In turn, the protection of these different and unequal abilities for acquiring property resulted in the possession among men of different degrees and

[1] There are innumerable editions of *The Federalist,* beginning as early as 1788. See *The Federalist: A Commentary on the Constitution of the United States,* ed. John C. Hamilton (Philadelphia, 1880). Beard edited *The Enduring Federalist* (Garden City, N.Y., 1948) but omitted numbers 13, 15-22, 50, 54, and 61.

kinds of property, which in turn influenced the sentiments and views of the owners, causing a division of society into different interests and parties.

Beard then omitted a section from No. 10 (Beard, p. 15, line 7), proceeding with Madison's statement that the most common and durable source of factions was the various and unequal distribution of property. Men with and without property and the creditors and debtors had always formed distinct interests in society. Landed, manufacturing, mercantile, moneyed, and many lesser interests of necessity developed in civilized nations, dividing men into different classes actuated by different views. The principal task of government was the regulation of these various and interfering interests, involving the spirit of party and faction in the necessary and ordinary operations of government. Beard called these views of Madison "a masterly statement of the theory of economic determinism in politics" (p. 15).

Since Beard said that *An Economic Interpretation* was based primarily on the philosophy of government expressed in No. 10, a further analysis of this particular number is important. And since we are especially interested in Beard's method, we should naturally be concerned first with what he omitted from the quotation.

When we examine No. 10, we find that the omission is rather important if we would understand Madison. What Madison said here was that the latent causes of faction are sown in the nature of man. Unfriendly passions and violent conflicts among men have been caused by zeal for different opinions on religion, government, and other things, by attachment to different leaders or others, and even by the most frivolous and fanciful distinctions. In short, it was necessary to omit this section from Madison's statement to make Madison an "economic determinist." It is quite true that Madison placed economic factors ahead of all others, but he did not rule out the noneconomic either here or in his other writings and statements, as we shall see later.

Furthermore, a close reading of Madison will show that even in his economic views Madison did not divide society the same way that Beard did in *An Economic Interpretation.*

29

Beard's division is primarily, although not completely, a horizontal division based on wealth. He leaves the impression with the reader that substantial men of property favored the Constitution while the debtor farmers, the poor town workers, and the disfranchised in general opposed it. Madison also had a horizontal division when he classified men as rich and poor, debtors and creditors. But Madison recognized that there were vertical divisions as well as horizontal—that society had landed, manufacturing, commercial, moneyed, and many lesser interests which might well come into conflict with each other. In other words, the division into upper and lower classes was not the only division, according to Madison, something which will be of special importance in our later analysis of the Convention debates. What Madison desired, and what he thought the Constitution provided, was the kind of government that would prevent the formation of factions as much as possible and would provide checks against the dominance of any one faction. If the nature of man made factions inevitable, the only cure was to control them.

*The Federalist*—all eighty-five numbers—certainly provides the best commentary on the Constitution aside from the debates in the Convention. But we cannot take a part of one number and say that this provides the correct basis for an interpretation. In order to single out one to the exclusion of the other eighty-four, Beard would have had to show that the one outweighed all the others, and that men at the time considered No. 10 the most important. Furthermore, it would also have been necessary to prove that Madison's views represented those of the Convention, a point which will merit some consideration later.

In spite of Beard's denial that he was an "economic determinist," it might be well to point out here that he did use the phrase several times in this chapter, whatever he meant by it, that people who read *An Economic Interpretation* are apt to get the impression that he was an economic determinist, and that even as late as 1939 writers such as Max Lerner still talked about him in terms of economic determinism. Historians must use words to convey ideas and if they use the phrase "economic determinism," readers are apt to believe that that is what they mean.

Beard concluded Chapter I with a statement of the requirements for an economic interpretation of the Constitution. Some men favored and some opposed the Constitution, he said, and if we could show that both groups owned about the same amounts and kinds of property, there could be no economic interpretation of the Constitution. But if most merchants, moneylenders, security holders, manufacturers, shippers, capitalists, financiers, and their professional associates supported the Constitution and most of the opposition came from non-slaveholding farmers and debtors, it would be fairly clear that the Constitution was the product not of abstract principles but of economic groups which expected to gain by its adoption. That farmers and debtors actually gained by the adoption of the new government, Beard said, did not alter the fact that the guiding purpose of the Fathers was not the general welfare. The direct, impelling motive, he declared, was the economic advantages which they expected from the Constitution (pp. 17-18).

Here Beard stated the first half of his thesis—that the Constitution was put over by personal property interests or capitalistic classes as opposed to small farmers and debtors. He did not contend, as many think he did, that the division in the country was between the owners of property, who favored the Constitution, and the propertyless, who opposed it. The split was more subtle: it was between personalty or personal property, the kind of movable property possessed by merchants, moneylenders, security holders, manufacturers, capitalists, and financiers, on the one hand; and realty or real estate owned by small farmers combined with debtors, on the other. The distinction is important, for it is not a Marxian division of society as we know it. Neither is it Madisonian, however, for Madison assumed that the various vertical property divisions would have clashing rather than similar interests, and he did not predicate his philosophy of government on an alliance between farmers and debtors.

31

The total impact of Chapter I is to answer some questions and to raise others. Here we have the basic ingredients for an economic interpretation, the use of "economic determinism," and the statement that the impelling motive behind the Constitution "was the economic advantages which the beneficiaries expected would accrue to themselves first"—to some, an erudite way of saying that the Fathers were out "to line their own pockets," though Beard in his 1935 Introduction denied having had this in mind. In terms of method we have the questionable use of *The Federalist* No. 10 to show Madison's "masterly statement of the theory of economic determinism in politics" and to provide the foundation for Beard's own interpretation. There is also the problem of whether American society was divided along the lines defined by Beard—whether the capitalistic classes were on one side and the small farmers and debtors on the other.

# "A SURVEY OF ECONOMIC
# INTERESTS IN 1787"

HAVING defined his hypothesis for an economic interpretation of the Constitution, Beard, in Chapter II, surveyed the prevailing economic interests of the country in 1787 to test his hypothesis. Since an economic interpretation presumes that progress is the result of contending interests in society, he said, we would need to know what classes and groups existed at the time the Constitution was adopted, and especially which groups, from the nature of their property, might have expected to benefit by a change of governments. In his summary of the chapter (p. 51) Beard concluded that personal property was the dynamic element in the movement for the Constitution. Let us examine the method by which he arrived at this conclusion.

Before he analyzed the various economic interests in 1787, Beard did an admirable job of pointing out what information was needed about the distribution of property before either a political or an economic history could be written. We would need to know the size, value, and ownership holdings of realty, which constituted a far larger proportion of wealth than it did in 1913. For personal property, we would need to know the geographical distribution and holders of money on hand and on loan, the distribution and ownership of public securities, the geographical distribution of mortgaged farms and their connection with paper money and schemes to impair contracts, the owners and operators of western lands, and the owners and distribution of manufacturing.

No one would quarrel with this excellent summary of work still to be done and essential to an economic as well as a political interpretation. But from the standpoint of historical method, there are some revealing statements accompanying Beard's summary. Such was the importance of this suggested survey of property distribution that it was strange that no attempt had been made to undertake it on a large scale. In fact, he said, not even a beginning had been made. Consequently, it would be necessary to rely on general statements of historians who had written on the period (p. 19).

If, as Beard said in 1935, the title of his book warned the reader of the book's approach, these statements should also warn the reader of his historical methods. Certain work must be done before an economic interpretation can be made, yet Beard said that he did not have time to do the work and that not even a beginning had been made by anybody else. Yet without this information, he planned to proceed on the basis of the work of other historians—who had not done the work either. In other words, the reader is warned that *An Economic Interpretation of the Constitution* is to be based primarily on secondary works whose authors had not done the spade work, that Beard himself did not go behind the scenes to the sources as he claimed in the 1935 edition, and that the thesis of the book—personalty vs. small farmers and debtors—had been arrived at before the author ever knew how property was distributed and who the debtors were. If the saying, "no evidence, no history," holds true, one might well question the validity of the Beard thesis at this point in the book. If we do not know what the property interests were, how can we say with any certainty that the conflict of these interests produced the Constitution?

Without having the evidence, however, Beard went ahead to discuss the various economic interests in the country in 1787. These included the disfranchised (presumably those who had little or no property), real estate owners, and personal property owners. On the basis of his discussion of these three groups, Beard arrived at some conclusions which are particularly important from the standpoint of historical method.

First Beard discussed the disfranchised, and here appeared the initial statement of the second part of the Beard thesis—that the Constitution was put over undemocratically in an undemocratic society. His classification of the disfranchised—slaves, indented servants, women, and the "mass of men" who could not qualify for voting because of property qualifications—is misleading. If slaves and women had to vote before there was democracy in this country, we did not have democracy until 1920. Actually the only group which concerned Beard in the remainder of the book was the free adult white men who were disfranchised by property qualifications. Half of the Beard thesis, that the Constitution was put over undemocratically in an undemocratic society, must therefore depend on proof that a "mass of men" were disfranchised by these property qualifications.

By his own statement, this second half of the Beard thesis should have been discarded on page 24. After saying that "the mass of men" were disfranchised, a phrase having the connotation of large numbers, and that these disfranchised were not represented in the Convention, Beard made this startling confession: "How extensive the disfranchisement really was cannot be determined." But of course determining the extent of disfranchisement is absolutely fundamental to half of the Beard thesis. We *must* determine the extent of disfranchisement before we can state that "the mass of men" were disfranchised and that the Constitution was put over in an undemocratic society. If Beard did not have the evidence, and if the problem cannot be solved, he did not have a valid interpretation.

One should also note the contradictions and the use of unsupported generalization on the remainder of page 24. Having said that many men could not vote, how many he could not tell, Beard proceeded to show that in some states, Pennsylvania and Georgia for instance, even propertyless mechanics in the towns could vote. This does not indicate extensive disfranchisement in two states, at least, and it would certainly imply that evidence was available on the number who could vote. Then Beard ended the paragraph with the unsupported generalization that in other states the freehold qualification "certainly excluded a great number of the adult males."

From the standpoint of method, these unsupported generalizations should be supported with evidence, since they are fundamental to the thesis, and the contradictions certainly ought to be resolved. We cannot have a "mass of men" disfranchised if the number cannot be determined. And if propertyless mechanics could vote in some states, why would the freehold qualifications exclude a "great number" of adult males in others? This latter statement should be particularly noted, for Beard later contradicted himself completely on the significance of the freehold qualification.

Judged by historical method, Beard's discussion of the "working-class" as part of the disfranchised was also unsatisfactory (p. 25). Without any evidence, primary or secondary, to support his statement, he said that this class was already sufficiently numerous to form a considerable portion of society. Yet he admitted that in the hundreds of pages of sources which he examined, he could not find any evidence of the existence or special problems of a working class. Sometimes the best evidence is the absence of evidence, for if the working class had been sufficiently numerous in 1787 to form a considerable portion of society, there should be some evidence to that effect. As we shall see later, the absence of evidence for a laboring class, as we know it, was due to the relative absence of the class. Hamilton's dismissal of the working-class problem with scant notice in his report on manufactures in 1791 should have been a warning to Beard.

As a matter of fact, Beard had, and quoted, the proper evidence but failed to see its significance (p. 25). When the question of the suffrage was before the Convention, he said, Madison warned the delegates of the "coming industrial masses." Madison favored the restriction of voting to freeholders (farmers), a point to be noted for future reference. Then Madison went on to say that "in future times" a great majority of the people would not have any property, and if the Convention enfranchised this group, property rights and public liberty would not be safe. But this is evidence for what would develop in the *future*, not evidence for a large laboring class in 1787. In the Convention Madison said what he implied here— that there was not much of a laboring class in the country in 1787.[1]

In the footnotes on page 25 there is an interesting use of

[1] *The Records of the Federal Convention of 1787*, ed. Max Farrand, 4 vols. (New Haven, 1937), I, 421-23. The *Records* were first published in 1911.

evidence judged by the standards of historical method. Workingmen in the cities were not disinterested spectators, Beard said, but if they had been enfranchised, they would doubtless have voted with the major interests in the cities in favor of the Constitution rather than with the farmers against it. In fact, he declared, they actually did this very thing in New York. If workers in New York voted for the Constitution, two conclusions are obvious: they *were* enfranchised, and others besides upper-class personalty interests must have favored the Constitution. Surely the propertyless mechanics in Philadelphia who had the vote and the workers in New York who voted did not represent substantial personalty interests.

In footnote 2, page 25, Beard also referred to an important item in Farrand, *Records*, ii, 204. In that note Madison supported the Beard thesis to a very limited extent in talking about the influence of property in government and how property should be protected in one branch of the government. But Madison included all property, real and personal, not just personal at the expense of real. Furthermore, Madison said that persons as well as property were essential objects of government, and that they also had a right to protection. This, of course, is not economic determinism. Then Madison made the significant statement that the United States had "not reached the stage of Society in which the conflicting feelings of the Class with, and the Class without property, have the operation natural to them in Countries fully peopled." As many other delegates were to do, Madison implied that the social structure in this country in 1787 had not developed to the stage where class conflicts were sharp.

Since the *Records of the Convention* are the best source of information on the Constitution, and since Beard cited the *Records*, it might be worth while to consult this source of information on these two important problems—the extent of disfranchisement and the approximate size of the working class in 1787. How democratic was the society which produced the Constitution, judged in terms of the adult white men, and what proportion of the people were laborers at the time?

In the first place, the *Records* show that probably most free adult men had the vote in 1787. Gerry of Massachusetts said the people of England would probably lose their liberty from the smallness of the number having the vote, while in America the danger came from the opposite extreme.[2] Sherman of Connecticut declared that an equal distribution of liberty among all ranks meant that the poor were equal to the rich in voting.[3] When the question of voting qualifications under the Constitution came up, Dickinson of Delaware argued that restriction of voters to freeholders would be popular because the great mass of citizens were freeholders and would be pleased by the restriction.[4] Gouverneur Morris supported this idea on the ground that nine-tenths of the people were freeholders who would favor a government which restricted voting to freeholders.[5] The implications here were that at least ninety per cent of the men were voters because they were freeholders. Certainly the evidence does not support Beard's statements that freehold qualifications must have excluded a great number of the adult men and that a "mass of men" were disfranchised. In fact, as we shall see later, Beard himself said that some ninety-seven per cent of the people lived in rural areas and that the freehold qualification admitted small farmers and debtors to the franchise (p. 71). It is unfortunate that Beard did not base his final conclusions on this statement.

But freeholders were not the only qualified voters in 1787. Attempts to limit voting to freeholders brought a great deal of opposition, showing that others could vote besides the ninety per cent or more who owned land. James Madison was politician enough to say that while the freeholders would be the "safest depositories of Republican liberty" (Beard, p. 25), his own reaction to restricting the vote to this group would depend on how much opposition came in those states where the franchise was exercised by every description of people.[6] Madison did not want to jeopardize the adoption of the Constitution by antagonizing nonfreeholders who had the vote already. Benjamin Franklin pointed out that the common people had

[2] *Ibid.*, p. 132.    [3] *Ibid.*, pp. 450, 457.    [4] *Ibid.*, ii, 202.
[5] *Ibid.*, p. 202.    [6] *Ibid.*, p. 203.

the vote and would resent any effort to deprive them of it. The country owed much to its common people, he said, and if they were denied the franchise, the country might lose their support.[7]

Other delegates also emphasized that the people in general had the franchise, not just the vast majority who were land-owners. Oliver Ellsworth of Connecticut said that the right of suffrage was a tender point strongly guarded by most of the state constitutions. The people would not readily subscribe to the new government if it disfranchised them, he said, which of course was another way of saying that they had the franchise.[8] George Mason of Virginia reminded the Convention that eight or nine states had already extended the suffrage to others besides freeholders, and what would these people say if they were disfranchised?[9] Nathaniel Gorham of Massachusetts, where the voting requirements were relatively high, said that there had never been any inconvenience from allowing non-freeholders to vote, though it had long been tried. Elections in New York, Philadelphia, and Boston, where merchants and mechanics voted, were at least as good as elections participated in by freeholders only. The people had long been accustomed to this right in various parts of America, Gorham concluded, and would never allow it to be abridged.[10] If ninety per cent or more of the men were freeholders and voters, and if merchants and mechanics voted in eight or nine states, where did the "mass of men" who were disfranchised come from?

We must realize that the delegates to the Convention were almost all practical politicians who had long faced the problems of being elected to office. As practical politicians, they undoubtedly knew what the electorate was, and whether the Constitution would be subjected to the vote of the few or the many. As Charles Pinckney of South Carolina said in that state's ratifying convention, the first job of the delegates had been to acquire a knowledge of the people for whom the system was to be formed, for it would be impossible to form a government without knowing their habits, opinions, and

[7] *Ibid.*, pp. 204-05, 210.   [8] *Ibid.*, p. 201.
[9] *Ibid.*, pp. 201-02.   [10] *Ibid.*, p. 215.

resources.[11] On this basis the views of these delegates on the extent of democracy at the time must have some validity, especially when they all agreed that American society was democratic in 1787. Some of them did not like democracy, but they had to recognize it as an important factor.

Space does not permit an inclusion of the views of all the delegates on democracy, but a few more will not be amiss. Elbridge Gerry said, "The evils we experience flow from an excess of democracy," and George Mason admitted that there had been too much democracy, but he did not want to go to the opposite extreme.[12] For notwithstanding the oppression and injustice experienced among them from democracy, he said, the genius of the people was in. favor of it and the genius of the people must be consulted.[13] "The democratick spirit runs high," said Paterson of New Jersey,[14] while Randolph of Virginia thought that "the democratic licentiousness of the state legislatures proved the necessity of a firm senate."[15] Hamilton could see evils operating in the states that would soon cure the people of their fondness for democracy, as he declared that the country needed to be rescued from democracy.[16] These are only a few of the many statements on the subject; others are to be found in the references.[17]

Being practical politicians, the Convention delegates recognized that they had to write a constitution which would meet the approval of the electorate. Perhaps the most convincing

[11] Jonathan Elliot, *The Debates of the Several State Conventions . . .*, 5 vols. (Washington, 1854), IV, 320.

[12] Farrand, *Records*, I, 48, 49.      [13] *Ibid.*, p. 101.

[14] *Ibid.*, p. 186.      [15] *Ibid.*, p. 218.      [16] *Ibid.*, pp. 291-310.

[17] *Ibid.*, pp. 48 Gerry; 49 Mason; 51 Randolph; 101 Mason; 132 Gerry; 134 Mason; 134-35 Madison; 158 Dickinson; 186 Paterson; 218 Randolph; 291, 301, 310, 362 Hamilton; 398, 402, 411 Pinckney; 422-23 Madison; 423 Sherman; 424 Hamilton; 432 Gerry; 450, 457 Sherman; 465 Hamilton; 512-14 G. Morris; II, 29 G. Morris; 35 Madison; 57 Gerry; 66 King; 111 Madison; 123 Dickinson; 201 G. Morris, Wilson, Ellsworth, Mason; 202 Dickinson, Ellsworth, G. Morris; 203-04 Madison; 204-05 Franklin; 205 Mercer; 210 Franklin; 215 Gorham; 217 Madison; 249 Rutledge, Franklin; 439 G. Morris; 476 Madison; 585 Sherman, Hamilton; 587 Madison; 626-27 King; 647 Gerry; III, 31 Knox; 32 Mason; 146 McHenry; 168 Baldwin; 307 Randolph; 326 Mason; 355 C. Pinckney; 356 Madison; 405 Madison; 409 Lewis; 412 Madison; 413 Hamilton.

evidence for the wide extent of democracy was the constant concern in the Convention for what the people would or would not accept. There was scarcely a feature of the Constitution which was not favored or opposed on the ground that it would please or displease the people. A few examples will suffice, as the reader can find others in the footnote references to the *Records*.

Randolph opposed a single executive on the ground that "the sentiments of the people ought to be consulted—they will not bear the semblance of monarchy."[18] But Wilson of Pennsylvania, on the other hand, argued just the opposite because he saw no antipathy of the people to a single executive.[19] Sherman believed that an executive council would be necessary to make the new government acceptable to the people.[20]

Again George Mason reminded the Convention that it must consider the prevailing democracy if it wanted to get the Constitution adopted:

"Do gentlemen mean to pave the way to hereditary monarchy. Do they flatter themselves that the people will ever consent to such an innovation? If they do, I venture to tell them they are mistaken. The people never will consent. And do gentlemen consider the danger of delay, and the still greater danger of a rejection not for a moment but forever, of the plan which shall be proposed to them. Notwithstanding the oppressions & injustice experienced among us from democracy; the genius of the people is in favor of it, and the genius of the people must be consulted."[21]

Butler of South Carolina opposed the court system in the Constitution on the ground that the people would also oppose it. Said he: "The people will not bear such innovations. . . . Supposing such an establishment to be useful, we must not venture on it. We must follow the example of Solon who gave the Athenians not the best Govt. he could devise, but the best they wd. receive."[22] Read of Delaware, on the other hand, countered with the argument that the people at large were

[18] *Ibid.*, i, 88, 90.    [19] *Ibid.*, p. 96.    [20] *Ibid.*, p. 97.
[21] *Ibid.*, p. 101.    [22] *Ibid.*, p. 125.

41

wrongly suspected of being averse to a general government.[23]
Paterson said the people of America were sharpsighted and not
to be deceived. The delegates must follow the people; the
people would not follow them. The plan of government must
be accommodated to the public mind—it must consult the
genius, temper, habits, and prejudices of the people.[24]

Gerry and Madison got into a little argument over the extent
to which the people should be consulted. Although Madison at
one point said that his view of restricting the franchise to
freeholders would depend on what the nonfreeholder voters
thought of the idea, at other times he argued that the Convention should not be guided by what the people thought, for no
one knew their opinions. What the Convention should do, he
said, was to devise the best government it could, regardless of
the people.[25] But Gerry answered that the Convention had to
consider what the people thought, as all legislators had done,
regardless of what it wanted to do.[26]

About the only dissenting voice in the Convention to the
general proposition that American society was democratic in
1787 was that of Hamilton, and Hamilton contradicted himself.
He did not say how many, but he did say that in all the states
some individuals were deprived of the right of suffrage by not
having sufficient property.[27] But this statement was offset by

[23] *Ibid.*, p. 137.    [24] *Ibid.*, p. 186.    [25] *Ibid.*, p. 215.

[26] *Ibid.*, p. 215. For additional evidence on the influence of the people
see *Records*, I, 49 Wilson; 50 Madison; 56 Mason, Madison; 80, 105
Wilson; 119 Rutledge; 132 Gerry; 143 Dickinson; 178 Paterson; 214
Gerry; 218 Pierce; 249-50 Lansing, Paterson; 253 Wilson; 258 Lansing,
Paterson; 282-91, 301, 303-04 Hamilton; 331 Wilson; 338-39 Mason;
360 Randolph; 361 Ellsworth, Wilson; 366 Hamilton; 372 Gorham,
Randolph, King; 377 Sherman; 403 Pinckney; 414-15 Ellsworth; 425
Gerry; 474 Hamilton; 490 Dayton; 491 Bedford; 528 Madison; 529
Butler, G. Morris; 569 Gerry; 570 Read; 583 G. Morris; II, 54 G. Morris;
82 Gerry; 119 Dickinson; 125 Langdon; 201 Ellsworth, Mason; 202
Dickinson; 203 G. Morris, Madison; 205 Franklin, Rutledge; 216
Gorham; 249 Rutledge; 275 Gerry; 278 Dickinson; 279 Randolph; 329,
388 Gerry; 451 Williamson, Mason; 455 Langdon; 477 Mason; 509
Gerry; 533 Hamilton; 539 King; 587 Mason; 614 Gorham, King; 623
Carroll; 643-44 Gorham, Washington; III, 30 Grayson; 53 Hamilton; 56
Washington; 60, 78 Madison; 85 McHenry; 210 Martin; 249 Pinckney;
271, 314-15 Madison.

[27] *Ibid.*, I, 465.

others expressing the opposite point of view. At one point he stated that he saw evils operating in the states which would soon cure the people of their fondness for democracy.[28] Again he declared that while the people now opposed both his own and the Randolph plan, they were gradually ripening their opinions of government and had begun to be tired of an excess of democracy.[29] Hamilton was dubious that the Randolph plan went far enough to rescue the country from democracy, for it only provided that a democratic house was to be checked by a democratic senate and both by a democratic executive.[30] But even Hamilton did not indicate that many men were disfranchised.

In addition to showing a great deal of political democracy in 1787, the *Records* also reveal that there was much economic democracy, or economic opportunity, at that time. Instead of quoting Madison to the effect that *in the future* there would be propertyless classes in this country, or instead of saying that the laboring class was already large enough to be important even though he could not find evidence for such a generalization, Beard should have consulted the Convention debates. There he would have found numerous statements that American society was predominantly middle-class in 1787, that there were few extremes of wealth and poverty, and that most men owned property. Charles Pinckney of South Carolina summed up this view very neatly:

"The people of the U. States are perhaps the most singular of any we are acquainted with. Among them are fewer distinctions of fortune & less of rank, than among the inhabitants of any other nation. Every freeman has a right to the same protection & security; and a very moderate share of property entitles them to the possession of all the honors and privileges the public can bestow; hence arises a greater equality, than is to be found among the people of any other country, and an equality which is more likely to continue, because in a new Country, possessing enormous tracts of uncultivated lands, where every temptation is offered to emigration & where

[28] *Ibid.*, p. 291.     [29] *Ibid.*, p. 301.     [30] *Ibid.*, p. 310.

43

industry must be rewarded with competency, there will be few poor, and few dependent—Every member of the Society almost, will enjoy an equal power of arriving at the supreme offices & consequently of directing the strength & sentiments of the whole Community. None will be excluded by birth, & few by fortune, from voting for proper persons to fill the offices of Government—the whole community will enjoy in the fullest sense that kind of political liberty which consists in the power the members of the State reserve to themselves, of arriving at public offices, or at least, of having votes in the nomination of those who fill them."[31]

Pinckney went on to say that the British constitution was the best, but that it could not be copied in America. There were few rich men here for a house of lords, and the genius of the people and their general mediocrity of situation would not favor a rapidly introduced distinction of rank. Elimination of entail and primogeniture, added to the influence of cheap land, would for a long time preserve the equality of condition which so eminently distinguished the people of America. Equality, he said, was the leading feature of the United States, and among the great body of the people there were few of wealth or poverty. He divided the people into three classes, professional, commercial, and landed—that is, vertical property interest groups rather than horizontal classes.[32] If Pinckney was correct, and apparently most of the delegates including Madison agreed that he was, we must explain the Constitution in the light of a democratic, middle-class society, not the class society suggested by Beard.

This rather lengthy analysis of democracy as revealed by the *Records* is simply designed to show a little of the evidence which was easily available. It was not necessary for Beard to base half of his thesis on the unsupported assumption of a large disfranchised element in the population, then to present several contradictions—that the extent of disfranchisement could not be determined, that practically all men could vote in Pennsylvania and Georgia, and that freehold qualifications

[31] *Ibid.*, p. 398.
[32] *Ibid.*, pp. 399-403, 410-11.

certainly excluded a large portion of the adult men from voting. We shall see from time to time what Beard did with this part of the thesis, and especially in Chapter IV, where the franchise will be dealt with at some length.

Beard then moved from the unenfranchised to the enfranchised in his survey of economic interests in 1787 with the unsupported statement that while there were no legal class distinctions or outward signs of special class privileges, every student of manners and customs knew that social distinctions were very sharp.

The treatment of the first of these enfranchised groups, the small farmers, raises many questions in relation to historical method (pp. 27-28). There is the implication that the inland areas were lower-class as they were peopled by mechanics, poorer whites, and immigrants. There is also no evidence to support this or to show how much of the inland area was settled by farmers and farmers' sons from older areas and how the inland agricultural areas differed from the settled agricultural areas.

In dealing with land speculation and its influence on small farmers, Beard could well be considered as having been guilty of a misuse of his source of information. He said the inland area had political doctrines derived from an antagonism to the seaboard group, one source of conflict being the possession of land. Speculators had taken up much of the land, he said, so that settlers were either squatters or purchasers from speculators. He then used Virginia as an illustration, quoting from Ambler's *Sectionalism in Virginia* to prove his point. In addition to the fact that Ambler is a secondary account, not a source, we should note that Beard did not use this account correctly.

What Ambler said was that there was a tremendous rush of settlers into the West after the war, but that the conflict of the frontiersman was not with eastern aristocrats, as Beard implied, but with savages, land companies, and individuals who claimed priorities to new lands. In this conflict the Virginia legislature favored the small holder. It annulled land grants made after 1763, reduced the price of land to two cents an acre, then granted each actual settler a settlement right to 400 acres and a preemption right to 1,000 acres adjoining. Ambler did say that Virginia's policy encouraged speculation, but he did not say that this happened before 1787. He cited debates in the Twenty-second Congress and showed in a footnote that there were large holdings in the West by 1791, but we still do not know how difficult it was for the individual to get land in western Virginia in 1787.[33] This is one of the pieces of research which would need to be done before land speculators could be injected into the story, and of course it would have to be done for all the states, not just Virginia. As Beard used this secondary work, we are left to believe that all this happened before 1787.

Beard also made a completely unsupported statement about debtor farmers and urban dwellers. Without any proof, he assumed that the farmers were "a large debtor class" who were dependent on the towns for capital to develop their resources (p. 28). Before we could make the farmers into a "debtor class," we would need much more information than we now have. My own study of Massachusetts shows that some farmers owed money, but most of them did not. There were debtors and creditors in both town and country, and more often than not the debtors and creditors were members of the same family. There was certainly no evidence in Massachusetts that the towns furnished operating capital for the farmers.[34] Richard Henry Lee made the statement that the great bulk of the people, the weight of the community, were men of middling property who were neither debtors nor creditors.[35] Readers of *An Economic Interpretation* should be aware that the use of the phrase "debtor farmers" throughout the work is not based on any evidence whatsoever.

In attempting to make the small farmers into a debtor class, Beard unwittingly contradicted his earlier contentions that

[33] Charles Henry Ambler, *Sectionalism in Virginia from 1776 to 1861* (Chicago, 1910), pp. 42-45.

[34] Robert E. Brown, *Middle-Class Democracy and the Revolution in Massachusetts, 1691-1780* (Ithaca, N.Y., 1955), ch. i.

[35] "Letters from the Federal Farmer . . .," in *Pamphlets on the Constitution . . .*, ed. P. L. Ford (Brooklyn, 1888). The Lee quotation can also be found in V. L. Parrington, *Main Currents in American Thought*, 3 vols. in 1 (New York, 1930), i, 291, and Louis M. Hacker, *The Shaping of the American Tradition* (New York, 1947), p. 290.

there was a disfranchised "mass" and that the freehold qualifications must have excluded a large number of men. Here,
these so-called debtor farmers apparently could vote, for they
controlled state legislatures and pushed through legislation to
help themselves. The use of Shays' Rebellion as an example is
misleading, for even if the followers of Shays were all debtors,
they comprised less than twenty per cent of the population in
the few counties where they were active (p. 59). Furthermore,
how do we explain the fact that the Shaysites and their sympathizers controlled the government of Massachusetts completely
after the election of 1787, yet they did not recall the Massachusetts delegates from the Convention and they later ratified
the Constitution? There were undoubtedly debtors and creditors in 1787, great and small, farmers as well as others, but we
do not know who they were, where they were, or how they
voted. It should also be noted that here the farmers were aware
of their interests and actively engaged in politics; yet to explain
why the Constitution was put over, Beard later had to make
them inert, ignorant, and indifferent (p. 64).

There are also inconsistencies and unproved generalizations
in the Beard explanation of other realty groups, the large landowners of the Hudson Valley region and the slave-owning
planters of the South (pp. 28-30). After saying that the
manorial lords of the Hudson Valley region constituted a
dominant aristocracy both before and after the Revolution, he
said that this aristocracy was unable or unwilling to block
issues of paper money. But if it were unwilling, its interests
must have been similar to those of the small "debtor farmers";
if it were unable, it must not have been a controlling aristocracy. He explained the apparent paradox of southern
planters forming an alliance with northern merchants by
saying that the planters who backed the Constitution were men
who were rich in personal property other than slaves. These
planters therefore had more in common with northern merchants than they did with their debt-burdened neighbors at
home. In Chapter V we shall consider how many of these
planters were rich in personalty other than slaves. As to the
fact that the planters' neighbors were more debt-burdened

than the planters themselves, that must remain strictly in the category of something yet to be demonstrated by historical research. Hamilton in *The Federalist* No. 35 assumed that the landed group, from the wealthiest landlord to the poorest tenant, had common interests that united it.

Although Beard himself implied that slaveholding was not a part of the personalty interests involved in the formation of the Constitution (p. 30), a further word is needed on whether slaves should be considered as personal property or as an integral part of a planter's agricultural operations. In Virginia before the Revolution, slaves on plantations were legally designated as real estate and could be entailed just as was real property.[36] Furthermore, one of the best reasons for docking the entail on land was that the planter had no slaves and therefore the land was a burden to him. Almost invariably the House of Burgesses permitted a planter to sell part of his entailed land so that he could buy slaves to work the remainder of his land. The slaves were then entailed in place of the land.[37] Unless a planter bought and sold slaves as a business, therefore, slaves should be considered as closely allied with agriculture rather than as strictly personal property. We shall want to know whether men such as Washington, the Pinckneys, and others were motivated by personal property or by agriculture and slaves.

The first half of the Beard thesis—that the Constitution was put over by important personalty interests—begins to crumble the first time it is tested on page 31 and following. First Beard said that the proportion of personalty to realty had never been and probably could not be determined, yet he went ahead ostensibly to show the importance of personalty in 1787. This, it would seem, is an important point for an economic interpretation, and one of the greatest weaknesses in Beard's

[36] *Statutes at Large* . . ., ed. William Waller Hening, 2nd ed., 13 vols. (New York, 1823), III, 333-35; IV, 222-28.

[37] *Ibid.*, IV, 36, 181, 240, 307-08, 377-79, 461-65, 534-37; V, 83, 214-16, 277-78, 392-400; VI, 311-14, 405-12, 443-52; VII, 157-59, 483-85, 488-90, 514-16, 630-36; VIII, 34-35, 54-57, 61-63, 66-68, 166-67, 174-76, 214-15, 224-27, 283-87, 289-93, 301-03, 436-38, 440-44, 457-60, 481-86, 631-35, 637-38, 641-43.

work. In the process of attempting to show the importance of personalty, however, he not only used questionable figures in a manner open to criticism, but he also used figures which, if they prove anything, actually refute his own generalizations.

First to be noted is that Beard used taxation figures and property values for various years from 1792 to 1804, not for the years 1785-1787, which would be proper for the background of the Constitution. In 1787 the public debt, state and Continental, was measured in securities which had depreciated to a fraction of their face value. After 1791 the value of these securities was increased tremendously by Hamilton's program of assuming state debts and funding the national debt. Figures after 1791 would represent this inflated value, not the value in 1787. If one argued that land values were also increased to balance the rise in securities, making the relative comparison of land and personalty valid, the question would immediately arise as to whether the farmers also expected to gain by a new government.

There is both a misuse of evidence and a drawing of unwarranted conclusions from the figures on New Hampshire, Massachusetts, and Connecticut (p. 31). The tax returns are for 1792, 1793, and 1795, making their usefulness in indicating conditions in 1787 at least questionable. The figures for Massachusetts and Connecticut do not show the value of realty, so we cannot tell the relative importance of realty and personalty. If we want to know how much personalty there was, we need a comparison with realty to get a true picture.

Actually, the figures for New Hampshire give us that comparison, and what do they prove? Realty was valued at £893,327, but Beard did not say whether this was assessed value or market value. If it were assessed value, as it probably was, we would need to know the assessment rate in New Hampshire to get the market value of realty. Money on hand or at interest was £35,985. On the basis of these figures, realty outweighed personalty by 96.13 per cent to 3.87 per cent, or more than 25 to 1. In short, what these figures show is that realty was overwhelmingly the predominant economic interest in New Hampshire in 1793. Furthermore, we do not know how much of this personalty was owned by the possessors of realty.

Even more convincing evidence that realty and not personalty was overwhelmingly the predominant economic interest in the country is to be found in Beard's figures and table on page 36. The table has a state-by-state account of land values and interest disbursed—$479,293,263 for realty and $1,180,909 for interest. If we just took those figures as they stand, the preponderance in favor of realty would be 99.75 per cent to 0.25 per cent. I hasten to add, of course, that these percentages are not valid because Beard's figures are not valid, but they do show what can be done with an uncritical use of figures. Beard did not say whether the ·figures represented full real estate values or only assessed valuation. Then he left out $140,000,000 in house values, as though real estate owners did not place any value on houses. Of course, the omission makes the figures for realty look less impressive than those for personalty. If we correct the figures—eliminating Vermont, Kentucky, and Tennessee, which were not states in 1787, adding the $140,000,000 for houses, and converting the $1,180,909 in interest to some $20,000,000 in capital at six per cent—the preponderance of realty over personalty is still 96.7 to 3.3. And again the generalization that personalty was important is not justified by the evidence.

Of course we might assume that the 96.7 per cent representing realty was not really an economic interest and that the more than 90 per cent of the people who were farmers were unique in not acting from economic motives. But if we accept Beard's contention that people are influenced by their economic goods, the farmers certainly should have been influenced by their realty. They certainly were if Beard's statement of their activities in their state legislatures was correct. As an alternative, we can simply accept at face value Beard's assumption— and it is an assumption—that the 3.3 per cent representing personalty put over the Constitution in spite of the 96.7 per cent representing realty. No politician in the farm belt today would make such assumptions, however, and expect to get elected. And if we would understand the Constitution, we must explain why the great bulk of the farmers, representing this vast realty interest, voted for the Constitution as they had to do if it were to be adopted.

Equally questionable are Beard's figures on the national debt (pp. 33-35) to show the importance public securities had for the Constitution. The total debt, $76,096,468.67, is not valid for his interpretation. To make his figures valid, he would first have had to eliminate the $13,745,379.35 in foreign debt, for this was to be paid to foreign countries, not to the members of the Convention. Next he would have had to eliminate the $18,271,786.47 in state debts which were assumed by the federal government under Hamilton. In the Convention the question of having the federal government assume the responsibility for paying off the state debts was brought up and discussed at some length. The main argument for such a move was that it would relieve the people of their state debts and incline them to favor the Constitution. A committee to discuss the proposition brought in a favorable report, but Gerry objected on the grounds that the states which had done most to pay their debts would not want to be saddled with the debts of delinquent states, and the motion to assume state debts was dropped.[38] The total for the foreign and state debts would be $32,017,166.22, leaving only $44,079,302.45 as the effective debt for consideration as far as the members of the Convention were concerned.

Then there are some questions about this *funded* $44,079,302 domestic debt, which amounted to $11.22 per person in 1790. Did the men in the Convention in 1787 know that Hamilton was going to fund the debt at full face value in 1791? Beard implied by using these funded figures that they did. Later he said that by September 3, 1787 Nicholas Gilman "had already discovered the probable effect of the proposed Constitution . . . upon the securities of the government" (p. 94), and that John Lansing was at the Convention long enough "to learn (what was not a very deep secret) the certain effect of an efficient government on continental securities" (p. 123).

[38] *Records,* ii, 6, 322, 327, 328, 355-56, 368, 377.

There is plenty of evidence to show that some members of the Convention expected or hoped that the price of securities would rise under the new Constitution, but none that I have seen to the effect that they knew the government was going to pay full face value. Franklin said he hoped and believed the value of securities would go up under the Constitution (p. xvi), and Gilman urged New Hampshire to buy up public securities, then selling in Philadelphia at 2*s*. 6*d*. on the pound, on the ground that the state might later have to pay six or eight times this amount for them. These two statements do not indicate certainty that the securities were going to be redeemed at full face value, for even Gilman would have said eight times instead of six or eight, for eight times 2*s*. 6*d*. equals a pound. Furthermore, as Beard said (p. 34), securities went up from 17*s*. to 22*s*. on the pound between March 5, 1791 and October 3, 1792. So men must not have known even as late as March, 1791 that the debt was to be funded at face value, or securities worth 22*s*. would not have been selling at 17*s*.

With the domestic debt of the Confederation government only $44,079,302, and the Convention rejecting the proposal to assume state debts, Beard's figure of $40,000,000 as the gain which came to security holders as a result of the adoption of the Constitution is certainly open to question. There is no doubt that some expected to profit, and that they did profit, by the increased value of the securities, but the lure was not $40,000,000. Furthermore, we would have to know how much of this anticipated gain went to men who were predominantly realty rather than personalty owners, and whether farmers might not also have expected to gain by increased prices for farm products under a stronger government.

Beard also gave an erroneous picture of the influence on the Constitution of personalty as represented by manufacturing and shipping (pp. 40-49). His assertion that a large amount of capital had been invested in various branches of industry would leave the impression of a substantial class of manufacturers. Actually, as his own evidence shows, most of the manufacturing was done by individual artisans or mechanics, not by manufacturers using hired labor. One should remember that a mechanic in 1787 was not a man who worked for wages in a garage. He was an artisan, a skilled worker who made shoes, hats, cloth, copperware, or one or more of a hundred other items (p. 45), and who was generally a businessman working for profit rather than wages. The probate records show that very few were "propertyless mechanics"—they usually owned their houses and shops, and in the small towns they almost invariably combined a trade with farming.[39] The petitions cited by Beard were signed by shipwrights and mechanics, and the articles for which they wanted protection were articles made by independent artisans, not made in factories. Twice he pointed out that the "mechanics and manufacturers" joined forces in asking for government protection, as though the two had common, not conflicting, interests (pp. 42, 43). Beard himself said the workingmen in New York City supported the Constitution. Of course they did. When has labor in this country not wanted protection from foreign labor, and why would shoemakers, hatmakers, weavers, and spinners not want protection for their products against foreign competition? But he who gets the impression that manufacturing in 1787 meant large-scale industrial production would certainly be misinformed.

Contrary to Beard, one would logically expect the commercial interests and the manufacturing interests to be opposed rather than in harmony. Shippers undoubtedly represented some substantial economic interests, since shipping was an established business. But would shippers and manufacturers both want a government which could impose a protective tariff? Shippers might want protection from countries which discriminated against them, but it is not likely that they would want a protective tariff, which would decrease trade. Were not the commercial interests the very ones which prevented the establishment of a protective tariff in 1789 and in 1791 when Hamilton in his report on manufactures advocated a protective tariff in vain?

[39] Brown, *Middle-Class Democracy*, ch. i.

In the light of this analysis, Beard had rather a curious conclusion to his chapter. He said the weight of various kinds of property in politics was determined not by the amount of property but by opportunities for gain and need for protection. This, presumably, would account for the fact that the three per cent of personalty dominated the ninety-seven per cent of realty, and Beard went on to say that personalty was under attack or failed to get proper governmental encouragement. But he had already made a great point of the fact that the so-called debtor farmers were "conscious of their status and actively engaged in establishing their interest in the form of legal provisions" (p. 28). Are we to assume that they suddenly lost interest in their economic well-being and supinely watched the personalty interests put over a government that would benefit personalty? Or could it be that Beard's analysis of economic interests in 1787 was wrong, and that small farmers and artisans also expected to benefit by hoped-for improved economic conditions under a new constitution?

Beard ended the chapter with the first clear statement of one phase of his thesis: that personal property, not just property in general, was "the dynamic element" in the movement for the new Constitution. This should be kept clearly in mind, both in the light of the demonstrated preponderance of realty over personalty and in the light of Beard's later analysis of the economic interests of the men in the Constitutional Convention.

From the standpoint of historical method, both halves of the Beard thesis on the Constitution ceased to have any validity in this chapter. We must have proof, not just assumptions, that the Constitution was put over in an undemocratic society by personal property interests. Evidence from the *Records* and elsewhere would seem to indicate that most men owned real estate and were voters. Until better evidence is produced, we must explain the Constitution in terms of a democratic society in which most men owned property. Not only did Beard fail to show how many men were disfranchised, but he also failed to account for the great agricultural interest of 1787.

By Beard's own admission, the ingredients for an economic interpretation of the Constitution were not even available when he wrote his book, much less the information that personal property, rather than property in general, was the dynamic element behind the Constitution. Having outlined so admirably the work that needed to be done, Beard should have stopped at this point. But since he did not stop, this critical analysis, perforce, cannot stop here either.

"THE MOVEMENT FOR THE

CONSTITUTION"

IN Chapter III Beard asked whether the government under the Articles of Confederation adversely affected the personalty interests of the country and whether the leaders of the move for the Constitution represented these interests. Both questions he answered in the affirmative. Capital as opposed to land— public securities, shipping, manufacturing, money at interest— suffered at the hands of the prevailing government, and men representing these interests were involved in the maneuvers. In addition, a new element is injected—the conspiracy theory of the Constitution. These personalty interests attempted to secure protection for their property through regular constitutional channels, but, failing to get the Articles amended, they set to work by a circuitous route ostensibly to revise the Articles but actually to put over a "revolutionary programme."

Since our primary interest here is method, let us see how Beard arrived at these conclusions.

On page 53 Beard cited a letter which he said summed up "concisely" the interests which were turning to the new Constitution. According to this letter, some men wanted roads and canals, but it is possible that even farmers could want these items, not just personalty interests. There were personalty groups included—trading and manufacturing interests, money-lenders, and public creditors—and of course these fit the Beard thesis. Two sections were omitted, leaving the reader to wonder, after the use made of The Federalist No. 10, what was left out. But at the end of the letter were two groups who should never have been included—embarrassed farmers and oppressed tenants, who wanted a strong government to protect them when they migrated to new lands. These were not personalty interests, but it is just possible that they would have voted for the Constitution for the very reason of protection.

Again, as he had done before, Beard gave an excellent out-line of the work that would have to be done before we could know whether the leaders in the move for the Constitution represented the personalty interests which he indicated. But again, from the standpoint of historical method, he arrived at a peculiar solution. Since the work in the sources had not been done, all that he could do was to give a "superficial" com-mentary based on the conventional secondary works on the Constitution. When we speak of Beard's methodology, we should keep in mind these statements which he himself made.

One method used in this chapter is that of reaching gen-eralizations by implication (p. 55). In 1781 Philip Schuyler in the New York Senate advocated a stronger government than the one under the Articles. Schuyler was a "large holder of depreciated securities," and the implication is that Schuyler wanted a strong central government primarily to protect his securities. Beard cited his own reference to Schuyler on page 109, but all we learn there is that Schuyler had large holdings in securities in *1791*, four years after the Constitutional Con-vention and at a time when many men were speculating in securities. From Beard's own evidence we do not know what Schuyler had in 1781, yet we are left to infer that he held these in 1781. On the other hand, if he had money and had not loaned it to the government during the war, he would probably have been accused of being a Tory.

When we check the citation on page 55 for other evidence, we find that it does not prove what Beard said it did. The reference was to Elliot, *Debates of the Several State Conven-tions*, I, 95, to show that ten leaders in Congress in 1783, all of whom held securities that were depreciating, voted to give the government power to raise money. These leaders were Gorham, Higginson, Ellsworth, Dyer, Boudinot, Fitzsimons, Williamson, Izard, Johnson, and King; and the implication is that these men were involved in the move for the Constitution.

What does this evidence prove? In Chapter V, where he gave the holdings of the delegates, Beard "surmised" that Gorham must have had some securities, for when he died in 1796 he had twenty shares of United States Bank stock. But he could have bought this at any time, as Beard said. There is no other evidence whatever that he had securities at any time—including 1783, when they presumably were depreciating. Higginson, Dyer, Boudinot, and Izard were not at the Constitutional Convention, and if Beard knew what securities they had in 1783, or whether they supported the Constitution, he did not disclose the source of his information. Ellsworth, an "excellent farmer" as well as a lawyer, had securities in December, 1791, but we do not know when he bought them or what he had in 1783. Fitzsimons was speculating in securities which he had "bought up," but we do not know when he bought them or whether he had them in 1783. Williamson also had securities in 1791, but again we do not know what he had in 1783. Johnson and King, according to Elliot, did not even vote on the proposition as Beard said they did.

So of the ten men cited by Beard as voting to give the government more power over finances in 1783, only eight actually voted; four were not at the Constitutional Convention, so we do not know their holdings; three had securities in 1791, but we do not know what they had in 1783; and Gorham may have had securities. Incidentally, Gorham was presumably one who was working for a rise in securities—that is, for his own interests—yet Gorham knew so little about what was going to happen under the new government that he and Oliver Phelps contracted in 1788 to buy a million dollars' worth of western land to be paid for in consolidated Massachusetts securities. When the securities rose in value, as according to Beard these men knew they would, Gorham, Phelps, Robert Morris, and others of the "Fathers" lost a great deal of money (pp. 99-100). Such events raise some questions about the motives of the Fathers and their certainty as to what the outcome of their work would be.

Beard's citation of Elliot on the vote in 1783 also raises some other questions about Beard's historical method in regard to a critical use of sources. According to Elliot, twenty-nine men voted on the measure, all but three voting yes. If these ten men (actually eight) cited by Beard voted for the measure, presumably because of their depreciating securities, why did eighteen others vote for it, too, and why did only three vote against it? Did the other eighteen have securities, or did they have other reasons for voting as they did?

Then we note a great surprise in this 1783 vote to strengthen the government. Both delegates from Rhode Island voted no, which might have been expected from Rhode Island's voting record, but who would guess that the third nay vote was cast by Alexander Hamilton of New York?

Is this analysis of the vote in 1783 proof that Beard should be especially praised for his historical method in *An Economic Interpretation?* It looks impressive—figures taken from sources and all that—but it simply crumbles to nothing when we examine it critically. What do we mean by a critical use of sources if sources can be put to such use as this?

Beard stated (pp. 55-56) that James Bowdoin urged a stronger union with enlarged powers and recommended a convention to deliberate on the matter. Beard said that Bowdoin was a large holder of securities, but the evidence for this statement does not appear on Beard's page 263, which he cited. We cannot tell from this what Bowdoin had. But if Bowdoin had securities and was motivated by a desire to enhance their value, why did the legislature of Massachusetts, representing scores of small agricultural towns, also resolve that the Articles were inadequate and advocate steps to strengthen the Union? Beard cited Ambler, *Sectionalism in Virginia*, page 48, for the statement that merchants in Virginia were learning their lessons in federalism, but Ambler emphasized trouble with Britain, not internal attacks on merchants' securities, and, to a lesser extent, trade restrictions among the states. Concern with British practices could be considered much more a manifestation of nationalism than of internal class conflict. The petition from Pennsylvania in 1781 against inflation (p. 57) could have represented many different interests, but the petition itself certainly does not signify personalty interests alone. The citation from Washington (p. 58) does not prove that Washington represented personalty interests or that his complaints about conditions at the time were due to attacks on personal property. From this quotation, there could have been any number of reasons for Washington's views, including poor agricultural conditions.

On the positive side, the quotation from General Knox (pp. 58-60) does show that Shays' Rebellion, in Knox's eyes, was a manifestation of class conflict. Knox was expressing a point of view, however, not the facts, and his predictions of dire consequences never materialized. Once the legislature of Massachusetts enacted measures demanded by the Shaysites, who had wide sympathy in the state, the rebellion collapsed. Furthermore, the Shaysites did not enact leveler or agrarian legislation when they captured control of the government in 1787, and it was the Shaysites and their supporters who elected the convention which ratified the Constitution in Massachusetts. The John Armstrong letter (p. 61) mentions disfranchisement as one punishment for the Shaysites, which is another way of saying that they had the franchise. And of course Shays' Rebellion was convincing evidence that farmers as well as personalty interests were hurt under the Confederation.

On the basis of the evidence presented in this chapter, we cannot say that personal property was the only economic interest that was hurt under the Articles, or that the men cited by Beard represented this personal property. If conditions were adverse to personalty interests, would they favor farmers and artisans? Beard did not prove that capital as opposed to land was adversely affected—he merely stated it. Was Washington a representative of realty or personalty, or, for that matter, was he acting from economic motives at all as far as Beard's evidence proves? Of particular interest in this chapter, of course, is the use made by Beard of the vote in 1783 to increase the powers of the government. All in all, does Beard's method justify his conclusions on page 63?

# "PROPERTY SAFEGUARDS IN THE ELECTION OF DELEGATES"

As THE title of Chapter IV indicates, Beard discussed here the significance of property qualifications for voting and office-holding as a protection for property, presumably meaning personal property, in the election of delegates to the Constitutional Convention. Since this involves the half of the Beard thesis that American society was undemocratic in 1787, we shall be interested in the evidence which he presented, particularly after seeing that the evidence from the Convention *Records* indicates a great deal of democracy at the time.

Again there appears the "conspiracy" theory that the leaders of the movement outwardly followed legitimate methods but actually worked in their respective legislatures to secure the election of the right kind of delegates, who would take the drastic steps demanded by the circumstances. In view of what Beard said on page 28 about the debtor classes being conscious of and actively engaged in passing laws to promote their own interests, the reader is not a little surprised here to find that the dynamic personalty groups were aided in their plot "by the inertness, ignorance, and indifference of the masses." Just when and how this change came about, and how Beard could account for Shays' Rebellion as a manifestation of inertness and indifference, we are not told. Neither did Beard explain why agrarian-dominated legislatures chose delegates who would favor personal property presumably at the expense of agriculture. Furthermore, if the masses were inert, ignorant, and indifferent, the problem of the Constitution is considerably different from what it would be if these same masses were actively aware of their interests but could not vote. In order to show why the personalty groups were anxious to change the government, Beard in one place had to make the masses active aggressors against personalty interests. Now, to explain why the legislatures elected the kind of delegates they did, he had the masses inert, ignorant, and indifferent.

Beard then explained the undemocratic features involved in the calling of the Convention. There were no special popular elections to complicate the choice of "the right kind of a convention." Then the delegates were elected not by the people, but by state legislatures, just as senators were elected, Beard pointed out, before the recent reform in 1913 providing for their direct election. Beard forgot to mention, however, that under the Articles of Confederation, the state legislatures elected all delegates to the Confederation Congress, and that no other form of election would have been constitutional. Finally, and an important item for our consideration, property qualifications for voting and officeholding placed an additional guard against too much democracy in the choice of delegates to the Convention.

To show precisely how these property qualifications for the suffrage and for holding office protected property, Beard then gave a state-by-state summary of the qualifications then imposed. What does this summary show?

In New Hampshire, apparently most men could vote and a very small amount of property qualified a man for office. The £200 freehold for senators and £100, half to be freehold, for representatives favored *realty*, not *personalty*, and, as I have shown elsewhere, a £200 freehold was a very small farm indeed.[1] As Beard himself said, the suffrage was widely extended to freeholders, taxpayers, and even those who paid a poll tax. So there was no mass of disfranchised men in New Hampshire and the qualifications did not favor personalty.

Beard's account of Massachusetts tells nothing except how much property was required for voting and holding office. A mere listing of qualifications tells only what the qualifications were. One might imply, and many writers have, that these qualifications restricted voting to a small percentage of the population, but it should be kept in mind that the listing of qualifications tells nothing about the number who were admit-

[1] Robert E. Brown, *Middle-Class Democracy and the Revolution in Massachusetts, 1691-1780* (Ithaca, N.Y., 1955), ch. II.

ted or excluded. I have already shown elsewhere that few men in Massachusetts were disfranchised.[2] As in New Hampshire, the qualifications for the Senate and House greatly favored realty rather than personalty, for the freehold qualification was only half as much as the personal property qualification.

As the voting qualifications in Connecticut were less than those for Massachusetts, and as the economies of the two states were similar, one might assume that as large a proportion of men were qualified in Connecticut as in Massachusetts. Beard did not say. He merely listed the qualifications, but that does not tell us how many men were voters.

The treatment of New York (pp. 67-68) provides a good test of Beard's historical method and shows the need for critical use of evidence and care in drawing conclusions from evidence. Beard said that the New York Senate represented property, but it was *realty*, not *personalty*, for a senator had to be a freeholder and electors of senators had to own freeholds worth £100—a small holding. Voters for members of the lower house had to own freeholds worth £20, or rent tenements worth 40s. annually, or be a freeman of Albany or New York.

Beard said that these qualifications "worked an extensive disfranchisement in New York." To prove his point, he cited a secondary writer, Henry P. Johnston, who did not give any sources whatever for his information. Johnston, however, said that the New York City census for 1790 gave 1,209 freeholders with £100 valuation, 1,221 with £20 freeholds, and 2,661 forty-shilling freeholders, a total of 5,091 qualified voters out of a total population of 30,000. Johnston said that "something like a landed aristocracy" controlled the municipal elections.[3] He did not say personalty.

At first glance these figures used by Beard—5,091 out of 30,000, or one out of six—indicate a restricted electorate. On second glance, however, the reader realizes that the 5,091 are qualified voters and the 30,000 are total population, including women and children. The big question is how many adult men

[2] *Ibid.*, ch. III.
[3] Henry P. Johnston, "New York after the Revolution, 1783-1789," *Magazine of American History*, XXIX (April, 1893), 311.

in New York City were disfranchised. Estimates of population before the census of 1790 give one adult man out of five or six people.[4] On this basis there would be between 5,000 and 6,000 adult men in the city. The census for 1790 gives 5,924 heads of families, of whom at least 673 were women and 135 were free Negro men.[5] This would mean 5,116 white male heads of families. So instead of showing "extensive disfranchisement" in New York City, Beard's figures, when subjected to critical analysis, show that there were 5,091 voters, not counting freemen who· had no property, out of some 5,116 white male heads of families or something between 5,000 and 6,000 adult males. The best percentage would be almost 100, the worst would be about 83⅓. In either case most. men in the city were voters, which is exactly what the members of the Constitutional Convention said.

In the end, all these figures, generalizations, and estimates for New York add up to nothing, anyway, for as Beard said (p. 67), the ratifying convention in New York was elected under the universal manhood suffrage rule.

The figures at the bottom of page 67 on the election of Richard Harrison from New York City do not prove how many men would have voted if there had been no property restrictions. Beard said that Harrison received 2,677 votes as a delegate to the ratifying convention, elected under manhood suffrage, but only 1,500 votes as a member of the state Assembly, when property qualifications were in effect. These were two different elections, with different issues at stake, so that a comparison of the two does not yield valid conclusions. If there were 5,091 or more voters, all that these figures prove is that slightly more than half of the qualified voters participated in one election and less than a third in the other.

In New Jersey the requirements for holding office favored realty over personalty, while the voting franchise of £50 proclamation money could be in any kind of property (p. 68).

[4] Evarts B. Greene and Virginia D. Harrington, *American Population before the Federal Census of 1790* (New York, 1932), *passim*.
[5] *Heads of Families at the First Census of the United States Taken in the Year 1790: New York* (Washington, 1908), pp. 9, 116-37.

But this still does not tell us how many men were disfranchised. In Delaware, members of the legislature also had to be free-holders, and again the voting qualifications of fifty acres of land with twelve acres improved or £40 lawful money do not give any information on the number of voters. Pennsylvania allowed any man who paid taxes to vote, and also included adult sons of freeholders even if they did not pay taxes, so there was no problem of a restricted electorate in the Quaker State.

In the southern states the evidence either reveals nothing about the disfranchised or shows that most men could vote and that the qualifications favored realty instead of personalty. Maryland required a freehold of fifty acres or property worth £30 current money. This latter was half the requirement in Massachusetts, where practically all men could vote. The £500 and £1,000 current money requirements for representatives and senators should have restricted officeholding to average small farmers at least, but as Gouverneur Morris said in the Convention, "All the guards contrived by America have not restrained the Senatorial branches of the Legislature from a servile complaisance to the democratic."[6] So apparently even the £1,000 qualification was not much of a safeguard against democracy.

Virginia's qualifications of twenty-five acres improved or fifty acres unimproved naturally favored realty but do not tell us how many men owned twenty-five or fifty acres. Artisans in Norfolk and Williamsburg could also vote, but this presumably would not benefit the wealthy personalty interests. North Carolina required its legislators to be freeholders, again favoring realty, the fifty-acre freehold for voting for senators had the same result, and the franchise for voting for representatives was given to all freemen who paid public taxes— not a very restricted electorate. South Carolina demanded a settled estate and freehold worth £2,000 currency for senators and £1,000 for representatives, which would probably have cut out the smallest farmers. But anyone could vote if he

[6] *The Records of the Federal Convention of 1787,* ed. Max Farrand, 4 vols. (New Haven, 1937), II, 512.

owned fifty acres of land or a town lot, or paid taxes equivalent to taxes on fifty acres of land. Georgia demanded 250 acres or £250 for the legislature, which would have been within reach of the small farmer; then, as Beard said, it extended the franchise widely to every white man having £10 and subject to payment of taxes or anyone who was a mechanic.

What conclusions can we draw from this state-by-state account of property qualifications for voting and officeholding? At the beginning of the chapter, pages 64 and 65, the reader gets the impression that Beard was going to show how many men were disfranchised. This is not so, however. In New Hampshire, Pennsylvania, North Carolina, and Georgia, as Beard said, there was little restriction on voting. In the other states he merely listed the qualifications, leaving the reader to infer that they were restrictive. If most men were independent freeholders, as the Convention delegates stated, these qualifications did not exclude many men, for a farmer could not have raised a family on a freehold too small to give him the vote. And finally, even though there were property requirements for voting and holding office, they were such that they tended to favor realty rather than personalty. There can be little doubt that property was a factor, but it was not the kind of property emphasized by Beard.

After starting the chapter with the impression that property qualifications were going to act as safeguards for personalty in the choice of Convention delegates, the reader is startled by the conclusions which Beard reached in the final two paragraphs, pages 71 and 72. The paragraph on page 71 has an almost complete contradiction in the first sentence. Beard said that these enumerated property qualifications "operated to exclude a large portion of the adult males from participating in elections," which is the conclusion one would expect. It should be noted, however, that this conclusion is reached by implication rather than by evidence—by jumping from the statement that there were qualifications to the conclusion that a large portion of the adult men were disfranchised without ever attempting to find out exactly how many men could or could not meet the qualifications.

66

Having said that these qualifications excluded a large portion of the adult men, Beard then contradicted himself by stating that "the wide distribution of real property created an extensive electorate and in most rural regions gave the legislatures a broad popular basis." When we add to this his statement (p. 242) that only three per cent of the population in 1790 lived in towns of 8,000 or over, the contradiction becomes even more apparent. Either the property qualifications excluded a large portion of the adult men or they created an extensive electorate in a country in which ninety-seven per cent of the people lived in rural areas. The choice is one or the other, not both, and all the evidence which Beard presented, here and later, points to the second conclusion of a broad electorate. It also coincides with statements made by the men in the Convention.

Furthermore, instead of protecting personalty, as one would expect, these same property qualifications actually gave the vote to what, according to Beard, were the most dangerous antagonists of personalty—"the small farmers and many of the debtors." And far from being inert, ignorant, and indifferent, these small farmers and debtors were now "the most active in all attempts to depreciate personalty by legislation," which is another contradiction. As for Madison's statement about the threat to property by freeholders, we shall see later that Madison offered many different views, some of which favored the restriction of voting to freeholders. We have already seen that many delegates favored the restriction of voting to freeholders on the ground that, having property, they would be the best safeguards for property. These delegates did not look on farmers as antagonists of property.

Then we find a new note in the last paragraph of the chapter. In spite of the fact that the country was ninety-seven per cent rural, that there was an extensive electorate which admitted small farmers and debtors, and that these farmers and debtors were active in depreciating personalty by legislation, the representatives of personalty "were able by the sheer weight of their combined intelligence and economic power" to secure the right kind of delegates. So property qualifications for voting and officeholding made no difference. What counted was the sheer weight of the intelligence and economic power of personalty.

If this were true, Beard should have eliminated the material in Chapter IV and should have produced the evidence that the personalty interests were successful because of sheer weight of intelligence and economic power. There is no evidence to substantiate this important generalization—merely Beard's statement that it was true. But if that is the important factor, not the franchise, the proper use of historical method would dictate that the author produce the evidence to back his statement.

Strange as it seems, the problem of democracy in this country before 1828 has received almost no serious attention from historians, and those who have dealt with it have sometimes been inaccurate and misleading. Many writers have been content to jump, as Beard did, from the fact that there were voting qualifications to the conclusion that a large number of men were disfranchised. Few have bothered to prospect the ground in between to see exactly how many men did or did not own enough property to be voters. It makes a great difference whether five or ninety-five per cent of the adult men could vote. Yet without this vital information, historians have built a whole interpretation of the period before Andrew Jackson on the assumption that democracy was limited.

A brief account of the work that has been done on the suffrage will perhaps explain why this fundamental problem has been neglected and why so much work still needs to be done.

Much of the blame for misconceptions about American democracy rests on a book by Albert Edward McKinley, *The Suffrage Franchise in the Thirteen English Colonies in America* (Philadelphia, 1905), and those who have misinterpreted McKinley. McKinley cited such writers as Bishop and Chandler, but Bishop merely gave the voting qualifications and Chandler assumed, but did not prove, that only a small percentage of the population could vote, although he did think that the suffrage in Virginia was more democratic than it was in New England.[7] Actually, McKinley did not attempt to ascertain the number of qualified voters in any of the colonies except Massachusetts and Pennsylvania, in both of which his estimates were either misleading or erroneous.

McKinley's treatment of Massachusetts furnishes a particularly good example of the care which must be taken in the use of secondary works. McKinley cited as his source of information an article by J. Franklin Jameson, "Did the Fathers Vote?" *New England Magazine*, New Series, I (January, 1890), 484-90. Jameson's argument was that Massachusetts was largely agricultural, that most men owned property, and that therefore few were excluded from the franchise. He estimated that twenty per cent of the people were adult men. Eliminating adult sons who were still living at home and the few men who did not have property, Jameson estimated that sixteen or seventeen per cent *of the population* could vote. Jameson really meant that sixteen or seventeen out of every twenty men were voters, which would be eighty or eighty-five per cent.

Jameson's conclusions are perfectly clear to anyone who reads the article, but McKinley did not explain what Jameson really meant. McKinley said that sixteen per cent *of the population* could vote in Massachusetts but failed to show that sixteen per cent *of the population* actually meant eighty per cent *of the adult men.* As a matter of fact, Jameson's estimate of eighty or eighty-five per cent of voters among the adult men was too low, as my own figures demonstrate, but from that day to this writers, including Beard, have cited Jameson and McKinley to prove how restricted the franchise was.

McKinley's error in colonial Pennsylvania (his pp. 287-92) was in confusing total value of property with assessed value. Voting in Pennsylvania was based on total value of property being £50, not on an assessed valuation of £50. Total value could have been as much as ten or fifteen times the assessed value, so all of McKinley's charts on Pennsylvania are worthless.

[7] Cortlandt Field Bishop, *History of Elections in the American Colonies* (New York, 1893); Julian Alvin Carroll Chandler, *The History of Suffrage in Virginia* (Baltimore, 1901).

A glance at some of the works from McKinley's time to the present shows that writers until very recent years have accepted the thesis that colonial and early American societies were undemocratic.[8] But recently there has been the beginning of a change. Several books, published within the past two years, have been written from the point of view that the suffrage was not restricted very much, although unfortunately most of these authors have failed to substantiate this generalization with adequate evidence.[9]

Interestingly enough, within the past few months two works based on the same thesis but with somewhat opposite conclusions have appeared. An article by Frederick B. Tolles on the Jameson thesis of the Revolution as a social movement raises some questions about the extent to which the Revolution was a social upheaval. Tolles also made the pertinent point that we must first discover how democratic colonial society was before we can determine how much democracy resulted from the

[8] In addition to works cited in footnote 29 on pages 18 and 19, see Frederick Albert Cleveland, *Organized Democracy; an Introduction to the Study of American Politics* (New York, 1913); Kirk Harold Porter, *A History of Suffrage in the United States* (Chicago, 1918); Homer Carey Hockett, *A Constitutional History of the United States* (New York, 1939); Harold Underwood Faulkner, *The American Way of Life: A History* (New York, 1941); Avery Odelle Craven, *Democracy in American Life: A Historical View* (Chicago, 1941); Alfred Hinsey Kelly and Winfred A. Harbison, *The American Constitution: Its Origins and Development* (New York, 1948); James Truslow Adams, *Revolutionary New England, 1691-1776* (Boston, 1923), and *New England in the Republic, 1776-1850* (Boston, 1926); Leonard Woods Labaree, *Conservatism in Early American History* (New York, 1948); Arthur Meier Schlesinger, *New Viewpoints in American History* (New York, 1922); Merrill Jensen, *The Articles of Confederation: An Interpretation of the Social-Constitutional History of the American Revolution, 1774-1781* (Madison, Wis., 1940); J. Franklin Jameson, *The American Revolution Considered as a Social Movement* (Princeton, 1926).

[9] Richard P. McCormick, *The History of Voting in New Jersey: A Study of the Development of Election Machinery* (New Brunswick, N.J., 1953); Theodore Thayer, *Pennsylvania Politics and the Growth of Democracy, 1740-1776* (Harrisburg, Pa., 1953); Robert J. Taylor, *Western Massachusetts in the Revolution* (Providence, 1954); Lee Nathaniel Newcomer, *The Embattled Farmers: A Massachusetts Countryside in the American Revolution* (New York, 1953); John A. Munroe, *Federalist Delaware, 1775-1815* (New Brunswick, N.J., 1954).

Revolution.[10] Elisha P. Douglass, on the other hand, frankly accepted the Jameson thesis at face value and based his work on the theory of an undemocratic society. Douglass did not challenge the old concept of a limited franchise.[11]

The works of two recent writers on Virginia leave the question of the franchise in that colony and state still very much of a question. Charles S. Sydnor estimated that only about one-third to one-half of the adult men were qualified voters.[12] But he also said there were only nine towns in Virginia in 1790 when as a matter of fact it is possible to count at least fifty-nine established before 1774, not to mention those established between 1774 and 1790. These towns started with between twenty-five and one hundred acres divided into half-acre lots, and many of them were added to from time to time as they grew.[13] Since voting qualifications were lowest in the towns, the whole problem of towns and town voting needs to be explored before a final answer is given to the question of voters in Virginia. Jackson T. Main has written two articles bearing on the vote in Virginia, but both Main and Sydnor neglect the town voters and also tenants who had leases and were voters.[14]

This brief survey of suffrage stresses the need for additional and detailed knowledge of the voting rights in each of the

[10] Frederick B. Tolles, "The American Revolution Considered as a Social Movement: A Re-evaluation," *American Historical Review*, LX (October, 1954), 1-12.

[11] Elisha P. Douglass, *Rebels and Democrats: The Struggle for Equal Political Rights and Majority Rule during the American Revolution* (Chapel Hill, N.C., 1955). Chapters 9, 10, and 11 on Massachusetts should be contrasted with my own work *Middle-Class Democracy and the Revolution in Massachusetts*.

[12] Charles Sackett Sydnor, *Gentlemen Freeholders: Political Practices in Washington's Virginia* (Chapel Hill, N.C., 1952), pp. 29-34.

[13] *Statutes at Large . . .*, ed. William Waller Hening, 2nd ed., 13 vols. (New York, 1823), III, 415-32; IV, 234-39; V, 106-07, 193-97, 199-202, 287-92; VI, 211, 265-66, 268-70, 273-77, 396-99; VII, 234-36, 285-86, 305-06, 406-09, 473-76, 597-601; VIII, 417, 421, 423-24, 616-19, 621-22, 665-67.

[14] Jackson Turner Main, "The Distribution of Property in Post-Revolutionary Virginia," *Mississippi Valley Historical Review*, XLI (September, 1954), 241-58, and "Sections and Politics in Virginia, 1781-1787," *William and Mary Quarterly*, 3 Series, XII (January, 1955), 96-112.

states. The Fathers thought their society was democratic and said so emphatically. My own examination of the problem in Massachusetts has proved that their conclusions were accurate for that state, the state with the highest qualifications. Until detailed research proves otherwise, then, perhaps we should accept contemporary opinion for the other states rather than unsupported estimates by modern writers.

In this chapter Beard did not prove that the voting qualifications "operated to exclude a large portion of the adult males from participating in elections." If his evidence proved anything, it proved his own statement that "the wide distribution of real property created an extensive electorate," including "the small farmers and many of the debtors," and thus in most rural regions, which was most of the country, "gave the legislatures a broad popular basis." In fact, Beard referred to page 242, where he repeated this generalization. All the evidence which I have seen substantiates this second generalization, not the first. And finally, voting and officeholding qualifications tended to favor realty, not personalty, and of course Beard recognized this when he said that the qualifications gave the vote to the most dangerous antagonists of personalty. It is unfortunate that Beard did not make these statements the basis for his general conclusions.

The major question emerging from this chapter is not how the Constitution was put over by personalty interests operating within a restricted electorate, but why it was adopted when realty was favored and when most men owned realty and were voters, according to Beard and the *Records*.

# CHAPTER V

# "THE ECONOMIC INTERESTS OF THE
# MEMBERS OF THE CONVENTION"

MANY reviewers of *An Economic Interpretation* as well as writers such as Lerner and Hofstadter have praised Chapter V as the heart of the book and the real foundation of the Beard thesis. Since so much emphasis has been placed on Beard's historical method in his Chapter V, a detailed survey of the chapter is essential. What he was attempting to do was to see whether the men in the Convention possessed the kind of personal property that would be increased in value or made more secure by their efforts in Philadelphia. On page 149 he concluded that "at least five-sixths, were immediately, directly, and personally interested in the outcome of their labors at Philadelphia."

At the risk of becoming tedious, I have followed his delegate-by-delegate approach to see whether his evidence actually justifies his generalization about the men in the Convention. While such an approach may not lend itself to fascinating reading, it is the only way to test Beard's historical method.

Before we start this delegate-by-delegate marathon, however, we should note Beard's denial of purpose on page 73. Here he said his aim was not "to show that the Constitution was made for the personal benefit of the members of the Convention" or "to discover how many hundred thousand dollars accrued to them as a result of the foundation of the new government." Yet he concluded on pages 17, 18, and 149, and in many other places in the book, that the delegates were not disinterested spectators and that they stood to gain by the new government. Furthermore, on pages 35-37 he went to great lengths to prove that the holders of public securities alone, and this included many delegates, stood to gain $40,000,000 by the adoption of the Constitution. The author should have been more consistent. Either the delegates were working for their own interests or they were not.

One other general criticism is essential before we analyze the main thesis of this chapter. In a footnote on page 75, Beard said he was assuming that when a member appeared on the funding books for redemption of public securities under the new government, the member was a public creditor in 1787 at the time of the Convention and had not purchased public securities for speculative purposes. The assumption appears to be unwarranted. Why would members of the Convention not buy public securities for speculation since anyone else could do so and there was no law against it? In fact, one might be surprised if they had abstained, especially if we assume that men act predominantly from economic motives. At the very least, this is one of the problems that Beard should have solved—whether the members of the Convention possessed what public securities they possessed at the time of the Convention, or whether they bought public securities later with the expectation that the value would increase.

Abraham Baldwin of Georgia had $2,500, probably in Continental paper, but there is no record of his holdings before April, 1792, so there is no way of telling whether he owned this in 1787 or bought it after the Constitution was adopted. Beard did not say what Baldwin held in real estate, so Baldwin as evidence proves nothing.

Richard Bassett of Delaware owned Bohemia Manor, an estate of 6,000 acres, as well as homes in Wilmington and Dover. There is no evidence that he held any public paper in 1787, and he held only a few hundred dollars' worth in 1796 and 1797. If anything, Bassett represented realty rather than personalty.

Gunning Bedford of Delaware was the son of a substantial landowner. The £16 tax paid by a Bedford of that name might well have represented considerable property if the tax meant 1*d.* on the pound of rating as it often did. This would mean a rateable estate of £3,840 and an actual estate of several times this amount. We do not even know whether in 1787 he still had the £400 certificate which he bought in 1779. Bedford proves nothing, but the odds would be in favor of realty.

74

John Blair of Virginia was apparently a man of some fortune, but Beard did not indicate whether it was realty or personalty. The record shows only £249 in paper before the writing and adoption of the Constitution, which would have been a very minor holding if he were a man of some fortune. What he did after the Constitution went into effect is not evidence, for many a man who opposed the Constitution bought government securities under the new government. We would need to know more about Blair's property to catalogue him, but £249 would not make him a large holder of personalty, so he does not prove much.

William Blount of North Carolina was the son of a man who owned a large estate, but we know nothing of Blount's property interests in 1787. Again, what he did after 1790 proves nothing for 1787. If he had large private means in Tennessee later, and had no securities, his wealth was probably in realty.

David Brearley of New Jersey had a grandfather who owned 1,600 acres near Newton, a 100-acre plantation in Delaware, and several thousand acres near Lawrenceville. How much of this Brearley inherited we do not know, but he had only a small amount of securities. The attempt to include Brearley's relatives proves nothing, for they, too, held few securities. The reader should note that much of Beard's information on Brearley came from secondary works, not sources, and that this is true throughout his account of the other delegates.

Jacob Broom of Delaware was the son of a blacksmith who rose to be one of the gentry—some evidence of economic democracy at work—and who had considerable substance in real estate, silver, and gold. Broom had lands and houses to rent and sell and money to lend on good security. What he did after 1787 is of no consequence, and from what we know of him before 1787, we could not put him definitely on the side of realty or personalty.

Pierce Butler was a gentleman of fortune from South Carolina, but the evidence does not prove that this fortune was personalty. His thirty-one slaves would suggest real estate, and he could easily have purchased securities after 1787 with which to buy United States Bank stock. That Butler was descended from the Duke of Ormond is irrelevant to the question of whether or not he owned personal property.

Daniel Carroll of Maryland had some securities, but Beard did not say what their value was. That Carroll made his chief profit out of the new system by selling land on which the capitol at Washington was located would support the notion of a realty rather than a personalty interest. But even so, Beard would have had to prove that Carroll knew in 1787 that the capitol was going to be located on his land. The $5,000 in paper recorded after 1790 proves nothing for 1787.

George Clymer of Pennsylvania is the first of the ten delegates discussed to this point who seems to have had a large personalty holding. But the fact that he held $3,000 worth of securities in 1791 does not prove what he held in 1787, and of course Beard did not say what realty Clymer owned. If the records do not tell us, we cannot "assume" that Clymer held deferred and funded securities and thus had over $10,000 worth of government paper.

William R. Davie of North Carolina owned a fine plantation at Tivoli and had close connections with the landed proprietors of his region, but Beard did not represent him as the owner of any personalty whatever. Davie's ability to pay $5,000 for a thoroughbred colt probably indicated an interest in improving his livestock. It is not evidence that he favored personalty over realty.

Jonathan Dayton of New Jersey speculated with associates in western lands. If Beard is correct, however, Dayton is a good example of a speculator who should not have wanted the Constitution. The speculators had agreed to pay for part of their land in certificates, the prices of which went up after the adoption of the Constitution, causing the speculators much financial hardship. So Dayton does not prove much for personalty, and his later activities mean nothing for 1787. What a man did in speculation in 1800 is quite a different problem from that of his holdings in 1787.

John Dickinson of Delaware was a member of one of the "established landed families," which ought to have put him on the side of realty. The description of his wife's father's house is strictly irrelevant information and does not in any way show how many securities Dickinson held—in fact, the house is just more realty. Beard admitted that there was no evidence whatever of Dickinson's personalty interests.

Oliver Ellsworth of Connecticut bought lands and houses, loaned money at interest, and in 1791 had some $6,000 in government securities. But we do not know whether he had these securities in 1787 or bought them for speculation between 1787 and 1791. We have no comparison of his realty and personalty, and all the irrelevant material from Brown's *Life of Ellsworth* does not resolve the problem.

William Few of Georgia was a small farmer who practiced law and acquired a plantation, and, as Beard said, his personal interest in the new government was probably rather small. Later he presented $2,170 in securities for funding, but he had purchased this amount from someone else. Beard did not indicate when he made the purchase, whether before or after 1787, for the fact that a certificate was of the 1779 issue does not mean that he bought it in 1779.

Thomas Fitzsimons of Pennsylvania combined mercantile and financial interests, so he could be put down as the second delegate clearly on the side of personalty. But his losses in the Robert Morris speculations do not support the view that the speculators gained by the Constitution, or that they were certain ahead of time that the new government was going to operate in their interests.

Benjamin Franklin was worth about $150,000, and at the beginning of the war he had loaned the government about £3,000 which had depreciated and which he hoped would increase in value under the new government (p. xiv). Just what the remainder of his property was is not clear, so Franklin as evidence proves nothing. In the Convention he was definitely on the side of the common people, so even if we proved that the bulk of his property was personalty, we could not use him as evidence that the Convention was rigging a government to favor personalty.

Nicholas Gilman of New Hampshire was a third delegate who definitely had personalty interests of consequence before the adoption of the Constitution. Far from working for a particular class, however, Gilman urged every town in New Hampshire to buy up public paper for a possible increase in price if the Constitution were adopted. We do not know what his realty holdings were, making it impossible to compare these with his personalty. Gilman's actions might well be considered economic, but they do not bolster a particular brand of economic determinism which pits personalty against realty.

Elbridge Gerry of Massachusetts was undoubtedly a large holder of public securities, some of them purchased before the Convention. The debates also show that he was interested in protecting the interests of public security holders—not only the wealthy ones, but also the soldiers who had been forced to sell their securities. Gerry believed that the new government should *be obliged* to pay off the debts of the Confederation government, not simply *have the power* to pay them. But as Beard pointed out, here was a man who was obviously a security holder, yet he opposed the Constitution. We also know that Gerry's father was a large holder of real estate, and we would need to know what Gerry himself had in realty to make a fair judgment. But even if we place him among the personalty interests, his presence there is of dubious value, since he opposed the Constitution and gave many reasons for his opposition, most of them noneconomic.[1]

Nathaniel Gorham of Massachusetts was a speculator in western lands in April, 1788, when the Constitution had already been ratified by several states, though there is no evidence that he had much in personalty before the Convention met. But Gorham is another example of a land speculator who did not understand what effect the Constitution was going to have. In April, 1788, Gorham and others contracted for a large tract of land for which they were to pay $1,000,000 in three annual installments in Massachusetts scrip, which was still selling below par at that time. When the price of the scrip went up, the speculators—including Robert Morris, who also was at the

[1] *Debates and Proceedings of the Convention of the Commonwealth of Massachusetts, Held in the Year 1788, and Which Finally Ratified the Constitution of the United States* (Boston, 1856), pp. 24-26.

Convention—suffered disastrous losses. But this speculation came after the Convention, not before, and the speculators did not prove to be good prognosticators.

Alexander Hamilton of New York, as Beard said, had little to do with the formation of the Constitution. But Beard nevertheless made Hamilton the colossus of the new system, the man who saw the economic interests necessary for the success of the new government and who shaped his policies for their benefit. There are weaknesses in Beard's arguments, however. One is that Hamilton did not get a protective tariff for manufacturers, as his report on manufactures in 1791 proves. The second is that the very land speculators who were supposedly helped by Hamilton's policies went bankrupt, evidence that they did not know how the new system would operate. Beard said that thousands of small farmers and debtors and laboring mechanics were opposed to Hamilton's policies, but that they were partly disfranchised and had no leadership. But again, as Beard said before, workingmen in the cities supported the Constitution, and farmers and debtors were in control of state legislatures. What these groups did after Hamilton's policies were adopted is another story, just as the election of Hoover in 1928 and his defeat in 1932 are two different stories. Furthermore, Beard admitted that Hamilton had only about $800 in securities, and that he did not profit personally from the new government. In fact, said Beard, it must be admitted that Hamilton was swayed "by large policies of government," not by personal interests. Does this mean that even the "colossal genius of the new system" actually acted from "principles" rather than from personal economic interests?

William C. Houston of New Jersey, a professor and lawyer, had no public securities apparently and had invested £20 in a land speculation venture. As evidence of either realty or personalty he is therefore worthless.

William Houstoun of Georgia is similarly worthless as evidence, for nothing is known of his holdings.

Jared Ingersoll of Pennsylvania also had no personalty interests which would benefit by the Constitution, and Beard did not give his realty interests.

Daniel of St. Thomas Jenifer of Maryland was a slaveowner and had at least two plantations. Beard's statement that he "probably" held a small amount of public securities is not evidence, so Jenifer must be counted among the realty interests. That his son Daniel had $6,000 in paper in 1790 does not prove that his father had it in 1787.

William Samuel Johnson of Connecticut cannot be placed in either category, real or personal. That he probably speculated in government securities through his son after the Constitution was adopted proves nothing.

Rufus King of Massachusetts probably had both realty and personalty, and his activities after the Constitution was adopted mean nothing for 1787.

John Langdon of New Hampshire could hardly be accused of operating from economic determinist motives, for win or lose, he was willing to put all of his property behind the Revolution. Beard's evidence on Langdon's security transactions, as with most of the men he dealt with, applies after the adoption of the Constitution, not in 1787. Like Gilman, Langdon wanted his state to benefit by acquiring securities.

John Lansing of New York funded over $7,000 in securities in 1791, but Beard did not say what he had in 1787, or what his realty interests were. In addition, Lansing opposed the Constitution, so even if he had $7,000 in securities in 1787, he could not be used as evidence for the influence of personalty. For future reference, the reader should note Beard's statement that Lansing was at the Convention "long enough however to learn (what was not a very deep secret) the certain effect of an efficient government on continental securities" (p. 123).

William Livingston of New Jersey had no securities as far as we know. What his son did in speculation after the Constitution was adopted does not prove anything, for even the men who opposed the Constitution took advantage of opportunities under the Constitution. If we can try to prove guilt by association, as Beard does by saying that some delegates married merchants' daughters, then Livingston should have favored the landed interests, because his wife's father had been a large proprietor of land. Both propositions are invalid, of course, unless backed by evidence.

James Madison of Virginia obviously belongs under realty, and judging by his disillusionment after the Constitution was adopted, he apparently was not aware of the results which the Constitution would produce. He soon became one of the chief architects of the party which opposed the Federalist interpretation of the Constitution.

Alexander Martin of North Carolina, a well-to-do planter and slave owner, should obviously be placed on the side of realty, for, as Beard said, his tastes did not turn to dealings in public securities, with neither the Treasury Department records nor those of North Carolina listing his name.

Luther Martin of Maryland affords an interesting study in the use of historical method. Because he sympathized with poor debtors and opposed the complete exclusion of paper money, Martin was a bitter opponent of the Constitution. Beard described Martin as owning "only six slaves" and holding public securities which "were apparently meagre—a few thousand dollars at most." Beard appeared to be playing down Martin's holdings in securities, since Martin opposed the Constitution, yet these same holdings were larger than those of the other men discussed by Beard. Martin's securities were also as of June, 1791, not as of 1787.

George Mason of Virginia was a large landowner and land speculator, married the daughter of a well-to-do Maryland merchant (which should have made him pro-personalty), but also opposed the Constitution. Mason's 300 slaves were by far the most enumerated by Beard for any member of the Convention. With $80,000 in personalty and debts due, and large areas of western land, he ought to have been an ardent supporter of the Constitution. Beard explained his opposition on the ground that the Constitution would restore British titles to land, which could certainly have been true; but that was not the only reason for Mason's opposition. As the debates in the Virginia ratifying convention show, his chief objection was that the Constitution would establish a national government which he feared would annihilate the state governments and threaten

81

the rights of the people. Particular items included powers of Congress over taxation, elections, and the military; lack of rotation in office for the president; failure to separate the functions of president and Senate; and absence of checks on the treaty-making powers.[1a]

James McClurg of Virginia was another example of the use of evidence after the Constitution was adopted presumably to prove something for 1787. This time, however, Beard admitted that most of the securities which he presented at the loan office had been bought for speculation and were not an original purchase. The same could easily have been true for most of Beard's examples, since most of his evidence comes from the period after 1790.

James McHenry of Maryland had both real and personal property, but there is no evidence, as Beard said, that he was an original holder of securities. If he had a debt of £5,000 due to him, and it was secured by bond, he should not have been interested in a government that would raise prices. What McHenry proves is difficult to say, except that he owned property of various kinds.

John Francis Mercer of Maryland is another example of the curious use Beard made of evidence. As mentioned before in dealing with Luther Martin, Beard said Martin's fortune was never very large for he owned "only six slaves" and had a "meagre" holding of at most a few thousand dollars in securities. But Beard changed his tone in speaking of Mercer. Mercer, he wrote, was "a man of some fortune," for he held "six slaves, and a moderate amount of public securities." Actually Beard should have attempted to show that neither owned any personalty, for they both opposed the Constitution.

Thomas Mifflin of Pennsylvania is still another example of misused evidence. Having said that Mifflin held only a "petty sum" of a few hundred dollars in Continental paper in common with Jonathan Mifflin, Beard then concluded that, on the basis

[1a] Jonathan Elliot, *The Debates of the Several State Conventions . . .* , 5 vols. (Washington, 1854), iii, 29-34, 262-72, 378-81, 402-05, 415-16, 425-26, 431-32, 441-42, 452-53, 472-73, 479-80, 484-85, 493-94, 496-97, 507-09, 521-30.

of this evidence, it was apparent Mifflin appreciated the position of the powerful class of security holders who looked to the Convention for relief, and that Mifflin had more than an abstract interest in the establishment of public credit. If Martin with a few *thousand* dollars' worth of securities did not appreciate the position of the security holders, why would a few *hundred* dollars' worth necessarily incline Mifflin in that direction? Perhaps Mifflin's interests were identified with those of artisans who also wanted protection for manufacturing.

Gouverneur Morris of Pennsylvania belonged to the "landed aristocracy" and did not hold any public securities. According to the Beard thesis, he should have opposed the Constitution, but he did not.

There can be little doubt from Beard's account that Robert Morris of Pennsylvania had varied economic interests, or that he was a large holder of personalty. We do not know how much he held, or what the relative weight of his personalty and realty interests were, but even so, if Beard could have proved that all the men in the Convention were Robert Morrises, his thesis would doubtless have been on pretty firm ground. There are no contradictions in the evidence, there is no reason to question the conclusions drawn from this evidence, and the *Records* tell us nothing. There is one problem with regard to Morris, however. Beard gives us the impression that these men in the Convention wanted a government that would help them in their speculative ventures, yet Robert Morris ended his career in poverty and debt after having served a term in a debtors' prison. We could account for this if the Antifederalists had controlled the new government and had adopted policies inimical to the interests of the speculators. Did Morris, like other speculators, promise to pay for western land in securities that rose in value, thus indicating that he did not know how the new government was going to affect economic conditions?

William Paterson of New Jersey was for a time a merchant, but Beard could find out little about his economic interests.

William Pierce of Georgia was likewise evidence for nothing in particular, since we know little about him.

Charles Cotesworth Pinckney of South Carolina, a lawyer and a "considerable" landholder in Charleston, had a country estate and forty-five slaves. His holdings of public securities after the funding system prove nothing, for they could have been original holdings or securities purchased for speculation between 1787 and 1791.

Charles Pinckney of South Carolina was also a large land and slave owner, which would place him on the side of realty. He was the man who pictured American society as particularly democratic, both economically and politically, in his long speech in the Convention, and who believed that all the Convention had to do was to design a reasonably stable government to fit this democratic society.

Edmund Randolph of Virginia furnishes another example of a curious use of evidence. Randolph's grandfather was Sir John Randolph, which seems irrelevant, and we do not know how burdened with debt the three farms, Negroes, and other property were which he inherited. Beard said that Randolph was apparently never very prosperous, yet he enjoyed a magnificent law practice which brought in considerable revenue, held £14,200 Virginia currency in money claims in 1801, and had 7,000 acres of land, several houses, nearly 200 slaves, and ten or fifteen thousand dollars' worth of public securities. Just what a man had to have to be prosperous Beard did not say, but it is interesting to note the contrast with Mercer, who was "a man of some fortune" with six slaves and a moderate amount of public securities, and Pierce Butler, who, with thirty-one slaves, was a gentleman of fortune. Randolph's refusal to sell his excess slaves might well have meant that economic motives were not the only ones. The letter to Hamilton (p. 140) does not necessarily mean that he owed Hamilton a considerable sum. It would appear likelier that Hamilton was negotiating the sale of some of Randolph's securities, for Randolph wanted to sell only a part of his holdings, the remainder to be kept for a rise in price. Beard failed to say that Randolph was one of the delegates who refused to sign the Constitution after it had been accepted by the

Convention, but perhaps this refusal accounts for his efforts to disparage Randolph's wealth.

George Read of Delaware was not a wealthy man. He owned a small farm and some slaves, and the records show that he invested $2,000 in securities in 1779, the darkest days of the Revolution and the days when the chances of getting back his money were at the lowest ebb. What he proves is difficult to say, for his farm might easily have been worth more than his securities.

John Rutledge of South Carolina was a plantation owner and had no securities. He should have opposed the Constitution if we follow the Beard interpretation to its logical conclusion.

Roger Sherman of Connecticut cannot be catalogued on the basis of Beard's evidence, for his securities were funded after Hamilton's program and there is no way of knowing from this account when he bought them or what he owned in realty.

Richard Dobbs Spaight of North Carolina was definitely on the side of realty, for he was "among the large planters of his state," held seventy-one slaves, and did not engage in public security transactions. But in spite of this, Beard pictured him as a supporter of personalty on the ground that "an old account of 3 per cents *for the sum of a few dollars*, shows that he was not unaware of the relations of public credit to stable institutions" (p. 143, italics mine). Just what such evidence shows about Spaight is anyone's guess.

Caleb Strong of Massachusetts likewise proves nothing, for he, too, could have purchased securities after the funding program seemed assured. Strong came from middle-class, agricultural Northampton, and the many members of the Strong family were ordinary middle-class farmers, as the tax records show.

Washington was undoubtedly the key figure in the whole movement for the Constitution. Without his prestige, there might not have been a Constitution, so we should be especially interested in Washington's holdings from the standpoint of the Beard thesis that personalty was the dynamic element. And it does not take more than a glance to see that Washington's wealth was overwhelmingly on the side of realty.

Much of Washington's western holdings had been acquired before the Revolution started. In 1754 Governor Dinwiddie of Virginia issued a proclamation granting lands to officers and soldiers who would enlist for the campaign against the French.[2] Before this land was actually granted, however, the British during the French and Indian War decided to stop all grants of land in the area.[3] This decision was reinforced by the well-known British Proclamation of 1763 dealing with governments, land, and Indians in the West, but the latter also provided for land grants to officers and soldiers who had served during the war. Field officers, of whom Washington was one, were to receive 5,000 acres.[4] In 1770 the grant of 1754 still had not been made, and many officers were selling their shares for a pittance, both because the grant itself seemed so uncertain and because they would have to invest a good deal of money to improve their lands in order to fulfill the terms of the grant. Washington was willing to gamble that the grant would eventually materialize, so he set out to buy twelve or fifteen thousand acres of these officers' grants at from £5 to £7 a thousand acres.[5] In 1771 the Governor and Council finally decided on a division of the 1754 grant, of which Washington received 15,000 acres.[6]

Washington's letters indicate that the grant would probably never have been made at all except for his persistent efforts and expenditure of money, and even then it took nearly twenty years. How much he bought in addition to the 20,000 acres he had coming as an officer would require further study, but in

[2] *Statutes at Large . . .*, ed. William Waller Hening, 2nd ed., 13 vols. (New York, 1823), vii, 661-62.

[3] *Journals of the House of Burgesses of Virginia, 1758-1761*, one of 13 vols., ed. H. R. McIlwaine and J. P. Kennedy (Richmond, 1905-15), pp. 283-84; *Acts of the Privy Council of England, Colonial Series*, ed. W. L. Grant and James Munro, 6 vols. (Hereford and London, 1908-12), iv, 475, 500, 544.

[4] Hening, *Statutes*, vii, 663-69. The Proclamation of 1763 may also be found in *Documents of American History*, ed. Henry Steele Commager, 3rd ed. (New York, 1943), pp. 47-50.

[5] Washington to Charles Washington, January 31, 1770, *The Writings of George Washington . . ., 1745-1799*, ed. John Fitzpatrick, 39 vols. (Washington, 1931-41), iii, 2.

[6] Washington to George Mercer, November 7, 1771, *ibid.*, p. 69.

1773 he was advertising that he had 20,000 acres on the Ohio which he would lease rent-free for a number of years to a tenant who would build on the land and clear a certain amount.[7] From this time until the Revolution, Washington worked feverishly to improve his land so that he could save it according to the terms of his grant. His aim was to get settlers on the land, not just to hold the land for a rise in price.[8] In fact, Washington bought, but very seldom sold, both land and slaves.

This account furnishes the background for an analysis of Beard's figures. These are for 1799, and as Washington never ceased acquiring property, they would necessarily have to be reduced somewhat to get the true amount in 1787. Even so, if we take the figures as they stand, we find that Washington owned 45,404 acres of land in addition to real estate in Washington, Alexandria, Winchester, and Bath, and that this real estate was valued at $266,819. Of personal property he held only $25,212. Using these figures alone, Washington's realty was 91.6 per cent and his personalty 9.4 per cent, or an advantage of nearly ten to one in favor of realty. In addition, however, we would need to add to the realty the $15,653 in livestock and the tremendous value of his slaves, for his total property amounted to $530,000. As I have said before, and as Beard acknowledged, slaves on plantations must be considered a part of realty. With these figures, the preponderance of realty over personalty is 95.44 to 4.56 per cent. If we emphasize government securities, as we shall see that Beard did, the ratio is 1.17 per cent for securities to 98.83 per cent for realty.

Washington had many financial interests, it is true, but these figures prove beyond doubt that his main economic interest was realty and agriculture, not personalty. No one can read the Washington *Diaries* without coming to this conclusion.[9] So the key figure in the whole move for the Constitution was on the side of realty—the wrong side according to the Beard interpretation.

[7] *Ibid.*, pp. 144-46.     [8] *Ibid.*, pp. 199-204, 280-83, 498-99.
[9] *The Diaries of George Washington, 1748-1799*, ed. John C. Fitzpatrick, 4 vols. (Boston and New York, 1925), I and II, passim.

A few minor points should be noted in Beard's treatment of Washington. If Washington was in arrears two years on back taxes because he could not sell his farm products, he must have been a debtor and he also must have been interested in doing something that would benefit agriculture. Furthermore, even the richest man in the country had been obliged to sell his certificates at the rate of twenty to one. On page 38 Beard made the unsupported statement that the Society of the Cincinnati, representing officers of some means, had not been forced to sacrifice their certificates as had the poor private soldiers. Yet Washington, the richest man, had sacrificed his certificates.

Hugh Williamson of North Carolina might well be placed on the side of personalty because of his mercantile activities, his $2,444.84 worth of securities, and his speculation in western lands. The securities, which of course could have been purchased between 1787 and 1791, were no more than those possessed by some men who opposed the Constitution, and Beard did not say what other realty interests Williamson had. But if Williamson's western lands would be enhanced in value by the new government, so would the lands owned by anyone else in the West.

James Wilson of Pennsylvania proves little, for most of the evidence on his activities came after the Constitution was adopted. Just what his stock in the Insurance Company of North America, 1792, or his speculations in Georgia land in 1795 have to do with 1787 is a problem that Beard did not explain. The only thing that counts is what he had in 1787, and Beard admitted that Wilson had only a "trivial" amount of securities.

George Wythe of Virginia is another example of realty rather than personalty interests. He inherited and married realty, and had only £513 of Virginia certificates which he had purchased from their original owners. His emancipation of his slaves and his provision for their future could mean that men had other than economic motives for their actions, for Wythe could certainly have sold his slaves.

Robert Yates of New York refused to enrich himself by speculating in confiscated estates, took no part in the transactions of public securities, and died poor. He also opposed the Constitution, so he really proves nothing as far as the Beard interpretation is concerned.

Having reviewed all this evidence on the economic holdings of the Convention delegates, the important question is whether Beard's historical method justified his conclusions that personal property was responsible for the Constitution. The answer must be an emphatic no. If we forget Beard's own generalizations and consider only his evidence, we find that actually only six delegates had personal property in excess of their realty (Clymer, Fitzsimons, Gilman, Gerry, Robert Morris, and Williamson), and further research into their holdings might show that even some of these held more realty than personalty. Two of these are of questionable value as evidence, Gilman because he presumably wanted farmers as well as personalty interests to benefit, and Gerry because he opposed the Constitution in spite of his holdings. In contrast with these six, and again strictly on the basis of Beard's evidence, eighteen delegates definitely had realty which greatly outweighed their personalty (Bassett, Bedford, Blount, Carroll, Davie, Dickinson, Few, Jenifer, Madison, Alexander Martin, Mason, Gouverneur Morris, Charles Cotesworth Pinckney, Charles Pinckney, Rutledge, Spaight, Washington, and Wythe). The other thirty (Baldwin, Blair, Brearley, Broom, Butler, Dayton, Ellsworth, Franklin, Gorham, Hamilton, Houston, Houstoun, Ingersoll, Johnson, King, Langdon, Lansing, Livingston, Luther Martin, McClurg, McHenry, Mercer, Mifflin, Paterson, Pierce, Randolph, Read, Sherman, Strong, and Wilson) really prove nothing in particular on the basis of Beard's evidence, for even he could not tell what these men had in the way of economic goods.

In evaluating Beard's historical methods, other criticisms mentioned in connection with the discussion of these various men should be summarized here. There is much material about their lives and background which is either irrelevant or the relevancy of which has not been made clear. A tremendous amount of Beard's material in this chapter comes from second-ary writers, not primary sources, including a great deal from uncritical biographers of the delegates. While much of the material on securities was taken from the Treasury records, most of it refers to holdings several years after the Convention met. We have seen that several of these men acquired their securities after the Convention, so we cannot assume, as Beard did, that they held these when the Convention met.

Anyone would concede that the Founding Fathers had education, property, and influence far greater than the average at that time, but the same would be true of colonial legislatures, the Confederation Congress, and legislatures today. Had Beard cited this evidence to prove that the Convention delegates represented property in general and were interested in a government which would protect property, he would have been on firm ground. All of the delegates believed in the sanctity of property; some even believed that the chief function of government was the protection of property. This was undoubtedly important, but it was not their only concern. Beard did not contend, however, that the Convention was rigged to protect property *in general.* What he emphasized was *personalty,* and in fact, a particular kind of personalty which did not include livestock and slaves. We shall see later that he even refined personal property to mean predominantly one kind of personal property—public securities.

In addition to the fact that the evidence in this chapter does not prove the predominance of personalty, the big criticism of this particular economic interpretation is the ease with which Beard dismissed the agricultural interest. Does this mean that farmers had no economic interests? Would a politician in the predominantly agricultural states of North and South Dakota ignore the farm vote in his state? Yet in 1787 all the states were more agricultural than the Dakotas.

As Shays' Rebellion and Washington's inability to pay his taxes demonstrated, the farmers as well as the holders of personalty were not enjoying prosperous times. Why not assume that perhaps they, too, expected conditions to be better under the new government? And why draw such a sharp distinction between realty and various forms of personalty? A man who owns realty is not necessarily less interested in his property than anyone else. The simple fact is that the farmers cannot be ignored in the adoption of the Constitution, for as we shall see, some of the most heavily agricultural states adopted the Constitution the most quickly and by the most nearly unanimous vote. He who leaves the farmers out of the picture of the Constitution is treading on thin ice indeed, especially when such an important man as Washington was so obviously on the side of realty.

# CHAPTER VI

# "THE CONSTITUTION AS AN
# ECONOMIC DOCUMENT"

---

HAVING proved to his own satisfaction that the delegates to the Convention were the representatives of personalty, Beard then went on to show that the Constitution was fundamentally an economic rather than a political document, designed above all else to protect personalty from the leveling attacks of democracy. The true nature of the Constitution is not apparent on the surface, he said, for it contains no property qualifications for voting and does not outwardly recognize economic groups or confer special class privileges. Only if we study the newspapers and correspondence of the time, or read *The Federalist* or the debates in the Convention, do we begin to understand the true nature of the Constitution. Our understanding is broadened by a study of such items as the structure of government or the balance of power, powers conferred on the federal government and denied the state governments, and the economics of international politics. These will convince us, said Beard, that the Constitution was not a piece of abstract legislation reflecting no group interests or economic antagonisms. It was "an economic document drawn with superb skill by men whose property interests were immediately at stake; and as such it appealed directly and unerringly to identical interests in the country at large" (p. 188).

We have already had occasion to note Beard's questionable use of Madison and *The Federalist* No. 10, but we need to examine more fully his interpretation of *The Federalist* in this chapter because he relied much on this source for his interpretation. Here, declared Beard, is presented in relatively brief and systematic form an economic interpretation of the Constitution by the men best qualified to expound the political science of the new government. In fact, he said, *The Federalist* was "the finest study in the economic interpretation of politics which exists in any language." When we combine this with his previous opinion that Madison's political philosophy in No. 10 was "a masterly statement of the theory of economic determinism in politics" (p. 15), we begin to appreciate Beard's concept of the importance of *The Federalist.*

The first question to be answered then is whether *The Federalist* presents merely an "economic interpretation of politics." Can Jay's arguments on the need for a stronger union as protection from foreign enemies, presented in Nos. 2 to 5, be considered strictly economic? Was the danger of civil war between the states, as expounded by Hamilton, all due to economic causes? Is an appeal for the preservation of liberty and justice simply an appeal to man's economic instincts? Were all the criticisms of the Confederation and all the attempts to allay fears about the form and powers of the new government or freedom of the press purely economic?

My answer to these questions is no, and I have little doubt that anyone who reads *The Federalist* without a propensity for the economic interpretation of history would find many noneconomic arguments in this document. This is not to deny that Hamilton, Madison, and Jay appealed to economic interests. On the contrary, there were many such appeals, as there naturally would be to a people the vast majority of whom were middle-class property owners. But nationalism and the fear of foreign domination can have a much broader appeal than merely the economic, and especially to a people who have just emerged from under British imperialism. We know there are people who have some concern over whether or not they have a voice in the selection of their governors, a matter certainly connected with the form of government. There have been studies showing that laboring men support their unions not merely because the unions work for better wages and hours, but also because they help to give the worker status as a human being. How much simpler life would be if people did operate strictly from economic motives.

But even if we granted that *The Federalist* appealed only to the economic man, which, of course, we do not, this still would not support the Beard thesis that *personal* property was responsible for the Constitution. If he had said that Hamilton, Madison, and Jay based their appeal on the protection of *property in general*, Beard would have been correct as far as he went. There are appeals to economic interests, *all kinds* of economic interests—merchants, farmers, moneylenders, land speculators, artisans, everybody. Hamilton, Madison, and Jay were astute politicians. They knew then, just as politicians know now, that a winning combination under popular government must appeal to many groups and many interests. They were too astute to think that the Constitution could be adopted by an appeal to only 3.7 per cent of the country's property, even if the appeal had been all economic. But as I have said before, why would farmers not be interested in expanded markets for their products, or in a government that could open western lands for settlement and the Mississippi as an outlet for western products? And why would artisans and mechanics not vote for a government that would protect them from foreign competition? But all this is not to say that *The Federalist* appealed only to economic instincts, and especially that it appealed only to personalty interests.

Then we return again to Beard's version of Madison's political philosophy in *The Federalist* No. 10 as the underlying political science of the Constitution. Madison *did say* that the most important function of government was to protect the diversity in the faculties of men, from which the rights of property originate, but he *did not say*, as the Beard thesis does, that the only property to be protected was personal property. Madison divided society both horizontally into those with and without property and vertically into various kinds of property interests, such as a landed interest, a moneyed interest, a manufacturing interest, a mercantile interest, and many others. In other words, he assumed not that these personalty interests would combine against agriculture, but that each had its own objectives and must be protected from the predatory actions of the others. This ability to ignore the influence of the landed interest and what it wanted by way of property protection was one of Beard's greatest failures. Furthermore, Madison was talking about the future, when there would be a landless proletariat; not about 1787, when the small farmers dominated the country.

A second point about Madison, as I have said before, is that he was not an economic determinist in *The Federalist* No. 10. He believed that there were many reasons for conflicts in society—religious differences, attachments to different leaders and different political ideas, and even frivolous contentions—and that the purpose of government was to control all these conflicting groups, whether religious, political, economic, or other. If this had not been true, Madison should have remained a Federalist rather than becoming a Republican.

In the light of Beard's emphasis on *The Federalist* No. 10, it is of some consequence to see what Madison believed as revealed by his statements in the Constitutional Convention and elsewhere. On occasion he talked of horizontal divisions in society—creditor vs. debtor, rich vs. poor—but in the same breath he included other divisions—followers of different demagogues and different religions, as well as landed, mercantile, manufacturing, and moneyed interests. Especially he said the landed interest oppressed the mercantile interest, and holders of one species of property oppressed holders of other species.[1] In speaking of the rich and poor, however, he said he was talking about a future day when American society would resemble that of Europe, not about society as it existed in 1787.[2] In fact, he claimed that the divisions in American society in 1787 were vertical rather than horizontal. The country was divided into three classes, the landed, commercial, and manufacturing, he said, with the latter two being very small compared with the landed interest. Farmers had more in common with each other, regardless of where they lived in the country, than they did with merchants or manufacturers, even if the latter were the farmer's neighbors. Each group had its rights, and the interests of one should not be sacrificed to the interests of another.[3] Or again he declared that the landed

---

[1] *The Records of the Federal Convention of 1787*, ed. Max Farrand, 4 vols. (New Haven, 1937), I, 108, 135, 421-23.
[2] *Ibid.*, pp. 421-23.    [3] *Ibid.*, II, 124.

interest was predominant, and should retain the power to check other groups when in the future America resembled Europe and had a propertyless laboring class.[4] This does not look like special consideration for personalty.

Sometimes Madison talked in terms of regional or sectional conflicts, in which apparently he thought that the various interests of one section combined to oppose similar interests in another section. He spoke of the division of eastern, middle, and southern states, or of commercial and noncommercial states.[5] He even believed that people would have attachments to their states, and that therefore there was a conflict of interests between large and small states.[6] But then he contradicted himself by saying that states had different manners, habits, and prejudices (all of which might be noneconomic), which prevented the combination of large states such as Massachusetts, Pennsylvania, and Virginia.[7] In short, Madison included many of the ideas found in *The Federalist*—all eighty-five numbers of it.

Having enumerated all these divisions in society, Madison finally got around to what he considered the most fundamental of all—and the one which actually proved to be the most fundamental. This was the division between slave and free states, between North and South. He contended that the states were divided in interests depending on whether or not they had slaves. The North against the South formed the great division in the United States, he said, and the great danger to the general government was this opposition of great northern and southern interests, as the sectional voting in Congress had demonstrated.[8] Later he declared that he had always conceived the great difference of interests in the United States to be between the two sections.[9] And finally he went so far as to say that it was pretty well understood in the Convention that the real difference of interests lay not between large and small states but between northern and southern, with the institu-

[4] *Ibid.*, I, 431; II, 124.    [5] *Ibid.*, I, 146.    [6] *Ibid.*, III, 125.
[7] *Ibid.*, I, 146, 321-22, 447-48.    [8] *Ibid.*, p. 486.
[9] *Ibid.*, p. 601.

tion of slavery and its consequences forming the line of demarcation.[10]

So we can use Madison to prove many things, in addition to what Beard said he proved. Given the Civil War, it would be better to use him as a basis for a political philosophy of sectionalism rather than economic class determinism.

Even if Beard had used No. 10 accurately, he would still have had to show that it was more important to the people at the time than the other eighty-four numbers of *The Federalist*. Perhaps some of the farmers actually believed that a stronger government would benefit them, as *The Federalist* suggested, by opening up western lands for settlement and by expanding the market for farm products. Perhaps the artisans and mechanics believed that a stronger government would protect the sale of their products by use of a tariff as they had asked in their petitions and as *The Federalist* promised would happen. The fact is that most of the people must have believed some of these arguments, for most of them had the vote, and we can assume that they did not vote for a government which would promote only the interests of personalty.

It follows from what has been said, then, that the balance of powers, or checks and balances, in the Constitution were not there for the reasons attributed by Beard. The Beard thesis follows the line that personalty was under attack and that it designed a system of checks and balances by which the majority, presumably including the propertyless, the debtors, and those with very little property, could not override the rights of the minority—"which minority is of course composed of those who possess property that may be attacked" (p. 160). The way to insure the rights of this minority, said Beard, was to have a government in which the different interests could check each other and thus head off any pernicious attacks. The House of Representatives, he continued, came from those people who were enfranchised, which did not include the disfranchised "mass of men"; the Senate was elected by state legislatures which were themselves based on property qualifications; and the president was to be chosen by electors, which would make him one step removed from the electorate.

[10] *Ibid.*, II, 10.

Different terms of office for each would make a complete over-turn in the government impossible at any given time. Then the keystone of the whole structure was a Supreme Court which was not elected, which held office during good behavior rather than at pleasure, and which had the final power of checking the other branches of the government by declaring laws unconstitutional.

If the class structure was not what Beard said it was, the corollary follows that checks and balances were likewise not as he pictured them. As I have already demonstrated, men in the Convention believed that there were all sorts of interests in the country, horizontal class interests, vertical property groups, states' rights, slave and free interests, and many others. Of course it is true that checks and balances were designed to allow these different interests to restrain each other. But we must remember that as recent colonists, the people in 1787 had experienced a system of government in which they did not have sufficient constitutional checks and balances. Even Jefferson believed that the main fault in the Virginia constitution was its failure to provide checks to a legislative tyranny by pitting different interests against each other. As for the Senate's being elected by state legislatures, we must remember that one of the big issues in the Convention was whether the government was to be national or federal, and those who advocated a federal government insisted that the Senate be elected by state legislatures to protect state interests. So while some looked on the Senate as a safeguard for property, others looked on it as the branch which would represent the states. Again, as I have said, some men did not think the people would accept a national government by giving up equal rights for states in the Senate.

That the judiciary, as a "check," was appointed during good behavior is not unusual. In fact, the very reverse is true, if we assume, as I do, that the Revolution was designed primarily to keep the prevailing social order rather than to change it. The colonies and states had long been accustomed to appointed judges. Furthermore, one of their strongest complaints against the British had come after 1760 when the British attempted to appoint judges during pleasure rather than during good behavior. The colonists had protested that their lives and property would not be safe in the hands of a judge who could be removed at the pleasure of the king.[11]

And finally, the authors of *The Federalist* were not simply justifying checks and balances. What they had to do was to assure the people that the Constitution really provided for checks and balances, for its critics claimed that it did not do this. In fact, *The Federalist* pointed out that the Constitution had the same system of checks and balances that the state constitutions had, especially that of New York, which had one of the better systems of checks.[12] One of the complaints of the colonists had been that they did not have checks on the British government, so checks and balances were nothing new.

A few quotations from the *Records* of the Convention will demonstrate what the members themselves thought of checks and balances. Madison said, as we have seen, that the landed interest dominated at the time; but in the future, when America resembled Europe, the landed interest would be outnumbered and it should have the power to check other interests.[13] The North Carolina delegates believed that the Constitution was devised in such a way to protect the interests of North Carolina's citizens.[14] Gerry agreed with Madison that the majority would violate justice if they had an interest in doing so, but he did not think there was any temptation for this in America because of cheap land.[15] Charles Pinckney thought there were three groups, landed, professional, and commercial, that they were mutually dependent on each other, and really had only one great interest in common. All that was needed, therefore, was to distribute powers of government in such a way as to provide a degree of permanency to the government—i.e. by checks and balances.[16] Gerry said the people had two great interests—land and commerce (including stockholders). Since the people were chiefly composed of the landed interest, to draw both House and Senate from the

---

[11] See Robert E. Brown, *Middle-Class Democracy and the Revolution in Massachusetts, 1691-1780*, Cornell University Press, 1955.
[12] *The Federalist*, Nos. 39, 47, 48, 66.    [13] Farrand, *Records*, I, 431.
[14] *Ibid.*, III, 84.    [15] *Ibid.*, I, 425.    [16] *Ibid.*, pp. 398-404.

people would not provide security for commerce.[17] Wilson answered that the election of the Senate by state legislatures would not reduce the power of the landed interest, for landed interests controlled state legislatures and there was no reason to suppose that they would choose someone different for the Senate.[18] Mason believed the purpose of the Convention was to devise a system that would obtain and preserve the protection, safety, and happiness of the people,[19] and even Hamilton said the great question was the kind of government which would be best for the happiness of the country.[20] King gave personal protection and security of property as one great object of government,[21] while Hamilton said there were three concerns of government—agriculture, commerce, and revenue.[22] There must be equality in the Senate to protect the small states, said Sherman, for states, like individuals, had their peculiar habits and usages.[23] Madison even proposed a check and balance system between slave and free states, for he considered the conflict between them to be the main conflict in American society.[24] "I do not, gentlemen, trust you," declared Bedford, and he went on to say that any group with power would probably abuse it, and that the small states must be protected from the large.[25]

So there were many views of society expressed in the Convention and many reasons given for checks and balances besides the protection of property and especially personal property. We cannot simply take one delegate's view, and only one of his many opinions, and say "This represents the thinking of the Convention," as Beard did.

After disposing of these elements of the check and balance system, Beard went on to give the reasons why another check on democracy, property qualifications for voting and office-holding, was omitted from the Constitution. Again the reason was economic, not political, and Beard's argument runs as follows: The personalty interests represented in the Convention could not see any "safeguard at all in a freehold qualification

---

[17] *Ibid.*, p. 152.  [18] *Ibid.*, p. 154.  [19] *Ibid.*, p. 161.
[20] *Ibid.*, p. 284.  [21] *Ibid.*, p. 302.  [22] *Ibid.*, p. 329.
[23] *Ibid.*, p. 343.  [24] *Ibid.*, p. 486.  [25] *Ibid.*, p. 500.

against the assaults on vested personalty rights which had been made by the agrarians in every state." On the other hand, they could not have gotten a personalty qualification written into the Constitution even if they had desired. The reason: "there would have been no chance of securing a ratification of the Constitution at the hands of legislatures chosen by freeholders, or at the hands of conventions selected by them" (p. 166). Distrusting the freeholders and unable to get the kind of voting qualifications they wanted, these personalty interests preferred to omit all property qualifications from the Constitution. Beard hastened to add, however, that there was really "little risk to personalty" in leaving the question of voting qualifications to the states, for there were other checks in the Constitution itself and most of the states already had voting qualifications (p. 168). Thus is the omission of property qualifications from the Constitution explained in terms of personalty interests.

The argument sounds plausible, so let us examine the evidence that Beard used to prove it, as well as some of the evidence in the *Records* that he might have used.

It is quite true, as Beard said, that Madison believed a small quantity of land as a qualification would be no security and a large quantity would exclude the representatives of those who were not landowners. But what else did Madison say about the franchise? He said "it was politic as well as just that the interests & rights of every class should be duly represented & understood in the public Councils. It was a provision everywhere established that the Country should be divided into districts & representatives taken from each, in order that the Legislative Assembly might equally understand & sympathise, with the rights of the people in every part of the Community. It was not less proper that every class of Citizens should have an opportunity of making their rights be felt & understood in the public Councils." These classes he defined as "the landed the commercial, & the manufacturing," and he wished that some qualification besides land could be devised to protect the interests of the last two.[26] But he did not say that commercial

[26] *Ibid.*, ii, 123-24.

and manufacturing interests were to be protected at the expense of landed interests. As I have said before, he also wanted to make sure that the landholders were able to protect their interests in the future when there would be a majority without land. In short, it was both politic and just for all groups to have a voice in government—which is not economic determinism, and especially economic determinism with a personalty flavor.

Later Madison elaborated even more fully on his views of the suffrage, again without supporting the Beard generalization. He said the right to vote was fundamental in a republican constitution. If this right were confined to property, persons would be oppressed, and if it were confined to persons, property would be oppressed. Both property and personal rights must be protected. Limiting the vote to freeholders would violate the vital principle of free government that those bound by laws should help make them. Madison even came to the conclusion, which is certainly not the result of an economic interpretation, that if the choice ever came between universal suffrage and limitation of voting to people with property, the decision would have to be for universal suffrage at the expense of property. But, he continued, the United States had a precious advantage in the actual distribution of property, especially land, and in the universal hope of acquiring property, for this created much sympathy in the country for property.[27] This, it seems to me, comes dangerously close to a political philosophy based on such old-fashioned principles as justice and right.

From the standpoint of historical method, Beard's generalization that "the other members also knew that they had most to fear from the very electors who would be enfranchised under a slight freehold restriction" (p. 165) and his citation of the *Records*, II, 201ff. for his reference constitute a misuse of evidence. If we turn to those pages of the *Records*, what do we find? Gouverneur Morris wanted to "restrain the right of suffrage to freeholders," who would approve the restriction because nine-tenths of the people were freeholders. Merchant

[27] *Ibid.*, III, 450-55.

Fitzsimons seconded his motion. Wilson did not want any qualifications in the Constitution because it would be difficult to make a uniform rule for all the states, the Convention should avoid innovations, and it would be hard and disagreeable for persons who could vote for state legislators to be excluded from voting for the national legislature. Ellsworth favored the qualifications as they were in the states, for the people would not adopt the Constitution if it disfranchised them.[28] Mason agreed. Eight or nine states allowed others besides freeholders to vote, and what would these people say if they were disfranchised? Butler agreed with Ellsworth and Mason that both freeholders and nonfreeholders should vote, but Dickinson wanted a restriction to freeholders "as the best guardians of liberty." Ellsworth then declared that every man who paid a tax should vote for the representatives who were to levy taxes, and this would certainly mean freeholders.[29] Then Mason went beyond his original position and declared that not only should freeholders and other property owners have the vote, but also "every man having evidence of attachment to & permanent common interest with the Society ought to share in all its rights & privileges." The electorate would not be restricted to freeholders or owners of other kinds of property but would include the parents of children, who obviously had a stake in society. Mason was really trying to break down the accepted idea that *only* freeholders could be trusted with the vote. Even Madison, Beard's great foundation stone for his personalty interpretation, said that "the freeholders of the Country would be the safest depositories of Republican liberty," and he implied that he would favor a restriction of the suffrage if he were sure that such a change would be accepted in those states "where the right was now exercised by every description of people."[30] To cite this evidence as proof that the Convention delegates feared the enfranchised small freeholders is gross misrepresentation.

The same misrepresentation carries over into Beard's citation of a part of Gorham's statement (p. 165) to bolster his own generalization that the delegates feared the freeholder vote.

[28] *Ibid.*, ɪɪ, 201, 203.　　[29] *Ibid.*, pp. 201-02.　　[30] *Ibid.*, p. 203.

Gorham *did not* say that he feared the vote of freeholders. What he was doing was attempting to head off the move by some of the delegates to restrict voting to freeholders because they thought freeholders were really the only ones to be trusted with the vote. To counteract this argument, Gorham said he had never seen any inconvenience from allowing non-freeholders to vote, a practice long tried in this country. He cited the elections in Philadelphia, New York, and Boston, where merchants and mechanics voted, to show that these nonfreeholders were just as capable of making good choices in elections as were the freeholders. Nowhere did Gorham say or imply that he feared the freeholders as voters.

Whether the historical method permits such a use of evidence is something that each reader must decide for himself. But if it does, the time has come for us to redefine it.

Numerous other statements made in the Convention emphasize the absurdity of attributing the absence of property qualifications in the Constitution to personalty influences. George Mason proposed a landed qualification for members of Congress and exclusion from Congress of anyone having unsettled accounts with the United States. Gouverneur Morris called this a scheme of the landed against the moneyed interest, and maybe it was. But we must remember that Morris was one of the most vocal advocates of the freehold qualification for voters, which could also be a scheme of the landed against the moneyed interest. John Dickinson, another proponent of the freehold qualification, sided with Morris against Mason. On the other hand Gerry, one of the few real representatives of personalty, was ready not only to support Mason's motion requiring land as a qualification, but to go much further than Mason.[31] The delegates simply were not consistent, for if Morris and Dickinson favored personalty, as Beard claimed, they should have championed a personalty instead of a freehold qualification for voting, and security holder Gerry should never have backed Mason.

If the omission of property qualifications from the Constitution was not due to the delegates' fear of freeholders and their

[31] *Ibid.*, pp. 121-23. The *Records* do not develop Gerry's position.

inability to get the kind of qualifications they wanted, what is the explanation?

John Dickinson offered two reasons, one based on interest, one based on principle. He was against "any recital of qualifications [for office] in the Constitution. . . . The best defense lay in the freeholders who were to elect the Legislature . . . . He doubted the policy of interweaving into a Republican constitution a veneration for wealth. He had always understood that a veneration for poverty & virtue, were the objects of republican encouragement. It seemed improper that any man of merit should be subjected to disabilities in a Republic where merit was understood to form the great title to public trust, honors & rewards."[32]

Like Madison, even Dickinson could talk in terms of "principles" rather than economic interest, though he certainly did not ignore the latter. Of course, if one argued that the delegates had tongue in cheek when they talked principles, but really meant what they said when they discussed economic interests, we would still need the evidence under the historical method.

As a matter of fact, the two reasons for the exclusion of property qualifications from the Constitution were political, not economic, and they are not difficult to find in the *Records*.

One reason was that there were different qualifications in effect in different states and the delegates simply could not agree on a uniform qualification that would be satisfactory to all. Some wanted a freehold, others wanted to include any property, and a few would eliminate practically all qualifications. There was no great opposition to property qualifications for voting either in the Convention or in the country at large, for as Dickinson and Morris said, nine-tenths of the people were freeholders and would be pleased if voting were restricted to freeholders. But while most of the delegates favored a voting qualification, they could not agree on what that qualification should be. Ellsworth explained the situation as follows: "The different circumstances of different parts of the U.S. . . . render it improper to have either uniform or fixed

[32] *Ibid.*, p. 123.

qualifications."[33] Wilson said it "was difficult to form any uniform rule of qualifications for all the states,"[34] and Rutledge said the committee considering the matter had omitted qualifications "because they could not agree on any among themselves."[35]

The second reason for omitting property qualifications from the Constitution was also political—the delegates were simply afraid that any innovations on this point might result in the rejection of the Constitution. Wilson wanted to avoid "unnecessary innovations," while Ellsworth thought the prevailing state qualifications were sufficient, and that "the people [would] not readily subscribe to the Natl. Constitution, if it should subject them to be disfranchised."[36] Men who wished for innovations on this point certainly were ignoring force of habit, declared Mason, for what would "the people say, if they should be disfranchised."[37] Franklin did not want to displease the common people by disfranchising them, for they had contributed much during the late war. Sons of substantial farmers would not be pleased at being disfranchised, he said, and if the common people were "denied the right of suffrage it would debase their spirit and detach them from the interest of the country."[38] Defending the habitual right of merchants and mechanics to vote, Gorham declared: "We must consult their rooted prejudices if we expect their concurrence in our propositions."[39] Rutledge explained why the committee had omitted the qualifications by saying its members could not agree among themselves for fear of displeasing the people if they made the qualifications high or having the qualifications be worthless if they were low.[40]

Since there were no personalty qualifications for voting in the Constitution, and since, as Beard said, the landed interests would control ratification either by state legislatures or by special conventions, the big question is this: Why was the Constitution ratified by the landed interests if it was designed to protect personalty? Beard never answered this question.

[33] *Ibid.*, p. 249.  [34] *Ibid.*, p. 201.  [35] *Ibid.*, p. 249.
[36] *Ibid.*, p. 201.  [37] *Ibid.*, pp. 201-02.  [38] *Ibid.*, pp. 205, 210.
[39] *Ibid.*, p. 216.  [40] *Ibid.*, p. 249.

Inconsistencies and the drawing of unjustified conclusions soon become obvious when we attempt to follow the tortuous trail of the Beard thesis into the powers conferred on the federal government. Why did rural interests have to be conciliated on the point of direct taxes to prevent manufacturing states from shifting the tax burden to sparsely settled agricultural regions, if these rural regions were not represented in the Convention? Does the quotation from the North Carolina delegates (p. 169) prove the influence of personalty? No. The delegates said they had protected "the Southern states in general and North Carolina in particular" on the tax question, but this represents a sectional or state interest, not personalty. These delegates were also looking out for the interests of North Carolina farmers, who, incidentally, had, on the average, land twice the value of that of the people in New England. And why did Hamilton have to conciliate "the freeholders and property owners in general" if the Convention represented personalty? Then there are the questions of whether military power and nationalism have nothing but economic connotations, even though everyone admits that economic factors accompany both.

One key to an understanding of the Constitutional Convention was provided by Beard himself in his discussion of the control of commerce (p. 175). His earlier use of petitions signed by mechanics and manufacturers was evidence that these skilled artisans wanted protection from foreign competition just as does organized labor today. But his final sentence in the paragraph is the important one—that merchants and manufacturing interests achieved commercial benefits, but "'they paid for their victory by large concessions to the slave-owning planters of the south." This is only one example of what is so evident to anyone who reads the *Records* without preconceptions. There were a multitude of conflicting interests in the Convention, some economic and some not, and there simply had to be a great deal of compromising of interests for anything to be achieved. As one delegate said, he did not trust the other gentleman, and they all did everything possible to insure that their interests and principles got a hearing and that others' were checked as much as possible. Nobody could have his own way completely.

That the Constitution did not confer on Congress the power to make direct attacks on property is not to be wondered at (p. 176). Given the America of 1787, in which most men owned property, the reverse would have been the more astonishing. A constitution which permitted an attack on property would not have received a hearing in a country that had fought a revolution for the preservation of life, liberty, and property. One of the colonists' chief complaints against Britain had been that the British, on whom the colonists had no check, were endangering the property rights of colonists. The opponents of the Constitution were not opposed to the protection of property rights. After all, were not the Antifederalists responsible for the adoption of the first ten amendments, and did not Articles IV, V, and VII provide for additional protection of property which these Antifederalists did not think the Constitution provided?

If Madison was any authority, and Beard seemed to think he was, then Beard greatly exaggerated the importance of agrarianism in the country (pp. 178-79). Beard used the term, not to mean agricultural, but to designate men who favored an equal or a more nearly equal distribution of land. Madison stated in the Convention that as yet there had not been any agrarian attempts in the country.[41]

Some interesting and significant points on obligation of contracts which Beard did not include in his discussion of the contract clause as a protection for personalty (pp. 179-83) were brought out in the *Records*. For instance, when King moved to add a clause prohibiting the states from interfering in private contracts, Gouverneur Morris objected. And his argument—shades of Oliver Wendell Holmes!—was that "within the State itself a majority must rule, whatever may be the mischief done among themselves."[42] Even Madison had his doubts about restricting the states on contracts, and Mason was strongly against it. Wilson then resolved the controversy with this answer: "The answer to these objections is that

[41] *Ibid.*, I, 423.    [42] *Ibid.*, II, 439.

*retrospective* interferences only are to be prohibited."[43] Instead of the original motion, then, the restriction was made that the state legislatures could not pass "retrospective laws," that is, ex post facto laws, and on this issue Connecticut, Maryland, and Virginia voted no.[44] Later, however, Dickinson said he had examined Blackstone's *Commentaries on the Laws of England* and found that "ex post facto" related only to criminal cases, and that legislatures could still pass retrospective laws in civil cases.[45] So the prohibition against violation of contracts was included, but to the members this meant only contracts already made.[46] It did not in any way restrict the right of legislatures to provide the conditions under which future contracts could be made.

Given this situation, Beard's account of Chief Justice John Marshall and the contract clause (pp. 181-83) was completely invalid, and could easily have been corrected by a reference to the *Records*. Beard said Marshall "doubtless" understood the full import of the obligation-of-contract clause better than any man of that generation. In 1827 the Supreme Court passed on the question of whether a bankrupt law which applied to contracts made after its passage impaired the obligation of those contracts. The majority on the Court upheld the law, but Marshall took "the high ground" that a contract was a contract and could not be changed by external legislation. Then Beard said that Marshall should have known what the framers of the Constitution intended better than any man on the Supreme Court, that is, that the Founding Fathers intended to ban "all legislation which affected personalty adversely." If the *Records* have any validity, this was not true. The majority of the Court which upheld the right of states to impair the obligation of *future contracts* was simply following the stated intent of the Founding Fathers as recorded in the *Records*. This explains why there was so little opposition to the Constitution on this particular score.

The *Records* also gave a different version of paper money than that given by Beard, who implied that the adoption of

[43] *Ibid.*, p. 440.  [44] *Ibid.*, p. 440.
[45] *Ibid.*, pp. 448-49.  [46] *Ibid.*, iii, 100.

the Constitution would put an end to paper money (pp. 178-80). He failed to point out that the adoption of restrictions against future emissions of paper money by the states did not annihilate paper money in the states or invalidate contracts that were to be paid in paper money. As Davie told the North Carolina convention: "The Federal Convention knew that several states had large sums of paper money in circulation, and that it was an interesting property, and they were sensible that those states would never consent to its immediate destruction, or ratify any system that would have that operation. The mischief already done could not be repaired: all that could be done was, to form some limitation to this great political evil. As the paper money had become private property, and the object of numberless contracts, it could not be destroyed or intermeddled with in that situation, although its baneful tendency was obvious and undeniable. It was, however, effecting an important object to put bounds to this growing mischief. If the states had been compelled to sink the paper money instantly, the remedy might be worse than the disease. As we could not put an immediate end to it, we were content with prohibiting its future increase, looking forward to its entire extinguishment when the states that had an emission circulating should be able to call it in by gradual redemption."[47]

This puts the paper money restriction in quite a different light, just as the *Records* put the contract clause in a different light. State legislatures did not have to retire the paper money that was circulating, and contracts in paper money were still valid. As long as the paper money party controlled the state legislature, that party could keep bills of credit in circulation. Parties to contracts could still make contracts in paper money, even if the legislature could not make paper money a legal tender, and in the future both parties to a contract would know the conditions under which the contract was to be fulfilled. This, too, explains the lack of opposition to the bills of credit clause. Further research in a later period would show how long bills of credit circulated in the states and whether state legislatures did not, in effect, get around the Constitutional restriction by chartering state banks which issued bank notes, just

[47] *Ibid.*, pp. 349-50.

as the colonists attempted to set up private land banks to replace the British-extinguished public banks.

In the last section of the chapter (pp. 183-88), Beard used Hamilton to prove a point that Hamilton did not prove, namely, that foreign and domestic controversies are based primarily on commercial antagonisms. What Hamilton appears to have been doing in *The Federalist* No. 6 was to convince the people that commerce was as important as other causes in the fomenting of wars. Hamilton was too realistic to make commerce the most important factor in war. The causes of hostility among nations were innumerable, he declared—love of power, desire of pre-eminence and dominion, desire for territory, jealousy of power, desire for equality and safety, and commercial rivalry, as well as private passions stemming from attachments, enmities, interests, hopes, and fears of leading individuals in their own communities. Even the caprices of women had caused wars. Sometimes countries engaged in wars contrary to their true interests, motivated by momentary passions and immediate interests rather than by general considerations of policy, utility, or justice. Men were subject to impulses of rage, resentment, jealousy, avarice, and other irregular and violent propensities. Was not the love of wealth as important a passion as love of power and glory, Hamilton asked? He implied that love of power and glory was important, and certainly he did not confine wealth to personalty. Hamilton did not rule out policy, utility, and justice as motivations, nor did he necessarily represent the views of other men in the Convention and the country at large.

So to prove that the Constitution was "an economic document drawn with superb skill by men whose property interests were immediately at stake," Beard had to violate the concepts of the historical method in many ways. These ran the gamut from omission to outright misrepresentation of evidence, and included the drawing of conclusions from evidence that not only did not warrant the conclusions but actually refuted them. To say that the Constitution was designed in part to protect property is true; to say that it was designed only to protect property is false; and to say that it was designed only to protect *personalty* is preposterous.

# CHAPTER VII

# "THE POLITICAL DOCTRINES OF THE
# MEMBERS OF THE CONVENTION"

AFTER examining the Constitution under the revealing light thrown on it by *The Federalist* and finding that the Constitution was an economic document reflecting the economic interests of the delegates, Beard posed this as the next problem: Did the members of the Convention have views about the political science of the new system similar to the views expressed in *The Federalist?* The reader can doubtless anticipate the answer: "The conclusion seems warranted that the authors of *The Federalist* generalized the political doctrines of the members of the Convention with a high degree of precision, in spite of the great diversity of opinion which prevailed on many matters" (pp. 189, 216).

Let us examine the views of the delegates, not only to see whether Beard's generalizations were justified from the evidence he presented, but also to see whether he gave a complete account of the delegates' political philosophies as found in the *Records.*

Even before he examined the political philosophies delegate by delegate, Beard placed himself in an untenable position. He declared that the leaders were not far removed from that frank recognition of class rights which characterized English society. And because of the "disfranchisement of the propertyless," they did not need to conceal their ideas of class conflict to the same extent that modern partisan writers do. Having no worries about the lower classes, who could not vote, they could express their ideas of essential economic antagonisms without fear of the political consequences. Of course these eighteenth century American political scientists did not express that sharp recognition of class rights which characterized feudal legists, he said, because there were divisions to be glossed over within those property interests which were represented in government.

There were also mutterings of unrest from the disfranchised, and these factors forced the supporters of the Constitution to be somewhat circumspect. But fortunately the debates were secret, allowing the delegates "to discuss with utmost frankness the actual politico-economic results which they desired to reach," and we have these debates in Farrand's *Records* (Beard, pp. 189-90).

Since the question of the franchise has already been discussed in Chapters I and IV, it should not be necessary here to deal with this assumption of a disfranchised mass at any length. Beard, himself, arrived at what appears to be the proper conclusions, that is, that the country was about ninety-seven per cent rural and that the freehold qualification gave the vote to the small farmers and many of the debtors. This conclusion agrees with the statements made in the Convention, where town mechanics as well as freeholders were included among the enfranchised, and with my own findings, which have already been cited. As for the delegates' ignoring the people, such a statement could be made only by someone who had not read the *Records*. One of the most striking features of the debates was the fact that practically every feature of the Constitution was subjected to the question of whether the people would accept it. If there was a single shaping factor more important than any other, it was the recognition by the delegates that they had to devise a constitution which the people would approve.

One other generalization needs to be made in connection with the political philosophies of the delegates. The Founding Fathers, like people of today, were not always consistent in their views. A man might well be liberal or democratic in his ideas about certain aspects of government, and conservative or undemocratic in his ideas about other aspects. As we shall see, delegates even expressed completely opposing points of view at different times, making it mandatory that we weigh all their expressions before we brand them as liberal or conservative. This generalization will become obvious as we assess the philosophies of the delegates from their remarks in the Convention.

In this chapter I have again followed Beard's organization of a delegate-by-delegate analysis in alphabetical order.

Little is known of the political philosophy of Baldwin of Georgia, and the fact that he wanted a Senate to represent property did not necessarily mean personalty as opposed to realty. Many men in the Convention, who wanted the Senate to represent property, also thought that the House should represent persons or human rights. The Massachusetts constitution, which Baldwin used as a model, represented both, and the fact that it was adopted by the vote of all adult men would indicate a widespread belief that the protection of property was one of the accepted functions of government. Furthermore, the big fight over the Massachusetts constitution was on religion, not economics.[1] Actually, Baldwin wanted a government that was more energetic than that provided by the Articles of Confederation, but he did not want the opposite extreme of a government that was too energetic.[2] His chief concern in the Convention was the protection of slavery.[3] In the following pages I am again assuming that slaves in general, though personal property, must be considered an adjunct of agriculture in the South, along with livestock, tobacco, and corn, which were also personal property.

Bedford of Delaware refutes the Beard thesis, as Beard's own evidence proves. As the Madison quotation says (p. 191), Bedford "opposed every check on the legislature" and said that the "representatives of the People were the best judges of what was for their interest, and ought to be under no external controul whatever." He was also adamant in his determination to protect the interests of the small states from the large, using the threat that the small states might be forced to seek the protection of some foreign power.[4] Bedford well recognized the influence of the people, for he declared that the Convention, like Solon, must draw up a constitution which the people would approve.[5] These do not prove a frank recognition of class

[1] Robert E. Brown, *Middle-Class Democracy and the Revolution in Massachusetts, 1691-1780*, Cornell University Press, 1955.

[2] *The Records of the Federal Convention of 1787*, ed. Max Farrand, 4 vols. (New Haven, 1937), I, 469, 475.

[3] *Ibid.*, II, 372.     [4] *Ibid.*, I, 167, 490-92.     [5] *Ibid.*, p. 490.

rights or the propensity of the delegates to ignore the people.

Broom of Delaware supported ideas favored by Jefferson and Luther Martin, which is confusing, to say the least, as Martin opposed the Constitution and Jefferson soon broke with the Federalists. If Broom advocated long terms of office, he also agreed to shorter terms; and if he favored a balanced democracy, as Beard said, he was somewhere in the middle with most of the delegates. The evidence does not prove that he wanted a government "balanced" in favor of personalty.

Butler of South Carolina believed that the Senate should represent *property*, as Beard said, but he did not say *personalty*, and he did say that representation should be based on both wealth and numbers.[6] He wanted to leave power with the states to balance divergent state interests, and he did not want extremes in government.[7] As with many other Southerners, Butler was mainly concerned with the protection of slavery, for he feared there was much sentiment in the Convention to abolish slavery.[8]

Carroll of Maryland either proved little, because he did not indulge in philosophical reflections and his system of political science is not apparent in the records, or he proved the opposite of the Beard thesis, because he favored the popular election of the chief executive (pp. 192-93). On this basis, even the three-fourths majority to override the executive veto, which he advocated, might be considered democratic since it would increase the difficulty of reversing the decision of a popularly elected president. Actually, Carroll at different times supported motions for electing the president (1) by the national legislature, (2) by the people, and (3) by electors elected by the people.[9] Carroll was obviously one of those delegates who changed his mind, and who could be made to appear liberal if we used one piece of evidence or conservative if we used another.

Beard did not offer any "evidence" on Clymer of Pennsylvania, but instead took all his information from a secondary work by Sanderson. Sanderson implied that Clymer did not believe in democracy because he thought a representative of the people should think for and not with his constituents, and

[6] *Ibid.*, p. 144.     [7] *Ibid.*, pp. 51, 53.
[8] *Ibid.*, pp. 580-81, 605.        [9] *Ibid.*, II, 105, 402, 404.

he opposed a clause in the Constitution allowing the people to instruct their representatives. I have not found this in the *Records*, but even if true, he also believed that the Constitution should be ratified by a majority of the people as well as the states.[10] Clymer apparently thought that the big difference of interests lay between sections rather than classes, as he feared that encouragement of the West would be suicide for the old states.[11] He also believed that there was a diversity of interests even within the commercial group, and that unfavorable commercial regulations by foreign countries would hurt the commercial states, not just the men engaged in commerce.[12]

Davie of North Carolina can be used as evidence for many views other than those that support the Beard thesis. He did not "expound any philosophy of government," so how do we know he agreed with *The Federalist*? Beard's evidence would prove that to Davie the real issue was North against South, free against slave states (p. 193). Furthermore, if Davie thought that wealth or property should be represented in the Senate and persons in the House, he thought the way a lot of other people thought in 1787—that government was designed to protect both property rights and human rights. But again I remind the reader that property rights do not mean merely personal property. Davie may have "fully understood the significance of the obligation of contract clause," but he also knew that the contract clause did not prevent future attacks on personal property by popular legislatures.[13] It may be true that Davie "undoubtedly understood and approved" John Adams' doctrine of balanced classes in government, but he did not favor personalty over realty. Furthermore, if he approved Adams' doctrine, Davie probably would also have believed that ninety-five per cent of the property in the country was in the hands of the common people, for this was what Adams believed. Adams did not advocate favoritism of personalty over realty or domination of the poor by the rich or the rich by the poor.[14] And if the "rabble" could have defeated Davie, as the quota-

[10] *Ibid.*, p. 476.    [11] *Ibid.*, p. 442.    [12] *Ibid.*, p. 450.
[13] *Ibid.*, III, 349-50.    [14] Adams, *Works*, IV, 359-60, *passim*.

116

tion in Beard said, there must have been democracy in North Carolina (p. 194).

John Dickinson should have been one of the last men to be used as support for the Beard thesis. Beard had maintained that the freeholders were the most dangerous antagonists of personal property. Here he said that Dickinson was among the members of the Convention who wanted to establish property qualifications for voting because he thought no other foundation would be secure. But did Dickinson want to exclude the dangerous freeholders? No, quite the contrary. He considered the freeholders as the best guardians of liberty, and he believed that *only* the freeholders should have the vote—and Beard quoted this evidence himself (p. 195). He also said that mechanics had the vote (p. 196), which, added to his statement that most of the people were freeholders, would make him good evidence for democracy in 1787. One might get the impression from Beard's statement that Dickinson advocated a monarchy for this country, but this is not what Dickinson said. What Dickinson said was that a *limited* monarchy was *one* of the best forms of government, but that it was out of the question for the United States because this country did not have the essential class structure that Europe had.[15] I have already cited Dickinson's statement that merit, not property, should be the qualification for officeholding. These points do not bolster Beard's hypothesis that the country was undemocratic, that the delegates feared the freeholders and were working for personalty, and that the delegates made frank statements of class rights.

Oliver Ellsworth's distrust of "levelling democracy" does not mean that he wanted to go to the opposite extreme, and what he believed after the French Revolution does not throw much light on his views in 1787. The *Records*, however, indicate many characteristics of Ellsworth and his times which Beard omitted. Ellsworth advocated winter meetings for Congress because he said most members would be connected with agriculture—not personalty.[16] He believed every state had its particular views and prejudices, which is not economic class

[15] Farrand, *Records*, I, 86-87.     [16] *Ibid.*, p. 200.

117

determinism,[17] and he thought Connecticut's delegates had taken good care of Connecticut's interests.[18] Restricting the suffrage to taxpayers, as Ellsworth advocated, would not have excluded many, as Beard admitted (pp. 65, 68, 70, 71). Beard could have quoted Ellsworth to show that there was actually a great deal of democracy in 1787, for Ellsworth said the right of suffrage was a tender point and the people would not readily subscribe to the Constitution if it disfranchised them— an indication that they had the franchise.[19] His protest against excluding merchants and manufacturers from the franchise did not mean that he wished to exclude freeholders. And if the Convention had been called by personalty, such a proposition would never have arisen.[20] He also proposed yearly elections because the people were fond of frequent elections, still another indication of democracy and the influence of the people on the Convention.[21] And in the end he thought that the Constitution represented a middle or moderate position, not that it represented strictly an effective check on democracy.[22]

What does the evidence prove when a man such as Fitzsimons of Philadelphia wanted to restrict voting to freeholders and at the same time wanted the federal government to have the power to erect piers and to maintain the navigability of harbors? Was he for the farmers? Was he for the merchants? Did he believe the farmers were opposed to the merchants? And especially what is proved when Fitzsimons from Philadelphia favored government power to help commerce and Gorham of Boston was against it?[23]

Beard should have omitted Franklin, for he obviously does not support the Beard thesis. Franklin is especially good evidence for democracy and the difference between the American and British societies. He did not want to deprive the common people of the vote, which would certainly be evidence that he thought they had the vote. In addition, he praised the part which the common people had played in the Revolution,

[17] *Ibid.*, p. 406.  [18] *Ibid.*, p. 240.  [19] *Ibid.*, ii, 201.
[20] *Ibid.*, p. 202.  [21] *Ibid.*, i, 361.  [22] *Ibid.*, ii, 375.
[23] *Ibid.*, pp. 201, 529.

attributing their patriotism to the difference in treatment of the common people here and in England, and feared that any restriction on their voting rights might result in a loss of their support for the government.[24] As Beard said (p. xiv), Franklin hoped and believed that public securities would rise in value under the new Constitution, but he also said the low value of these securities was not due to a lack of honesty in the government but to a lack of ability because of war exhaustion.[25] If Franklin ever opposed the Constitution, as Beard said, that opposition is not apparent in the *Writings*.[26] On April 22, 1788, he said that he did not approve of everything in the Constitution but that nevertheless he hoped it would be adopted.[27] Beard got his information on Franklin's position from Scharf and Westcott, *History of Philadelphia*, who did not explain what Franklin's stand was or why he was placed on the opposition ticket.

Like Franklin, Gerry was another delegate who expressed many points of view in addition to those enumerated by Beard, and like Franklin, too, Gerry is not good evidence for the Beard thesis. On the contrary, as the Beard quotation shows, Gerry furnishes some of the best possible proof that there was a great deal of democracy in the country in 1787. He said that the evils of the time came from an "excess of democracy" and that while the people of England stood to lose their liberties because so few people there had the suffrage, over here the danger was from the opposite extreme.[28] Does this mean that a "mass of men" were disqualified from voting because of property qualifications? Gerry did not want to swing from extreme democracy to the opposite extreme and declared that, while he had been too republican, he was also against aristocracy and monarchy.[29] He reminded the delegates that they had to consider what the people would accept regardless of what the delegates themselves wanted, and he advocated

[24] *Ibid.*, pp. 205, 208, 210.
[25] Benjamin Franklin, *The Writings of Benjamin Franklin*, ed. Albert H. Smyth, 10 vols. (New York, 1907), ix, 635.
[26] *Ibid.*, pp. 619, 637-38, 645.    [27] *Ibid.*, p. 645.
[28] Farrand, *Records*, i, 48, 50, 123, 132.
[29] *Ibid.*, p. 132.

annual elections as the only defense of the people against tyranny.[30] While there is no doubt that Gerry represented personalty and believed that personalty, like other property, should be protected, he opposed the assumption of state debts by the federal government,[31] and even more important, he finally opposed the adoption of the Constitution itself.

Gilman of New Hampshire was characterized by Pierce of Georgia as modest, genteel, and sensible; not brilliant or striking, but respectable and worthy.[32] The *Records* give nothing else, and just where Beard got his information that Gilman was more interested in public securities and western lands than in political theory remains Beard's secret. Gilman signed the Constitution without protest, so he must have approved in general.

Gorham is another delegate who proves the opposite of the Beard thesis. As Beard said, Gorham was against property qualifications for voting, which would place him on the democratic side. Beard's long quotation on Gorham shows Gorham's desire to prevent domination of the executive by the judiciary, which would also place him on the democratic side since the executive was to be elected by freeholders, mechanics, and merchants. Beard could have used Gorham to prove many points, most of them refuting the Beard thesis. Gorham was a Boston merchant, but he opposed government help for commerce.[33] He thought the conflict of interests was among states, not classes.[34] As I have said before, Gorham offered particularly good evidence that democracy existed in 1787. He opposed restriction of voting to freeholders on the ground that mechanics and merchants had always voted in Philadelphia, New York, and Boston, and that their judgment was just as good as that of freeholders. He also showed the influence of the people on Convention delegates when he said that the people had long been accustomed to the right of voting in various parts of America and would never allow it to be abridged.[35] He did not want the Constitution to contain provi-

[30] *Ibid.*, pp. 214-15.  [31] *Ibid.*, ii, 356.  [32] *Ibid.*, iii, 87.
[33] *Ibid.*, ii, 201, 529.  [34] *Ibid.*, p. 453.  [35] *Ibid.*, p. 215.

sions which would excite the enmity of the people, or innovations which would upset established customs and increase the people's opposition.[36] It was Gorham who proposed one representative for every 30,000 instead of 40,000 inhabitants, a proposal seconded by Washington in his only speech in the Convention, and the reason for Gorham's proposal was to eliminate as much ground for objections to the Constitution as possible.[37] And he favored interference by the national government in state rebellions, not to put down democracy, but to prevent the establishment of monarchy.[38]

One can quote Hamilton, as Beard did, to show that society was divided into the rich and the poor, the few and the many. He is one of the small number who made such a statement. But he can also be quoted to show that Europeans of moderate fortunes would be considered wealthy in this country;[39] that the three great objects of government were agriculture, commerce, and revenue;[40] that the people of a state often had a community of interests;[41] that the country divided between North and South, commercial and noncommercial, and large and small states, and that the Constitution was a compromise of all these clashing interests;[42] that society in 1787 was democratic;[43] and that the Constitution provided for a democratic house checked by a democratic senate and both checked by a democratic executive.[44] Hamilton said he favored an executive and senate elected for life, but that most men in the Convention opposed this and the people were fond of democracy.[45] He favored the British government as a model, but admitted it could never be established in America.[46] Though he advocated a vigorous government, he wanted the House of Representatives laid on a broad foundation to protect the liberties of the people.[47] And he believed the people favored a strong government.[48] So one can prove many things by Hamilton, not just the class conflict. But if he is used as

[36] Ibid., I, 372; II, 614.
[37] Ibid., II, 643-44.
[38] Ibid., p. 48.
[39] Ibid., p. 268.
[40] Ibid., I, 329.
[41] Ibid., p. 466.
[42] Ibid., III, 332.
[43] Ibid., I, 291, 301.
[44] Ibid., p. 310.
[45] Ibid., pp. 281-91.
[46] Ibid., pp. 303-04.
[47] Ibid., p. 533.
[48] Ibid., III, 53.

evidence, it must be done with William S. Johnson's qualification that "though he has been praised by every body, he has been supported by none."[49]

Houstoun of Georgia might well have opposed the democratic Georgia constitution, which is evidence of democracy in 1787, but that does not prove that he wanted to go to the opposite extreme, or that he favored personalty over realty. There is not much evidence on Houstoun in the *Records*, except that he was active in looking out for Georgia's interests.[50]

Ingersoll of Pennsylvania does not prove much of anything, either from Beard's secondary evidence or from the *Records* themselves.

Beard's evidence that King of Massachusetts favored a balanced government does not mean that he favored one balanced in favor of upper-class personalty interests. On the other hand, King's statement that an "extreme caution in favor of liberty" might weaken the government they were forming certainly shows that he favored a stronger government, but at the same time is evidence that some of the delegates were motivated by some principle called "liberty" rather than economic interests. As with other delegates, King expressed many views at different times. He declared that property was the primary object of political societies, but he did not say personal rather than real property.[51] On another occasion he said that one object of government was personal protection and security of property.[52] He agreed with Madison and others that the differences of interest were not between large and small states but between eastern and southern, or free and slave.[53] He was willing, however, to compromise for the mutual benefit of both,[54] and he recognized that the Convention must consider the reaction of the people in drawing up a plan of government. Beard stated that King believed in judicial control to check popular attacks on property, but again this did not mean exclusively personal property. And if King made the motion to prohibit interference with contracts, as he did, he also

49 *Ibid.*, I, 363.    50 *Ibid.*, I, 568; II, 64.    51 *Ibid.*, I, 541.
52 *Ibid.*, p. 302.    53 *Ibid.*, p. 566.    54 *Ibid.*, p. 562.

knew from the debates that the restriction applied only to past contracts, not to future ones.[55]

Livingston of New Jersey was somewhat contradictory as a political philosopher. If he considered John Adams' views as conservative and branded them as a humiliating admission that man could not govern himself, he could be considered liberal. At the same time, however, he did not want to go to the opposite extreme of complete democracy. What he wanted was a government in which powers were delegated to elected officials, but in which the elected officials were so checked that no man or group could control. This did not mean that he wanted to deprive the people of their right of election, and there is certainly nothing here that would indicate a preference for personalty as a force in government. We do know, however, that he favored the Paterson plan to protect the small states.[56]

The treatment of McClurg of Virginia is a good example of the care which must be exercised in the historical method in order not to use evidence out of context. Beard said that McClurg proposed that the term of office for the executive should be changed from seven years to "good behavior" and that McClurg was anxious to have the executive independent of the legislature. On the face of it, this makes McClurg look very conservative. But the real situation, which Beard neglected to explain, was this: At the time McClurg made his proposal, the Convention had decided that the president was to be elected by the *national legislature*, was to serve for seven years, and was to be eligible for reelection.[57] Under those circumstances McClurg believed that the executive would be under the complete control of the legislature, and that the only way to make the executive independent of the legislature, if he were to be elected by that legislature, was to have him serve during "good behavior" rather than for seven years.[58] When the mode of electing the president was changed from the national legislature to electors appointed by state legislatures, McClurg did not advocate "good behavior" as the term of office for the

[55] *Ibid.*, p. 372; ii, 439-40.  [56] *Ibid.*, iii, 496.
[57] *Ibid.*, ii, 32.  [58] *Ibid.*, pp. 33, 36.

president.[59] That McClurg wanted the executive as a check on the legislature was quite true, but it was also true of Mason, of Jefferson, and, as McClurg said, of "the most zealous republicans."

Beard did not offer any evidence from the Convention on McHenry of Maryland, though there was plenty of evidence available. McHenry believed the Confederation could be altered sufficiently to meet the purposes of a central government, and that a new national government was not necessary. The controversy over this point in the Maryland delegation shows how far from unanimity the Convention was on various points.[60] McHenry was obviously more concerned about Maryland's interests than he was about class interests,[61] and he was fully aware of the importance of the people in the adoption of a new government.[62] He thought commerce itself should bear the expense of erecting lighthouses and cleaning out harbors.[63] McHenry is an excellent example of the compromising attitude which entered into the construction of the Constitution. He said he opposed many parts of the system but signed it and meant to support it because (1) he distrusted his own judgment, which had not always been right, and especially distrusted it when men of ability and patriotism composed the majority confronting him; (2) the system could be altered if it proved defective; (3) the new system promised more benefits than the old.[64] In the Maryland ratifying convention he cited Franklin to answer the charge that if the qualifications for voters were the same as in the state governments, the federal government would be involved in all the disorders of democracy—further evidence of democracy in 1787.[65] Nowhere in the Convention did McHenry propose that the new government was to benefit personalty alone.

Madison of Virginia, as I have already said, had many views besides those expressed in Beard's version of *The Federalist* No. 10. One could cite him as maintaining that the landed interest—not personalty—controlled the system then and that the

---

59 *Ibid.*, pp. 50, 57-58.   60 *Ibid.*, p. 191.   61 *Ibid.*, p. 211.
62 *Ibid.*, p. 212.   63 *Ibid.*, p. 504.   64 *Ibid.*, p. 649.
65 *Ibid.*, III, 146-47.

system should be so constructed that the landed interests could always check the others.[66] Madison also said that one kind of property had oppressed other kinds,[67] that the conflict of interests was between commercial and noncommercial states,[68] that states and sections had different interests,[69] and especially that the main conflict was between slave and free states,[70] a prediction which proved all too accurate.

Alexander Martin, former governor of North Carolina, had little to say in the Convention. He tried to increase North Carolina's representation, but this would prove only that he was concerned with his state's interests, not with promoting the position of personalty.[71]

Luther Martin of Maryland, a champion of paper money and debtors' laws, refused to sign the Constitution and voted against its ratification. To this extent he supports the Beard thesis, but he also expressed other views in the Convention which would refute Beard. For example, Martin thought the economic conflicts were vertical rather than horizontal, and that slavery was a big issue.[72] He said he would never agree to a plan which abolished equality of states, a position he adhered to tenaciously.[73] Martin thought the people in general believed in a government to protect life, liberty, and property,[74] so the protection of property was not peculiar to personalty interests, if he was any judge.

Mason of Virginia. Beard insinuated that George Mason fitted into the Beard thesis, when actually he is good evidence for refuting it. In the first place, Mason said the American people differed from the people of any other nation, so the Convention could not draw conclusions from other people's experiences. He believed that the purpose of the Convention was to devise a system which would preserve the safety and happiness of the people.[75] He proposed land, not personal property, as a qualification for holding office.[76] He also thought

[66] *Ibid.*, i, 423.
[67] *Ibid.*, p. 135.
[68] *Ibid.*, p. 146.
[69] *Ibid.*, pp. 321-22, 447-48, 458.
[70] *Ibid.*, i, 476, 486, 601; ii, 10.
[71] *Ibid.*, i, 568.
[72] *Ibid.*, iv, 25.
[73] *Ibid.*, i, 324, 340, 437, 444.
[74] *Ibid.*, p. 341.
[75] *Ibid.*, p. 161.
[76] *Ibid.*, p. 121.

the country had a great diversity of interests, and especially that the interests of the northern states differed from those of the southern.[77] Mason thought the country had been too democratic, but he did not want to go to the opposite extreme.[78] As further evidence of democracy in 1787, he felt that the Convention would have to fit a government to the people. He said: "Notwithstanding the oppression & injustice experienced among us from democracy; the genius of the people are in favor of it, and the genius of the people must be consulted."[79] He warned the Convention not to alter the franchise, for the people would oppose the Constitution if they were disfranchised.[80] Time and again he emphasized that the delegates must consider what the people would accept.[81] Naturally he believed in a "balanced government," as did most other men at the time, and naturally he believed in the protection of property, for he had a lot of it to protect. But he did not advocate merely the protection of personal property, and he was among those who opposed the Constitution.

Mercer of Maryland is also a good example of what can be done with evidence if it is quoted out of context or only part of it is quoted. Beard gave the selection which shows that Mercer was against elections by the people. Actually, Mercer apparently wanted the franchise limited to freeholders to prevent urban domination of the rural areas.[82] The day after he made this statement, however, Mercer said he did not object so much to an election by the people at large including nonfreeholders as he did to their being left to make their choice without any guidance. He hinted that candidates should be nominated by state legislatures, but when the question came to a vote, he voted with all other members to allow the franchise to voters who could vote in their states.[83] Obviously his objections were not very strong. Like other delegates, Mercer was often a compromiser. At one stage he said he did not like the Constitution but he would go along with the Maryland dele-

---

[77] *Ibid.*, ɪɪ, 251, 362.      [78] *Ibid.*, ɪ, 49.
[79] *Ibid.*, p. 101.      [80] *Ibid.*, ɪɪ, 201-02.
[81] *Ibid.*, ɪ, 101, 338-39; ɪɪ, 201-02, 451, 477, 587.
[82] *Ibid.*, ɪɪ, 205.      [83] *Ibid.*, p. 216.

gation on points in question and with the Convention if it would not back his own ideas.[84] While almost everyone else complained that there was too much democracy, Mercer said he considered the existing state governments as aristocracies, but aristocracies of officeholders, not of personalty interests.[85] All this, plus the fact that Mercer finally opposed the Constitution, shows how difficult it is to force Convention delegates into a set pattern.

Mifflin of Pennsylvania, according to Beard and the *Records*, took little part in the debates and so cannot be used to prove much of anything.

Gouverneur Morris of Pennsylvania, whom Beard quoted at length, actually did not prove the Beard thesis as Beard implied. Morris wanted the suffrage restricted to freeholders, whom Beard had called the greatest enemies of personalty, and he said nine-tenths of the people were freeholders, an indication that there was much democracy in 1787. Furthermore, Morris, like Madison, was talking about the development of a proletariat in the future and did not say there was a propertyless proletariat at the time the Convention met.[86] He did not want to set up an aristocratic government, as has generally been assumed. What he wanted was an aristocratic senate based on personalty to check a democratic house based on realty. He believed the influence of the rich must be guarded but that a pure democracy was equally oppressive to the lower orders.[87] He also thought that the western states would have interests different from those of the eastern[88] and that love of fame was one of man's strongest passions.[89] Again he declared that all the guards contrived by America—that is, property qualifications for voting and officeholding—had not prevented the state senates from being dominated by the democratic houses, an indication that society at the time was democratic.[90] He also wanted the executive elected by the people at large, by the freeholders of the country,[91] for he thought such a feature in the Constitution would make it "extremely palatable"

[84] *Ibid.*, p. 212.    [85] *Ibid.*, p. 284.    [86] *Ibid.*, pp. 202-03.
[87] *Ibid.*, I, 512-14, 518.    [88] *Ibid.*, pp. 533, 583.    [89] *Ibid.*, II, 53.
[90] *Ibid.*, I, 512.    [91] *Ibid.*, II, 29.

to the people.[92] Within the state itself, he declared, the majority must rule regardless of the mischief done.[93] All these points of view do not add up to Beard's statement that Morris always showed "his thorough distrust of democratic institutions." Perhaps Morris was only an unwilling democrat because the social order of the time forced it upon him, but some of these statements, at least, make him look like a democrat. Even if Morris proved the Beard thesis, which he did not, the fact still would remain that his views were about as little representative of the Convention as were those of Hamilton, and Hamilton's plan was not even seconded.[94]

Robert Morris of Pennsylvania, as Beard indicated, revealed little of his political philosophy, so he cannot be used as evidence of anything in particular. He did support a motion for senators to serve during good behavior,[95] but he also signed the Constitution without this provision and made no great effort to get the motion adopted.

Paterson of New Jersey did not prove the Beard thesis, as Beard himself said. His concern was the protection of small states against large, not personalty, and he can be cited many times to prove that there was democracy in 1787. He said that the democratic spirit ran high,[96] that the delegates must follow the people in drawing up a government, for the people would not follow the delegates,[97] and that the object of the Convention was to devise not the best government, but the one their constituents had authorized and would approve.[98] What he really wanted was a modified democracy.[99]

Pierce of Georgia does not prove anything according to Beard's account. Actually, he thought in terms of state interests, for he wanted the House elected by the people and the Senate by the states to preserve state sovereignty,[100] and he advocated three-year terms for senators, which would place him on the democratic side.[101] He also believed that men were motivated more by state and local considerations than they were by class advantages.[102]

[92] Ibid., p. 54.    [93] Ibid., p. 429.    [94] Ibid., I, 293, 301.
[95] Ibid., p. 409.   [96] Ibid., p. 186.    [97] Ibid., pp. 176, 186.
[98] Ibid., p. 250.   [99] Ibid., p. 186.    [100] Ibid., pp. 59, 137.
[101] Ibid., p. 218.  [102] Ibid., p. 474.

Beard's analysis of Charles Pinckney of South Carolina shows what can be done by choosing only a small part of the available evidence. At one point Pinckney proposed a high property qualification for president, legislators, and judges, which certainly was conservative. Rutledge seconded the motion, but said the committee had omitted qualifications for fear of displeasing the people by making them high or rendering them worthless by making them low. But as Madison said, "The Motion of Mr. Pinkney was rejected by so general a *no*, that the States were not called."[103] From the evidence I have seen, Pinckney came very close to a correct analysis of American society at the time. He said the chief characteristics were equality and mediocrity, few rich and few poor, few excluded by lack of sufficient property from participation in politics. He divided the people into three groups—professional, commercial, and landed—and said that the landed interest was and should be the governing interest. He also agreed that the Convention must design a government to fit this American society, to have some permanency while reserving to the people the right of election, which they would not and should not relinquish.[104] Pinckney's letter to Madison, quoted by Beard, gives just the opposite view—little faith in elections by the people— so it apparently depends on which Pinckney quotation we use. Pinckney believed that people were motivated by religious and political prejudices, not just economic interests,[105] and that the real conflict of interest was between North and South rather than between horizontal classes.[106]

C. C. Pinckney of South Carolina, as Beard said, moved that senators should not receive pay since the Senate was to represent the wealth of the country. He was seconded by Franklin, which is confusing to say the least. It should be noted, however, that Pinckney did not specify personalty.[107] He also proposed election of the House by state legislatures, then changed and advocated election by the people.[108] He favored four-year terms for senators on the ground that the states had different interests, especially the northern and southern, and he feared

[103] *Ibid.*, ii, 248-49.  [104] *Ibid.*, i, 398-404.  [105] *Ibid.*, iii, 254.
[106] *Ibid.*, i, 510.  [107] *Ibid.*, pp. 426-27.  [108] *Ibid.*, pp. 358, 360.

that long terms in office would cause a senator to lose touch with his state's interests.[109] As with most of the southern delegates, he was a strong defender of slavery interests.[110] At one point he reminded the Convention that the southern states had to have security against emancipation of slaves and taxes on exports.[111]

Randolph of Virginia undoubtedly believed in some checks on complete democracy, as the quotation in Beard shows, which in itself is evidence that there was democracy. He did not say, however, that the check was primarily for the protection of personalty over other forms of property. Randolph can be quoted to prove many things, in fact. He believed a stronger government was needed to pay the debt to France as well as to pay officers, soldiers, and those who had lent the government money.[112] He also declared that Virginia had fought the Revolution "under a democracy almost as pure as representation would admit," evidence that democracy operated in that state.[113] He was against a single executive because he thought the people should be consulted and would oppose anything that looked like monarchy,[114] and he wanted representatives to serve two rather than three years because the people were attached to frequent elections.[115] Later he changed his mind and declared that the Convention was going too far in consulting popular prejudices.[116] But then he went back to the idea that the people would oppose an aristocratic senate and president, and stated that his main object was to prevent popular objections which might defeat the Constitution.[117]

With some qualification, two of the three points made by Beard on George Read of Delaware are correct, though they do not represent Read's complete political philosophy. What Read's desire to discard the Articles of Confederation means will depend on the way one interprets the Articles. If they seem democratic, Read can be considered conservative. But

[109] *Ibid.*, p. 421.
[110] *Ibid.*, I, 580, 592, 593; II, 371.
[111] *Ibid.*, II, 95.
[112] *Ibid.*, I, 262.
[113] *Ibid.*, III, 307.
[114] *Ibid.*, I, 90.
[115] *Ibid.*, p. 360.
[116] *Ibid.*, p. 372.
[117] *Ibid.*, II, 279.

if a system which provided for equal votes of states regardless of size, for a majority of nine out of thirteen to pass important legislation, and for unanimous consent for amendment is considered undemocratic, Read was liberal; and the Articles had these provisions. Read favored an absolute veto for the president but he received little support from his colleagues on this motion, and his proposal that senators serve during good behavior was defeated overwhelmingly, nine to one.[118] Actually, Read's chief concern in the Convention was to protect the interests of the small states, such as his own state of Delaware, which is not the kind of economic interpretation that Beard emphasized.[119]

The material presented by Beard on Rutledge of South Carolina is sufficient in itself to refute the Beard thesis. Rutledge wanted representation based on *both* wealth and population, not just wealth, and certainly not in a way that would favor personalty. Of course Rutledge was "one of the most ardent champions of the rights of property" in the Convention, but this is not the Beard thesis. If Beard had based his thesis on *property* and not *personalty*, he would have been on much safer ground. Furthermore, and again as Beard shows, Rutledge's chief concern was slavery, and his division of interests was slave vs. free states, not personalty vs. small farmers and debtors. He was also perfectly aware of the influence of "the people" on the Convention and realized that the Constitution had to be fashioned to meet their approval.[120]

Sherman of Connecticut did maintain on one occasion that the people should have as little to say about government as possible, but he said many other things too. He contended that government was designed to protect the liberties of those who lived under it, and that frequent elections were necessary to guarantee the good behavior of officials.[121] With others, he was a defender of the rights of small states, contending that states like individuals, had their peculiar habits and usages.[122] Sherman was not aware of a mass of disfranchised, for he

[118] *Ibid.*, p. 200.
[120] *Ibid.*, ii, 205, 249.
[122] *Ibid.*, p. 343.
[119] *Ibid.*, i, 37, 137, 424, 463.
[121] *Ibid.*, i, 423.

said the poor man was equal to the rich in voting because of the equal distribution of liberty among all ranks.[123] In the formation of laws, he believed the opinions of the people who were to be governed should be followed, which looks like a direct contradiction of his previous statement.[124] He, too, was guided in his ideas by what the people would approve.[125] There is nothing in the evidence on Sherman which would indicate that American society was undemocratic in 1787 or that Sherman favored personalty over realty or even over political "principles."

Spaight of North Carolina, from the evidence presented by Beard, does not seem to prove anything. He favored a long term for the president, denounced judicial control, and claimed the Constitution was not aristocratic. But he also believed that the national legislature should be based on population,[126] moved that the Senate should be appointed by state legislatures,[127] changed his mind and withdrew his motion,[128] advocated a seven-year term for senators,[129] voted against equality of the states in the Senate,[130] wanted the executive chosen by electors elected by state legislatures,[131] changed his mind and wanted the executive elected by the national legislature,[132] moved that the president serve seven years and be ineligible for reelection,[133] and then spoke of election of the president as being "crammed down" as though he disapproved the method.[134] In a letter to the Governor, he and the other North Carolina delegates asserted that they had guarded and promoted the interests of North Carolina in particular and of the South in general, especially protecting them from unequal and heavy taxation.[135] Surely North Carolina was not one of the states with large personalty interests. On the whole Spaight was conservative, but he was often voted down, an indication that the Convention did not support him.

Strong of Massachusetts certainly does not bolster the Beard thesis on the basis of Beard's evidence. As Beard said, Strong

[123] *Ibid.*, pp. 450, 457.  [124] *Ibid.*, II, 585.  [125] *Ibid.*, I, 377.
[126] *Ibid.*, p. 36.  [127] *Ibid.*, pp. 51, 58.  [128] *Ibid.*, p. 52.
[129] *Ibid.*, p. 218.  [130] *Ibid.*, II, 15.  [131] *Ibid.*, p. 95.
[132] *Ibid.*, p. 99.  [133] *Ibid.*, I, 71; II, 525.  [134] *Ibid.*, II, 526.
[135] *Ibid.*, III, 83-84.

seconded Ellsworth's motion for one-year terms for representatives because the people were fond of frequent elections,[136] and he voted against seven-year terms for the president and senators.[137] He was also against ineligibility of the executive for a second term[138] and favored origination of money bills in the House.[139] Since Strong advocated these democratic or liberal measures and yet supported the adoption of the Constitution, he must not have considered the Constitution much of a check on democracy.

As we shall see eventually, George Washington may have come much closer to a correct interpretation of the Constitution than Beard did. Washington characterized the Constitution as "the offspring of our own choice, uninfluenced and unawed, adopted upon full investigation, and mature deliberation, completely free in its principles, in the distribution of its powers, uniting security with energy" (Beard, p. 215). He opposed a seven-year term for the president,[140] voted for origination of money bills in the House of Representatives,[141] was for adoption of the Constitution by seven states,[142] and, as Beard said, favored a rural (realty) rather than an urban (personalty) society. Washington seconded Gorham's motion that representation in the House be apportioned on the basis of one member for 30,000 people instead of 40,000, as the Constitution originally provided. He said this would decrease objections to the plan as well as increase the security for the rights and interests of the people.[143] On the strength of this evidence, Washington would fall somewhere near the "middle of the road" between the extremes of liberalism and conservatism.

Williamson of North Carolina does not help the Beard thesis much either. He was against election of the president by electors,[144] and he opposed a motion to restrict the franchise to freeholders only, even though that should have been an advantage to agricultural North Carolina.[145] In both "opinion & practice" he was against slavery, yet he did not want the

[136] *Ibid.*, I, 361, 368.  [137] *Ibid.*, pp. 72, 219.  [138] *Ibid.*, II, 100.
[139] *Ibid.*, p. 297.  [140] *Ibid.*, p. 121.  [141] *Ibid.*, p. 280.
[142] *Ibid.*, p. 482.  [143] *Ibid.*, p. 644.  [144] *Ibid.*, I, 81.
[145] *Ibid.*, II, 201.

union to break up over the slavery issue.[146] He apparently thought an election of representatives by the people would be less open to corruption than an election of senators by state legislatures.[147] And he believed that wealthy immigrants did more harm by their luxurious example than they did good by the wealth they brought with them.[148] Williamson was one of the North Carolina delegates who assured the Governor of that state that they had safeguarded the interests of the South in general and North Carolina in particular.[149]

Wilson of Pennsylvania, as Beard said, favored such democratic practices as annual election of representatives by the people, popular election of senators, popular election of the president, and no property qualifications for voting. Obviously he is not good evidence for the Beard thesis. In addition, Wilson said the Convention could not set up a government like the British government because this country had no laws of primogeniture and no distinction of families, and the partition of estates destroyed the influence of the few.[150] He said he did not see how the landed interest would be made less prominent in the Senate by election through state legislatures rather than the people, for if the state legislatures now sacrificed commercial to landed interests, why suppose that they would choose someone different for the Senate.[151] No government could long subsist without the confidence of the people, he declared, and he wanted a government broadly based on the people.[152]

Wythe of Virginia proves practically nothing, both from Beard's evidence and from the *Records*.

These were the delegates whose political philosophy Beard considered, but he could have analyzed the views of others in the Convention with the same results as the following examples show. Bassett of Delaware opposed federal veto of state laws, presumably because he wanted to protect the interests of the small states.[153] Blair of Virginia first opposed and

[146] *Ibid.*, pp. 415-16.   [147] *Ibid.*, p. 239.   [148] *Ibid.*, p. 268.
[149] *Ibid.*, III, 83-84.   [150] *Ibid.*, I, 159.   [151] *Ibid.*, p. 154.
[152] *Ibid.*, p. 49.   [153] *Ibid.*, p. 168.

then favored a single executive,[154] approved the veto of state laws,[155] and voted against the exclusive right of the House to originate money bills.[156] Brearley of New Jersey was a strong advocate of the rights of small states, but there is not much evidence on his other views.[157] Dayton of New Jersey was also pro-small state,[158] thought the people would reject the Constitution,[159] believed there was a division of interests between slave and free states,[160] and seconded Gouverneur Morris's strong stand against slavery.[161] Houston of New Jersey proves nothing. Jenifer of Maryland proposed three-year terms for representatives on the ground that too frequent elections promoted indifference among the people,[162] but otherwise it is difficult to tell what he thought. Johnson of Connecticut was willing to take a compromise position between the large and small states by allowing the states representation in the Senate.[163] He also made the statement that for his ultra-conservative plan of government, Hamilton had been praised by everybody but supported by none,[164] and believed that numbers were the best measure of wealth and representation, including slaves as well as free men.[165] Langdon of New Hampshire favored election of the president by joint vote of House and Senate even though such a procedure would not benefit the small state of New Hampshire,[166] and he kept an eye on what the people would accept in a constitution.[167] Lansing of New York wished to protect the interests of small states by amending the Articles of Confederation,[168] believing that great differences of interest existed among the states.[169] In stating his reasons for leaving the Convention and not favoring the Constitution, Lansing emphasized states' rights rather than property rights.[170] Yates of New York was in agreement with Lansing and also left the Convention.

[154] *Ibid.*, I, 97; II, 121.
[155] *Ibid.*, I, 168.
[156] *Ibid.*, II, 280.
[157] *Ibid.*, I, 176-77; II, 402-03.
[158] *Ibid.*, I, 445, 490; II, 5.
[159] *Ibid.*, I, 490.
[160] *Ibid.*, p. 567.
[161] *Ibid.*, II, 223.
[162] *Ibid.*, p. 214.
[163] *Ibid.*, I, 354-55, 407, 415, 461, 470.
[164] *Ibid.*, p. 363.
[165] *Ibid.*, p. 593.
[166] *Ibid.*, II, 402.
[167] *Ibid.*, p. 125.
[168] *Ibid.*, I, 242.
[169] *Ibid.*, p. 337.
[170] *Ibid.*, III, 244-47.

Judged by historical method, what does all this information prove? Beard said it proved that the authors of *The Federalist* generalized the political doctrines of the delegates to a high degree of accuracy despite the diversity of opinion in the Convention. That is very nearly true, if he meant all eighty-five numbers of *The Federalist*. But if he meant only a distorted version of Madison's No. 10, then the answer is no. The delegates acted from all sorts of motives and with all kinds of interests and principles in mind, both liberal and conservative. As Madison said, the delegates reasoned clearly on most points but drew different conclusions because they reasoned from different principles.[171]

If Beard meant that the delegates reflected his own thesis—that the Constitution was put over by personalty and put over because of an absence of democracy—the answer again is no. Naturally the delegates believed in the protection of property as one function of government, as Beard's evidence in this chapter proves. But that is not the Beard thesis, though it has often been so considered. As I have said so often, Beard would have been on safer ground if he had stuck to property in general, not personalty. Then he would simply have had to show that most of the people were property owners and also believed in the protection of property. This would have gotten him much closer to a more nearly accurate interpretation of the Constitution than his emphasis on personalty. And of course Beard's evidence and all the other evidence from the *Records* prove that there was something close to complete democracy among free adult men in 1787. Even the fact that some of the members themselves were not democratic—and some were not —does not invalidate the conclusion that society was democratic. The truth is that even such a conservative as Hamilton knew that the Constitution had to meet the approval of a democratic society.

If we would understand the political philosophies of the men in the Convention, we must accumulate everything they said on every point, then add it all up to see what it means. We cannot simply pick out those statements which appear to prove

171 *Ibid.*, I, 147.

a thesis. Above all, we should not choose evidence that actually disproves what we say it proves, as Beard did. And when we collect this evidence, as I have done in this chapter, we find that the delegates represented all kinds of interests and all sorts of political philosophies, not just the interests and philosophy contained in Beard's interpretation of Madison and *The Federalist* No. 10.

# CHAPTER VIII

## "THE PROCESS OF RATIFICATION"

BEARD attempted to show in this chapter that the process of ratifying the Constitution represented a political revolution accomplished by somewhat underhanded methods. The Articles of Confederation provided that any alteration in government should be made by the Confederation Congress and approved by *all* the state legislatures, and the delegates to the Convention had been sent with instructions to amend the Articles. Instead, they drew up an entirely new plan of government, then provided that it would go into effect when ratified by conventions, not legislatures, of *nine* instead of thirteen states. If such revolutionary processes had been performed by a Caesar or a Napoleon, Beard said, "they would have been pronounced *coups d'état*" (pp. 217-18).

Before we see what happened at Philadelphia, we need to examine the meaning and connotation of the term *coup d'état*. The word is defined in Webster as either a sudden decisive exercise of force whereby the existing government is subverted or an unexpected stroke of policy. The question, then, is whether or not the process by which the Constitution came into being can be characterized as a *coup d'état*.

No one would deny that some of the leaders of the Convention intended to scuttle the Articles of Confederation and construct a new government. In fact, I would go even further than Beard on this point. If we can believe George Mason and other delegates, "the most prevalent idea" among the delegates even before the Convention met was "a total alteration of the present federal system, and substituting a great national council or parliament."[1] But does this signify a *coup d'état*?

Before we brand the overthrow of the Articles and the adoption of the Constitution a revolutionary *coup*, we need to

[1] *The Records of the Federal Convention of 1787*, ed. Max Farrand, 4 vols. (New Haven, 1937), III, 23-26, 30, 32.

have in mind some salient points about both documents. First, the Articles of Confederation were neither democratically adopted nor did they represent democratic processes. They were ratified by state legislatures, not by the people; they provided that each state would have one vote, regardless of size; important acts had to be passed by nine out of thirteen states; and amendment could be accomplished only by the unanimous consent of the thirteen state legislatures. Madison pointed out that, under the Articles, one state with one-sixtieth of the population (Rhode Island) could and did block the desires of twelve states representing fifty-nine-sixtieths.[2] If the argument is offered, as it has been, that the Articles were democratic because they did not permit interference with democracy in the states, all Beard's material on the limitation of democracy in the states by property qualifications will have to be discarded. Then there are the statements made in the Convention of a general feeling among the people that the Confederation was inadequate and would have to be changed,[3] and also that the people expected something substantial from the Convention.[4] It is perfectly true that the members of the Convention were not democratically elected by the people, either. They were chosen by state legislatures just as delegates to the Confederation Congress were chosen. But as Gorham said, the actions of the Convention were not binding, and the states could reject any plan it submitted.[5] The Constitution was to be ratified, after due debate, by conventions elected specifically for that purpose rather than by state legislatures, which were not elected on the issue of ratifying the Constitution. And the people were fully aware, when they chose their conventions, that they were voting on whether to discard the Articles of Confederation.

In view of the Beard thesis, we need to consider further the idea that the Convention recommended bypassing the state legislatures to get adoption by state conventions elected

[2] *Ibid.*, p. 257.
[3] *Ibid.*, I, 261; III, 37, 54, 124.
[4] *Ibid.*, I, 261; II, 90; III, 23, 32, 36, 37, 60, 73.
[5] *Ibid.*, II, 462.

specifically on the question of ratifying the Constitution. Theoretically, the Convention should have wanted ratification by state legislatures, for Beard said in Chapter IV that the qualifications for officeholding provided safeguards in these legislatures. Why should the Convention subject the fate of the Constitution to the freeholders if the Convention was motivated by personalty interests and the freeholders were the most dangerous antagonists of personalty? One would think, on the basis of Beard's particular economic interpretation, that the delegates would try to eliminate "the people" as much as possible from any consideration of the Constitution, and would restrict discussion of the Constitution to the state legislatures, where property supposedly predominated. Why, then, did the Convention specify ratification by special conventions rather than by state legislatures?

The answers which Beard gave to this question (p. 221) are rather interesting in view of his thesis and the *Records*. The first, that such a procedure permitted the disregard of the principle of unanimous approval by the states, would be valid only if the Convention were following the procedures laid down by the Articles of Confederation. The Convention could have specified ratification by state legislatures of nine states as easily as it specified ratification by conventions of nine states. Beard's second reason, that ratification by special conventions would give the Constitution a firmer foundation than ratification by state legislatures, is correct as far as it goes. There was included also the idea that "the people were . . . the fountain of all power," and if the people sanctioned the Constitution through conventions, "all disputes & doubts concerning the legitimacy of the new Constitution" would be obviated.[6] The third reason, that state legislatures would oppose the Constitution because they would lose power, is quite correct, but it seems to me that all three of these reasons have elements of the political as well as the economic in them. The fourth reason, that one leading purpose of the Convention "was to pay the public debt at par," I have already discussed at some length. The statement is certainly open to question from the evidence I have presented. And furthermore, did the Convention expect the freeholders to

[6] *Ibid.*, pp. 92, 476.

be friendlier on this score than the state legislatures? I think the process of reasoning from Hamilton's funding and assumption programs backward to the Convention is twenty-twenty hindsight and needs proving.

In the last line of the paragraph (p. 221) the conspiracy motif reappears. Beard said "the urgent necessities of the advocates of the new system could not permit such a mere technicality" as the requirement in the Articles for unanimous approval "to stand in their way." Why should the Convention abide by one part of the Articles since it was obviously discarding the rest of them for a new system? As Gouverneur Morris said, some delegates erroneously supposed that the Convention was proceeding on the basis of the Confederation, but he concluded: "This Convention is unknown to the Confederation."[7]

There is no question that the whole procedure from the meeting of the Convention to the adoption of the Constitution was illegal from the standpoint of the Articles of Confederation. The only question is whether the process of deliberating three months and then submitting the Constitution for ratification by the people constitutes a *coup d'état*. Some of the delegates had qualms about their methods while others justified their actions on the ground that a revision of the Articles would not be adequate. The facts remain, however, that, as Gorham said, the people could reject any plan offered by the Convention, and that the Constitution was submitted to the people for ratification. Furthermore, they ratified it in spite of all the charges that it was illegal, so they certainly knew what they were doing. If all this constitutes a *coup d'état*, perhaps we need to revise our meaning of the word, for the method involved neither force nor sudden action.

When we turn from the discussion of the *"coup d'état"* to Beard's state-by-state account of ratification, we find that the author used some extremely interesting methods. To get the full impact of these methods, the reader needs to have in mind a complete picture of the order in which the states ratified and the vote or margin of victory in each in favor of the Constitution. This information will be found in Table I.

[7] *Ibid.*, p. 92.

TABLE I

| ORDER OF RATIFICATION | DATE OF RATIFICATION | VOTE ON RATIFICATION | |
|---|---|---|---|
| | | *For* | *Against* |
| 1. Delaware | Dec. 7, 1787 | 30 | 0 |
| 2. Pennsylvania | Dec. 12, 1787 | 46 | 23 |
| 3. New Jersey | Dec. 18, 1787 | 39 | 0 |
| 4. Georgia | Jan. 2, 1788 | 26 | 0 |
| 5. Connecticut | Jan. 9, 1788 | 128 | 40 |
| 6. Massachusetts | Feb. 6, 1788 | 187 | 168 |
| 7. Maryland | April 28, 1788 | 63 | 11 |
| 8. South Carolina | May 23, 1788 | 149 | 73 |
| 9. New Hampshire | June 21, 1788 | 57 | 46 |
| Vote after nine states had ratified | | 725 | 361 |
| 10. Virginia | June 25, 1788 | 89 | 79 |
| 11. New York | June 26, 1788 | 30 | 27 |
| Vote of states forming Union when Washington took office, 1789 | | 844 | 467 |
| 12. North Carolina | Nov. 21, 1789 | — | — |
| 13. Rhode Island | May 29, 1790 | — | — |

The first feature of Beard's discussion of ratification to strike the reader is the fact that he did not take up the states in the order in which they ratified. Instead, he discussed them on somewhat of a geographical basis, starting with New Hampshire and going to Georgia, with the exception that he did place Rhode Island last. In Table II the reader can see at a glance the order used by Beard, together with the order in which the states actually ratified and the vote.

Why did Beard take up the states geographically instead of in the order in which they ratified? A geographical approach is irrelevant, since there is no correlation whatever between geography, the order of ratification, and the vote. On the other hand, a discussion of the states in the order in which they ratified would have been perfectly logical. Then we would have the same information that the people of the time had: that is, when Pennsylvania ratified, it was known that Delaware had ratified unanimously; and when Massachusetts ratified, everyone knew that five states had ratified, three unanimously and two by large majorities. But Beard did not choose to discuss

142

TABLE II

| ORDER IN WHICH BEARD DISCUSSED RATIFICATION | ORDER IN WHICH STATES RATIFIED | VOTE ON RATIFICATION | |
|---|---|---|---|
| | | *For* | *Against* |
| 1. New Hampshire | 9 | 57 | 46 |
| 2. Massachusetts | 6 | 187 | 168 |
| 3. Connecticut | 5 | 128 | 40 |
| 4. New York | 11 | 30 | 27 |
| 5. New Jersey | 3 | 39 | 0 |
| 6. Delaware | 1 | 30 | 0 |
| 7. Pennsylvania | 2 | 46 | 23 |
| 8. Maryland | 7 | 63 | 11 |
| 9. Virginia | 10 | 89 | 79 |
| 10. North Carolina | 12 | — | — |
| 11. South Carolina | 8 | 149 | 73 |
| 12. Georgia | 4 | 26 | 0 |
| 13. Rhode Island | 13 | — | — |

the states in their logical order. We can never know why, but an analysis of the vote on ratification and experiments with students lead to some interesting speculations.

The reader's impression of the ease or difficulty of ratification depends on the order in which the states are discussed. I have found that students get the notion that ratification was easy if the states are discussed in order of ease of ratification, with the easiest ratification first, and that it was difficult if the states are discussed in order of difficulty of ratification, with the most difficult ratification first. Beard's general interpretation was that the Constitution was put over by questionable methods only after a strenuous political battle. He started his discussion with New Hampshire and Massachusetts, the only two of the first nine where the vote was even remotely close, then skipped lightly over Connecticut to New York, a state where the vote was extremely close, but a state which was not even among the first nine to ratify. Not until the reader reaches New Jersey does he realize that the vote was not close in some states. But by then he has the impression that ratification was difficult in three out of the first four states, and he does not stop to see whether these were actually the first four states to ratify.

Had Beard taken up ratification in its logical order, that is,

143

the order in which the states ratified, the reader might be tremendously impressed by the lack of opposition to the Constitution.

A glance at Table I gives a much different impression from that created by Beard with his account. Here we find that the vote in the first nine states to ratify was close in only two, Massachusetts and New Hampshire, or numbers six and nine respectively; that it was unanimous in three of the first four, Delaware, New Jersey, and Georgia; and that the margin of victory was overwhelming in the others. The total vote for the first nine ratifiers was 725 to 361, or 66.75 per cent to 33.25 per cent—a margin that would satisfy almost any politician— while the vote of the eleven states which put the Constitution in operation was 844 to 467, or a comfortable percentage of 64.37 to 35.63. This is not to deny that the vote in Massachusetts, New Hampshire, Virginia, and New York was fairly close, but it does place the vote of all the states in its proper perspective.

If the Beard thesis were correct—that the Constitution was put over by personalty and opposed by small farmers and debtors (realty)—one might expect to find some correlation between the quickness and ease with which the Constitution was ratified, on one hand, and the amount of realty and personalty in the various states, on the other. To show this correlation, in Table III I have combined Table I with Beard's figures on realty and interest values (p. 36). My comparisons will show what can be done if generalizations are followed to their logical destinations. A few brief explanations will perhaps help the reader who is not statistically inclined.

The first five columns should be self-explanatory. They give the order and vote by which the states ratified, the amount of taxable land (not including houses) in the states, interest paid on the public debt in each state, and how this interest, which represents personalty, compares with a state's realty.

Columns 6, 7, 8, and 9 are the important columns as far as correlations are concerned. Column 6 shows how the states should have ratified if there is a close correlation between the speed with which states ratified and the amount of opposition

144

## TABLE III

### COMPARISON OF RATIFICATION, LAND VALUES, AND INTEREST DISBURSED

| States by order of ratification (1) | Vote on ratification (2) | Valuation of land, not including $140,000,000 for houses (3) | Interest disbursed, presumably on public debt (4) | Percentage of interest disbursed to total value of land and interest (5) | States by order of ease of ratification (6) | Order in which states should have ratified on basis of land values (7) | Order in which states should have ratified on basis of interest disbursed (8) | Order in which states should have ratified on basis of percentage of interest to total (9) |
|---|---|---|---|---|---|---|---|---|
| 1. Delaware | 30-0 | $ 4,053,248 | $ 2,980 | 0.074 | 1. N.J. | 1. Del. | 1. N.Y. | 1. S.C. |
| 2. Pennsylvania | 46-23 | 72,824,852 | 86,379 | 0.119 | 2. Del. | 2. R.I. | 2. Mass. | 2. Mass. |
| 3. New Jersey | 39-0 | 27,287,981 | 27,350 | 0.101 | 3. Ga. | 3. Ga. | 3. S.C. | 3. N.Y. |
| 4. Georgia | 26-0 | 10,263,506 | 6,800 | 0.067 | 4. Md. | 4. S.C. | 4. Penn. | 4. R.I. |
| 5. Connecticut | 128-40 | 40,163,955 | 79,600 | 0.198 | 5. Conn. | 5. N.H. | 5. Conn. | 5. Md. |
| 6. Massachusetts | 187-168 | 54,445,642 | 309,500 | 0.573 | 6. S.C. | 6. Md. | 6. Md. | 6. Conn. |
| 7. Maryland | 63-11 | 21,634,004 | 74,000 | 0.341 | 7. Penn. | 7. N.J. | 7. Va. | 7. Penn. |
| 8. South Carolina | 149-73 | 12,456,720 | 109,500 | 0.872 | 8. N.H. | 8. N.C. | 8. R.I. | 8. Va. |
| 9. New Hampshire | 57-46 | 19,028,108 | 20,000 | 0.105 | 9. Va. | 9. Conn. | 9. N.J. | 9. N.H. |
| 10. Virginia | 89-79 | 59,976,860 | 63,300 | 0.106 | 10. Mass. | 10. Mass. | 10. N.H. | 10. N.J. |
| 11. New York | 30-27 | 74,885,075 | 367,600 | 0.489 | 11. N.Y. | 11. Va. | 11. Ga. | 11. Del. |
| 12. North Carolina | — | 27,909,479 | 3,200 | 0.012 | 12. N.C. | 12. Penn. | 12. N.C. | 12. Ga. |
| 13. Rhode Island | — | 8,082,355 | 31,700 | 0.391 | 13. R.I. | 13. N.Y. | 13. Del. | 13. N.C. |

in the state. In short, the states with the least opposition to the Constitution should have ratified soonest and by the largest vote, and on this score there is a fair correlation.

Column 7 shows how the states should have ratified if there was a close relationship between land values and ratification. If the opposition came from agriculture, we might expect to find states with the least value in land ratifying first while those with the most land would ratify last. The correlation is perfect for Delaware, almost completely reversed for Rhode Island and Pennsylvania, fair for Georgia, Maryland, Virginia, and New York, but not very close for the others.

From the standpoint of the Beard thesis, columns 8 and 9 are the most important. Here we have the way the states should have ratified on the basis of total interest paid and the way interest compared with realty. If interest represented securities, those states receiving the most interest should have ratified the most quickly and easily, as should also those states where interest formed the largest percentage of total wealth. The correlation in column 8 is not very significant. Connecticut and North Carolina are perfect, but Delaware is completely reversed and Georgia is off considerably, while New York and Massachusetts, where the vote was close, should have been the first two to ratify. Similarly, the correlation in column 9 has little significance. South Carolina, Massachusetts, New York and Rhode Island should have ratified first but actually ranked well down the list. New Jersey, Delaware, and Georgia rank among the last four but were among the first four to ratify.

If we use as a basis for correlation the per capita figures for land values and interest disbursed instead of total values (Table IV), there is no significant correlation, again assuming that the states with the largest per capita realty would have opposed the Constitution and those with the largest per capita interest would have favored it. On land values, Massachusetts correlates perfectly and Delaware, New Hampshire, and New York are close, but the other states are almost reversed. Elimination of slaves would raise the per capita value of land for whites in the southern states but probably would not change the order very much. On the basis of interest disbursed,

146

## TABLE IV

### PER CAPITA VALUES OF LAND AND INTEREST DISBURSED

| States by order of ratification | Population in 1790, including slaves | Per capita value of land not including $140,000,000 for houses | Per capita value of interest disbursed | Order in which states should have ratified on basis of per capita land values | Order in which states should have ratified on basis of interest per capita |
|---|---|---|---|---|---|
| 1. Delaware | 59,096 | $ 68.41 | $0.05 | 1. S.C. | 1. N.Y. |
| 2. Pennsylvania | 434,373 | 121.61 | 0.20 | 2. Md. | 2. Mass. |
| 3. New Jersey | 184,139 | 159.05 | 0.15 | 3. Del. | 3. R.I. |
| 4. Georgia | 82,548 | 124.33 | 0.08 | 4. N.C. | 4. S.C. |
| 5. Connecticut | 237,946 | 168.79 | 0.34 | 5. Va. | 5. Conn. |
| 6. Massachusetts | 475,327 | 114.56 | 0.65 | 6. Mass. | 6. Md. |
| 7. Maryland | 319,728 | 67.66 | 0.23 | 7. R.I. | 7. Penn. |
| 8. South Carolina | 249,073 | 50.01 | 0.44 | 8. Penn. | 8. N.J. |
| 9. New Hampshire | 141,885 | 134.10 | 0.14 | 9. Ga. | 9. N.H. |
| 10. Virginia | 747,610 | 80.22 | 0.08 | 10. N.H. | 10. Va. |
| 11. New York | 340,120 | 220.17 | 1.08 | 11. N.J. | 11. Ga. |
| 12. North Carolina | 393,751 | 70.88 | 0.01 | 12. Conn. | 12. Del. |
| 13. Rhode Island | 68,825 | 117.43 | 0.46 | 13. N.Y. | 13. N.C. |

the correlation is perfect for Virginia, New Hampshire, and Connecticut, and close for Maryland and North Carolina. But it is almost reversed for New York, Rhode Island, Georgia, and Delaware. Georgia and Virginia had the same per capita interest, $0.08, yet one ratified quickly and unanimously while the other ratified late and by a close vote. New York and Virginia both ratified late and by a close vote, but they were completely unlike in security holding.

For all practical purposes there is no correlation between ratification, on the one hand, and realty and personalty, on the other.

Still another element in the Beard technique should be noted in relation to his discussion of ratification. This was the relatively large amount of space he gave to states where ratification was close or the methods were questionable, and the small amount of space he accorded to the states which ratified unanimously or by overwhelming majorities. For an understanding of the Constitution, it seems to me that we need to know not only why the vote was close in some states, but also why it was not close in seven of the first eleven to ratify.

For his interpretation of New Hampshire, Beard relied on the word of a secondary writer, J. B. Walker. Walker said in his *History of the New Hampshire Convention* that a majority of the ratifying convention were undoubtedly opposed to the Constitution, but that some of them, though converted by the discussions, would not vote for its adoption without first going back to their towns and consulting their constituents. The convention first met in February, 1788, and then adjourned for discussion between delegates and constituents until June. The vote was close, 57-46 or 55.3 per cent to 44.7 per cent, but the process certainly appears to have been deliberate and democratic. That both sides tried to win converts among the delegates would signify only that American political practices were operating in 1787.

Beard's use of innuendo in footnote 2, page 226, was completely unjustified. He cited Walker to the effect that there was "a pretty well authenticated tradition" that a prominent Federalist was entertaining several delegates "reckoned" as opponents of the Constitution at the very time the vote was being taken. If this was true, the delegates were remiss in their duty to their constituents, but in any event the historian should document such an important point and not accept hearsay evidence or traditions.

Beard's uncritical use of secondary works again appears in his discussion of ratification in Massachusetts, and here the reader will note that he made no pretension of going to the sources. He quoted Harding's *The Federal Constitution in Massachusetts* to show that the Constitution would have been defeated if the ratifying convention had voted as soon as it met. As a matter of fact, Harding could not have known this, for many towns sent uninstructed delegates. How did Harding know that the nine delegates whose names were returned to the convention were "mainly" from Antifederalist towns, or that enough of the forty-six towns which were not even represented were Antifederalist and would have defeated the Constitution if they had sent delegates? If they did not send delegates, how do we know how the towns divided, and why not assume that the unrepresented towns would have split their vote about the same way other towns did? The only conclusion we can draw from the fact that fifty-four towns were not represented is that there was not much enthusiasm one way or the other in these towns. The neglect could not have been for financial reasons, for the state paid delegates' expenses.[8] If "eloquence, logic, and pure argumentation" lay on the side of the Federalists, as Beard said (p. 227), why not conclude that these factors explain the adoption of the Constitution? Also, why introduce the accusation that members of the Massachusetts convention were bought by New York money if such charges, as Beard pointed out, have been proved baseless?

To explain the adoption of the Constitution in Massachusetts, Beard would have had to account for many factors which he did not mention. For one thing, the Shaysites and their sympathizers had won complete control of the legislature in 1787,

[8] *Debates and Proceedings of the Convention of the Commonwealth of Massachusetts, Held in the Year 1788, and Which Finally Ratified the Constitution of the United States* (Boston, 1856), pp. 22-24.

and they could have stopped the calling of a convention or defeated the Constitution in the convention if they had desired. Minot, the contemporary historian of Shays' Rebellion, described democracy in Massachusetts as follows: "So small are the qualifications of voters that scarce a single man is excluded from his equal share in creating the first magistrate in the community."[9] In this connection it should be noted that the opponents of the Constitution were the ones who demanded property qualifications in it.[10] A few samples will show the difficulty of telling where the towns of this state stood on adoption. Andover, an eastern town, voted 124 to 115 against acceptance of the Constitution *as it was*, but then voted not to instruct its delegate.[11] One might conclude that he was to hear the arguments pro and con, then decide the question himself. Great Barrington, a western town, elected William Whiting, Esq., and a committee instructed him to vote against the Constitution. But the town rejected the instructions, reconsidered the election of Whiting, then elected Elijah Dwight and sent him uninstructed.[12] Hadley in the Connecticut Valley sent Elisha Porter uninstructed,[13] and Malden in the East sent Captain Benjamin Blaney uninstructed.[14] Sheffield, another western town, voted 86 to 78 for the Constitution, voted to send only one delegate though the town could have sent more, could not elect one at that meeting, and then elected John Ashley over John Hubbard by 133 to 129;[15] and Springfield in the Connecticut Valley sent three delegates uninstructed.[16] Just what certain conclusions on Federalists and Antifederalists anyone could draw from these town records I am not sure.

Beard passed lightly over ratification in Connecticut with the explanation that the legislature was determined "not to

[9] George Richards Minot, *History of the Insurrections* . . . (Worcester, 1788), p. 23.
[10] *Massachusetts Convention Debates, 1788*, pp. 133-34.
[11] Andover Town Records, January 31, 1788.
[12] November 26, 1787, Whiting MSS, Mason Library, Great Barrington.
[13] Hadley Town Records, II, 224. November 30, 1787.
[14] Malden Town Records, II, 187. December 17, 1787.
[15] Sheffield Town Records, II, 52-53. December 10 and 17, 1787.
[16] Springfield Town Records, IV, 595. November 20, 1787.

be behindhand" in its approval of the Constitution. The vote, 128 to 40, did not signify much opposition in Connecticut, but we would still want to know why the Connecticut vote was so lopsided while the Massachusetts vote was close.

New York ratified after ten other states had already insured the adoption of the new government. We would need to know why two-thirds of the ratifying convention opposed the Constitution when it first met, yet the Federalists won 30 to 27, and just what "'manoeuvering" Beard hinted at but did not explain.

New Jersey ratified unanimously and so received little attention from Beard. Again we would want to know why agricultural New Jersey ratified unanimously.

Delaware also ratified unanimously, at the desire of great numbers of people, but this does not explain what these people saw in the Constitution to approve.

When he reached Pennsylvania, where he characterized the proceedings as "precipitous" and almost "irregular," Beard had a great deal to say. He seems to have approved by implication the minority's tactics of staying away from the legislature to prevent the majority there from calling a ratifying convention, and he seems to have condemned by implication the majority for bringing the minority back forcibly to form a quorum so the majority could act. He hinted that the Federalists were in such a hurry that they could not allow a delay, and so resorted to high-handed methods. The reader should note that Beard got all his information on Pennsylvania from a secondary source, McMaster and Stone's *Pennsylvania and the Federal Constitution*, but that none of it explains why the vote was two to one (46 to 23) for the Constitution in that state. Beard's accusation that the Federalists used "precipitous actions" does not square well with Franklin's statement that the Constitution was being adopted "after the fullest discussion in convention, and in all the public papers, till everybody was tired of the argument."[17] On the other hand, Beard's own evidence that only 13,000 voted out of 70,000 entitled to vote would seem to support Franklin's view that the people were tired of the

[17] Benjamin Franklin, *The Writings of Benjamin Franklin*, ed. Albert H. Smyth, 10 vols. (New York, 1907), ix, 658. June 9, 1788.

argument. If they did not vote, after all the propaganda pro and con, who was to blame?

The Maryland legislature unanimously voted for a ratifying convention in spite of Luther Martin's "masterly indictment" of the Constitution. With the meeting in April, 1788, there could be no charge of precipitous action, and the nearly six-to-one vote, 63 to 11, should be ample evidence of popular support for the Constitution in that state.

There apparently was nothing underhanded about the way Virginia ratified, even though the 89-79 vote was close and Virginia did not ratify until nine states had already accepted the Constitution.

North Carolina did not ratify until after the new government went into operation, and again Beard relied on secondary authority for his material.

South Carolina ratified by more than two to one, 149 to 73, after having had ample time to deliberate, so there is little question about the methods in that state.

Georgia ratified unanimously, a point which Beard forgot to make.

Rhode Island held out until after the Constitution was adopted and the new government was set up. As he did with other states, Beard depended on secondary works rather than sources for his main interpretation.

Given this analysis, we naturally conclude that Beard's generalizations were open to question.

It is true that Rhode Island and North Carolina refused to ratify until after the new government went into operation. But did they ratify because powerful economic forces were used against them, as Beard said, or because the government had agreed to amendments which they demanded, including such noneconomic items as freedom of religion, freedom of the press, and freedom of speech, as well as provision for better protection of property than the Constitution originally provided?

I have already shown by a few examples from the town records that the popular vote on the Constitution in Massachusetts cannot be determined, and Beard did not offer any evidence that it ever had been in New York and New Hampshire.

Beard's conclusion that the popular vote was doubtful in Virginia is completely unwarranted from his evidence and discussion on that state. He did not even mention the popular vote, and until more work is done on Virginia we can only assume that the final vote on the Constitution, 89 to 79, was a proximate reflection of popular sentiment.

There is much innuendo in the paragraph on Connecticut, New Jersey, Georgia, and Delaware (p. 238). Beard implied that action in these states was quick, but said that "this facility of action may have been due to the general sentiment in favor of the Constitution; or the rapidity of action may account for the slight development of opposition." All the evidence he presented pointed to general sentiment in favor of the Constitution, and even there the evidence was extremely thin. But if the Constitution was put over because of haste, as he implies, he should have produced the proof.

There is both innuendo and inconsistency in saying that deliberation and delays in Maryland and South Carolina resulted in an undoubted majority in favor of the Constitution. There is simply no evidence in his discussion of these two states to warrant the conclusion that delay favored the Federalists. If speedy adoption favored the Federalists in some states, why would not deliberate action favor the Antifederalists in others?

There is no logic, either, in Beard's references to the popular vote in the various states. For instance, he said that in New Hampshire, New York, and Massachusetts the popular vote as measured by the election of delegates was unfavorable to the Constitution. But as Beard himself stated, we do not know what the popular vote was (p. 240). Then he said the popular vote in Virginia was doubtful, but if we do not know what the vote was, how can we know that it was doubtful? Instead of accepting such undocumented generalizations, could we not as easily assume that popular sentiment was roughly reflected in the ratifying vote, which in the eleven states combined was nearly two to one for the Constitution?

Instead of assuming that the Constitution was ratified through a conspiratorial *coup d'état* by conservative personalty interests, why not start with some of the following points? The Constitutional Convention was not democratically elected by popular vote, but it was composed of some of the most important men of the country, it deliberated for some three and a half months, and, though its debates were secret, the knowledge that it was considering changes in government was widely disseminated throughout the country. There is evidence of extensive dissatisfaction with the prevailing system and of the belief that great things were expected from the Convention. Most men could vote, the arguments for and against the Constitution were long and in some instances bitter, and the people were perfectly aware that they were voting to overthrow the Articles of Confederation even though the Convention did not have authorization to design a new government. The vote was unanimous in three states, overwhelming in some others, and close in four states, two of which ratified after nine states had already accepted the Constitution. The total vote in the eleven states which established the new government was nearly two to one for the Constitution, and there is very little correlation between personalty and ratification.

Maybe the following sampling of statements actually represented the prevailing situation. Franklin said that seven states had ratified and that others were expected to do so, after the fullest discussion in convention and in all the public papers, until everybody was tired of the argument.[18] Elbridge Gerry opposed the Constitution, but if the people wanted it in spite of his objections, he said, he would support it.[19] Most of Gerry's objections were political, not economic, and included lack of adequate representation, ambiguous powers granted to the government, *failure of the Constitution to provide adequate separation of powers*, the nature of treaty powers, no bill of rights, and the fact that the Constitution set up a national rather than a federal government.[20] In the Massachusetts convention the leading opponents of the Constitution acknowledged that

[18] *Ibid.*, ix, 658. June 9, 1788.
[19] *Letters of Members of the Continental Congress*, ed. Edmund C. Burnett, 8 vols. (Washington, 1921-36), viii, 680n.
[20] *Massachusetts Convention Debates, 1788*, pp. 24-26.

they had been fairly beaten by a majority of wise and understanding men in a body as completely representative of the people as could be convened. And their statements were that while they had opposed ratification, a majority had decided and they would abide by majority rule.[21]

The diary of John Quincy Adams gives us a great deal of insight into what some people thought about the Constitution at the time, who supported it, and what the losers thought about their defeat:

February 7, 1788. "This day, at about noon, the news arrived in this town [Newburyport, Massachusetts] that the Federal Constitution was yesterday adopted and ratified by a majority of nineteen members in our State Convention. In this town the satisfaction is almost universal; for my own part, I have not been pleased with this system, and my acquaintance have long since branded me with the name of an *antifederalist*. But I am now converted, though not convinced. My feelings upon the occasion have not been passionate nor violent; and, as upon the decision of this question I find myself on the weaker side, I think it my duty to submit without murmuring against what is not to be helped. In our government, opposition to the acts of a majority of the people is rebellion to all intents and purposes; and I should view a man who would now endeavour to excite commotions against this plan, as no better than an insurgent who took arms last winter against the Courts of Justice."

February 8, 1788. "This afternoon the delegates from Newbury and from this town returned home from Convention. A number of very respectable citizens, and a number who were not very respectable, went out on horse-back to meet the members and escort them into town; as they came along the bells at the different churches were set to ringing, and this noisy expression of joy was continued with some intermissions till eight o'clock in the evening. The mob huzza'd, and one would have thought that every man from the adoption of the Constitution had acquired a sure expectancy of an independent

[21] *The Debates of the Several State Conventions . . .*, ed. Jonathan Elliot, 5 vols. (Washington, 1854), II, 181-83.

fortune. I pass'd the evening at home in reading and writing."[22]

Adams' views were certainly like the views on politics of many people today, and it would be of some importance to know how many men at the time thought as he did.

Beard's story of ratification fails to explain why some of the agricultural states adopted the Constitution unanimously and why, after so much discussion, the country in its ratifying conventions taken as a whole favored the new government by a two-to-one vote. Certainly there is little correlation between ratification and personal property. An interpretation picturing a country in which most men were middle-class property owners, however, obviates many of Beard's difficulties. Under such circumstances it is not difficult to see why agricultural states voted for the Constitution. No one would deny that the conflict over ratification in some places was probably bitter, or even that the infighting was not always the cleanest. But when has there been an election in this country for which the same charges would not be true, except, perhaps, in 1788 and 1820?

[22] John Quincy Adams, "Diary of John Quincy Adams," Massachusetts Historical Society *Proceedings,* 2nd Series, xvi, 378-79.

# CHAPTER IX

# "THE POPULAR VOTE ON THE CONSTITUTION"

IN LINE with his thesis, Beard attempted to show through his discussion of the popular vote on the Constitution that the Constitution did not result from what we consider the democratic process. By now, of course, the reader realizes the danger of interpreting the Constitution as the product of an undemocratic society, but we still need to examine this chapter to see how Beard has used his evidence and arrived at his conclusions.

We need to dwell for a moment on Beard's contention that the question of holding a convention was not submitted to popular vote and was not an issue in the election of legislatures which selected the delegates. A popular election of a convention to amend the Articles of Confederation would have been unthinkable in 1787. In the first place, it would have been unconstitutional, for the Articles set up a federation which could act only on states, not on individuals, and a popular election of a convention to alter the Articles would have been out of the question. The calling of the Constitutional Convention by state legislatures was perfectly legal under the Articles: the departure from legal processes came when the delegates abandoned their instructions to amend the Articles, adopted a new system, and then had it ratified by conventions rather than state legislatures. As far as I have been able to tell, the people in 1787 were about as agitated over the fact that they did not elect the delegates to the Constitutional Convention as the American people are in 1955 that they do not elect this country's delegates to the United Nations.

Neither was it unusual that the Constitution was not submitted to popular ratification. The calling of the First Continental Congress had not been submitted to popular vote; the calling of the Second Continental Congress had not been submitted to popular vote; the Declaration of Independence had not been submitted to popular vote; and the Articles of Confederation had not been submitted to popular vote. With this precedent, why would we expect the ratification of the Constitution to deviate from accepted practice? In fact, Mason in the Convention argued that ratification by nine states would be acceptable to the people because all important questions under the Confederation had required the consent of nine states, and he "was for preserving ideas familiar to the people." The other states supported Mason's motion 8 to 3, so other men must have thought the same.[1]

As usual, the *Records* supply the answer to the question of popular ratification of the Constitution. For one thing, the delegates seem to have thought that ratification of the Constitution by conventions expressly chosen by the people for that purpose was ratification by the people. When the Convention considered the resolution calling for ratification by state conventions, many delegates expressed opinions which would indicate that they considered this method to be practically the same as a popular referendum. George Mason "considered a reference of the plan to the authority of the people as one of the most important and essential of the Resolutions. The Legislatures have no power to ratify it. . . . Whither then must we resort? To the people with whom all power remains that has not been given up in the Constitutions derived from them."[2] Gerry opposed because "great confusion he was confident would result from a recurrence to the people."[3] Ellsworth explained it this way: "As to the 1st. point, he observed that a new sett of ideas seemed to have crept in since the articles of Confederation were established. Conventions of the people, or with power derived expressly from the people, were not then thought of. The Legislatures were considered competent. Their ratification has been acquiesced in without complaint."[4] We might easily say that ratification by conventions elected expressly for that purpose was as radical an approach as the initiative and referendum were in 1913.

When we get to Beard's discussion of the voters themselves

---

[1] *The Records of the Federal Convention of 1787*, ed. Max Farrand, 4 vols. (New Haven, 1937), ɪɪ, 477.

[2] *Ibid.*, pp. 88-89.  [3] *Ibid.*, p. 90.  [4] *Ibid.*, p. 91.

(p. 240), we again encounter that horrible specter, the disfranchised. With the aid of Beard's own evidence, plus innumerable citations from the records, we killed and buried this ghost in Chapter IV. All we need to note here is that Beard dragged him forth again when he contended that "a considerable portion of the adult white male population was debarred from participating in the elections of delegates to the ratifying conventions by the prevailing property qualifications on the suffrage."

After citing the qualifications for the election of ratifying conventions (the same as the qualifications for election of state representatives, except in Connecticut, where all voters in town meetings were enfranchised, and in New York, where manhood suffrage prevailed) Beard answered his own question about how many men were disfranchised. He said "that only about 3 per cent of the population dwelt in towns of over 8000 inhabitants in 1790, and that freeholds were widely distributed, especially in New England." We have already seen that a larger percentage of the population in North Carolina than in New England were freeholders and that their land was on the average worth twice as much as the freeholders' land in New England.[5] If, as I contend, a farmer could not have made a living on a freehold small enough to disfranchise him, Beard is really saying here that most men were farmers and therefore qualified voters. His other evidence from sources will support this generalization, not only for farmers but for "city" dwellers as well.

Actually, Beard confused the issue by his statement that "far more were disfranchised through apathy and lack of understanding of the significance of politics" (p. 242). In the first place, a man is not "disfranchised" if he has the right to vote but does not use it. The term disfranchised means that he has been deprived of the right, not that he simply failed to exercise his right. In the second place, the problems of whether a man *can* vote, but does not, are quite different from those of whether he *cannot* vote, but wants to.

When he stopped talking about those who *could not* vote and started talking about those who *did not* vote, Beard was

[5] *Ibid.*, III, 84.

on sound historical ground from the standpoint of historical method. One of the master keys to an understanding of the Constitution is not how many men could not vote, but why so many having the vote did not use it. Beard used evidence that is absolutely correct when he generalized about the "noteworthy fact that only a small proportion of the population entitled to vote took the trouble to go to the polls until the hot political contests of the Jeffersonian era." When we stop talking about the "mass of men" who *could not* vote on the Constitution and start talking about the "mass of men" who *could* vote but did not bother to do so, then, and only then, will we understand the Constitution and its adoption.

Beard unwittingly gave the answer to this political apathy. On page 242 he implied that the journey to the polls and delays at elections were troublesome, thus accounting for the smallness of the vote. This had little to do with the problem. The governing factor was whether or not there was an issue, or whether the people thought there was an issue, and how important it was. Beard gave figures to show that few people in Massachusetts voted in 1786, before Shays' Rebellion, but that in 1787, after Shays' Rebellion, the number trebled. This is correct, and anyone can chart the importance of the issues of the day by checking on the vote. In other words, the people exercised their right to vote when they thought something was at stake, and failed to vote when they were not particularly interested.

Innumerable examples could be used, but one will suffice to show what I mean when I say that the people voted when they thought something was at stake. In Sheffield, Massachusetts, strong Shaysite country, the town voted 86 to 78 in favor of the Constitution. But in voting for a man to represent it in the ratifying convention, the town split its vote as follows: John Ashley, Jr., 79; Lieutenant John Hubbard, 78; John Fellows, 1. No one had a majority, so a new election was held. It is obvious that the candidates had not taken a clear stand for or against the Constitution, or the one for would have had a majority. In the second election, seven days later, the vote was 133 for Ashley, 129 for Hubbard, and 1 for Anthony

Austin.[6] One would presume from this increase in the vote that the issue was probably a personal one between Ashley and Hubbard, and that both candidates beat the bushes for voters between elections. But the point is that the voters did turn out in numbers, even though it was December in the Berkshires.

As Beard said in a footnote, page 243, information for a detailed study of the vote is available, and not only in Connecticut, as I have shown by evidence cited from some of the town records in Massachusetts. Such a study, now in progress, should enable us to tell within limits how many people voted for and against the Constitution, and how many towns simply sent uninstructed delegates who would use their own judgment after hearing all the arguments. This is the kind of thing Beard should have done, since he knew where to find the sources.

Again I would like to remind the reader that the use of percentages of the whole population in a discussion of voters for 1787 is misleading. Only about 18 or 19 per cent of the people were adult men, and there is no point in including the women and children. For example, Beard's statement that 16 or 17 per cent of the Massachusetts population was entitled to vote actually meant that about 80 to 85 per cent of the adult men were enfranchised, since less than 20 per cent of the people were adult men. In reality, the evidence shows that even this estimate is low and should be revised upward into the high 90's.

Beard's discussion of voting on the Constitution furnishes examples of the need for critical analysis of evidence if we are to arrive at valid conclusions. In Boston, he said, "where the fight was rather warm," only 760 out of 2,700 qualified voters actually voted on the Constitution (p. 244). The people of Boston were not inhibited by inability to get to the polls or by lack of knowledge of the issues, yet only a little more than a quarter of the voters bothered to ballot. My interpretation of that evidence would not be that it was indicative of a warm fight, but that, as is true with most elections today, it signified

[6] Sheffield Town Records, II, 52-53. December 10 and 17, 1787.

a great deal of indifference. Furthermore, if there were 2,700 qualified voters in Boston, which had only 3,174 polls or males over sixteen years of age in 1784,[6a] there were not many "propertyless mechanics" or a disfranchised mass of men in the town, for 2,700 should have included most of the town's adult men.

The account of Philadelphia is even less logical than that of Boston (p. 247). Beard characterized Philadelphia as "the scene of perhaps the hottest contest over the election of delegates that occurred anywhere." What was the evidence that this was the "hottest contest"? The candidate who stood highest at the polls, George Latimer, received 1,215 votes, and his leading opponent received 235 votes. Furthermore, Philadelphia with a population of 28,000 should have had between 5,000 and 6,000 qualified voters, yet only 1,450 votes were cast. We know that in 1765, twenty-two years before the Constitution, a "hot" political battle in Philadelphia had attracted nearly 4,000 votes, yet at that time the qualifications for voting were higher and the population of the town was much less.[7] Would a Philadelphia election today in which only a fourth of the voters voted and in which the leading candidate won by better than five to one be a "hot" contest?

The tables (pp. 244-45) on the Federalist and Antifederalist vote mean very little as they now stand. The only thing they show is that except for Suffolk and Washington counties, the Federalist counties had fewer people per delegate than did the Antifederalist counties. Other than that, the tables merely raise questions. Given the fact that many people in other states were undecided and many delegates to the ratifying conventions went uninstructed, we would want to know whether New York's delegates were instructed, and if so, how, or whether they were merely to use their own judgment. Beard's figures on the vote are obviously incomplete and practically worthless, yet without the popular vote, we cannot say that the

[6a] Evarts B. Greene and Virginia D. Harrington, *American Population before the Federal Census of 1790* (New York, 1937), p. 40.

[7] William B. Reed, *Life and Correspondence of Joseph Reed* (Philadelphia, 1847), I, 36-37.

people of New York were overwhelmingly against ratification. It we accept the figures in the tables at face value, the Constitution was defeated 41 to 23 in spite of inequitable representation. What we need to know is why it was ratified 30 to 27, and this Beard did not explain.

The long Antifederalist quotation on page 246 contains some ideas that are worthy of comment. The Antifederalists claimed that more than 70,000 freemen were entitled to vote in Pennsylvania, yet that only 13,000 had voted for the ratifying convention. This, of course, is indicative of a great deal of political indifference. The Antifederalists advocated that the government should not be changed unless a majority of the people approved, not just a majority of those who voted. Such a position was untenable unless there was compulsory voting. We assume, and the assumption was the same then, that the decision is to be made by a majority of those who vote. If the qualified non-voters do not approve, they can become voters, for as Thomas Paine said, a man who fails to exercise his right to vote has no one to blame but himself. Hence all this evidence on the failure of voters to vote in 1787 must be taken to mean that they did not consider the issue of great moment.

If there were more than 70,000 qualified voters in 1787 and the population of the state was 434,373 in 1790, the ratio of voters to people would be slightly less than one to six, which would certainly mean that most adult men were voters.

The evidence on Baltimore and Maryland simply adds more weight to the idea that the Federalists won by a substantial majority and that there was a great deal of indifference in the state. The total vote in Baltimore, 1,347, was a little more than half the estimated number of adult men in the city. McHenry won by 962 to 385, or 71 per cent to 29 per cent, which is not even as close as the average present-day national election in Maine. That only 6,000 voted in the state out of 25,000 qualified voters does not signify much of a contest in Maryland. The insinuation that the Federalists won because the "common people" were not informed and that severe winter weather curtailed the dissemination of information on the Constitution does not stand examination. The elections were held in April,

1788, and as we shall soon see, winter was not much of a factor in that state's decision on the Constitution.

Since Beard himself admitted that a careful study of South Carolina could give an accurate picture of the vote in that state (footnote, p. 249), his attempt to suggest that the opposition vote there may well have represented a majority is simply guesswork. In fact, he had previously made the point (p. 238) that the popular vote in South Carolina had never been figured out. Until it is, all we are justified in saying is that the state ratified by a convention vote of more than two to one after the people had been given the whole winter and spring to consider the Constitution.

Another example of an unwarranted conclusion from the evidence presented appears in the paragraph in the middle of page 249. The evidence is that in the election of 1788 the vote was only 2.8 per cent of the population in New Hampshire, 2.7 per cent in Madison's district in Virginia, 3.6 per cent in Maryland, and 3 per cent in Massachusetts. These figures mean only that few people were sufficiently concerned to exercise their right to vote. Yet out of this kind of evidence, Charles Oscar Paullin conjured, and Beard accepted without criticism, the following conclusion: " 'The voting was done chiefly by a small minority of interested property holders, a disproportionate share of whom in the northern states resided in the towns, and the wealthier and more talented of whom like a closed corporation controlled politics.' " The evidence does not justify this conclusion under a proper use of historical method. One is reminded of the lawyer who told the jury: "Out of these conclusions I draw my facts."

Given all this discussion, we can only conclude that Beard's estimates of the total vote on the Constitution are mere guesses (p. 250). Since we do not know how many people voted, we are not justified in saying that 100,000 voted for it and 60,000 voted against it. But if we did accept those figures, we could say that 62.5 per cent of those who voted favored the Constitution and 37.5 per cent opposed it, which is a substantial majority. Franklin D. Roosevelt received only 62.22 per cent of the popular vote in 1936, but I am sure most people would consider this a smashing victory in American politics.

As for the men who did not vote, we can only conjecture about their views on the Constitution. If they had held strong opinions one way or the other, they probably would have gone to the polls. A logical assumption would be that the actual vote was a fairly close representation of the views of the total voting population, and that if every man had voted, the result would not have been much different from what it was, except in number. At any rate, democracy means a majority of those who vote, at least until we have compulsory voting, and there can be little doubt that the Constitution received that majority.

On page 251 Beard has a particularly clear statement of his interpretation. Here he said the disfranchisement of the masses through property qualifications, ignorance, or apathy contributed to the victory of the personalty interests. The latter were alert, knew as a matter of dollars and cents the value of the new Constitution, were informed, were unified in their purposes, and well understood in advance the nature of the conflict. They resided in the towns, where they could act effectively; the talent, wealth, and professional abilities were on their side; and they had the money to spend for propaganda, pamphlets, parades, and demonstrations. The opposition, on the other hand, had difficulty in marshaling its forces. The backwoods vote, Beard claimed, was gotten out with difficulty because of long journeys to the polls and bad weather, the elections having been held in the late fall and winter. They had little money, they were poor and uninfluential, and the wonder was that they did as well as they did.

Let us examine these generalizations in more detail.

First there is again the confusion of issues as to whether "the disfranchisement of the masses" was the result of property qualifications, or whether the problem was "ignorance and apathy." Beard often confused the two, yet they are quite distinct problems.

Beard then made the statement that the representatives of personalty knew, "as a practical matter of dollars and cents, the value of the new Constitution." Did this mean that the advocates of the Constitution were working for their own pockets? Beard denied such an implication earlier, but his use of this particular phrase certainly has this connotation.

There is something of a contradiction between the statements at the bottom of page 251 and other generalizations throughout the book. In many places Beard gave the impression that ratification was hurried through with unseemly haste before the people really knew what had happened to them. On this page, however, we have the wealthy spending what is implied to be a sizable sum for pamphlets, parades, demonstrations, and newspaper space in their campaign of education for their cause.

If, as Beard said on page 252, the debtors and small farmers had opposed the Constitution as a group, there would have been no Constitution. We do not know how many debtors there were, but if Richard Henry Lee was correct, there were not many. We do know that ninety-odd per cent of the people were farmers or closely connected with farming, and that most of these were small farmers qualified to vote. As the votes in such agricultural towns in Massachusetts as Andover, Sheffield, and Great Barrington show, some small farmers were for the Constitution and some were against it. That is a typical phenomenon in American political history. Given the fact that these farmers were property owners and the Constitution was designed in part to protect property, the reason for a good deal of support is not difficult to understand.

Two generalizations on page 252 yield some interesting results when we compare them with the evidence. One is that the opponents of the Constitution were handicapped by the difficulty of getting out the vote in the "backwoods." If we compare the 263 votes in the small Berkshire town of Sheffield with the 760 votes in Boston, or the 106 votes in the Berkshire town of Great Barrington with the 196 votes in seaport Marblehead, we may easily come to the conclusion that the real difficulty lay in getting out the vote in "backwoods" Boston and Marblehead. Furthermore, Sheffield voted for the Constitution[8] and Great Barrington rejected the town committee's instruction for the delegates to vote against the Constitution.[9]

The other generalization concerns the handicaps of the Antifederalists because "the elections were held in late fall and winter," when the weather was apt to be bad. This generalization calls for the solution of two problems: When were the ratifying conventions held? and What kind of weather prevailed in 1787-88? The following list shows when the elections were held:

Massachusetts—after October 24, 1787
Pennsylvania—November 6, 1787
Delaware—between November 10 and 26, 1787
Connecticut—November 12, 1787
New Jersey—November 27, 1787
Georgia—December 4, 1787
New Hampshire—between December 14, 1787 and the second Wednesday in February, 1788
Virginia—March, 1788
North Carolina—last Friday and Saturday in March, 1788
Maryland—first Monday in April, 1788
South Carolina—April, 1788
New York—last Thursday in April, 1788

As we can see from the above, five states—Massachusetts, Connecticut, New Jersey, Delaware, and Pennsylvania—held their elections in the fall before November 27, that is, during our present football season in that part of the country. New York, Maryland, North Carolina, and South Carolina held their elections in the *spring*, not the fall or winter. Georgia held its election on December 4, which is late fall, but I doubt a time of severe weather in Georgia. That leaves New Hampshire and Virginia as the *only* two where elections could have been held in the winter, and March in Virginia is not apt to be severe.

On the second problem, the weather in 1787-88, the following evidence would seem to indicate that there was not much difference in the weather in 1787 and 1955; and if anything, the winter of 1787-88 was much milder than usual for that time.

[8] Sheffield Town Records, ii, 52-53; Marblehead Town Records, iv, 528.
[9] Whiting mss, Mason Library, Great Barrington. November 26, 1787.

There was an early frost reported in September in New England, but not in New York and New Jersey.[10] The writer has seen frost in New York before Labor Day. From Halifax, Nova Scotia, came word that as of November 16, 1787, the weather was "yet very mild," for the previous year there had been a heavy snow by this date.[11]

Massachusetts seems to have had a particularly mild winter. John Quincy Adams said that the weather was uncommonly warm on October 22 and "dull" on November 20, the day delegates were elected to the ratifying convention. Two days later, November 22, 1787, he said that the weather was "remarkably mild for the season." There was no snow by December 15, not unusual in· Massachusetts, although by December 20 there was snow and colder weather. But the threat failed to last, for on December 22 Adams said the weather was "quite moderate." There was cold and snow from December 23 to January 8, when it moderated. Snow turned to rain "and before the weather cleared up the snow was almost gone." Some 300 members met at the convention in Boston on January 10, 1788, so apparently the mild weather continued.[12] The weather was so mild that Marblehead boasted of not losing a single fisherman during the fall and early winter because of bad weather, apparently an unusual occurrence for the town.[13]

Adams also recorded that the weather was reasonably good for the New Hampshire convention. From Newburyport he wrote on January 19, 1788, that the weather had been "very favorable," that winter was "already far advanced" and was "now rapidly passing away." He lamented that the country seemed "fated to have no lasting snow this winter," for snow that day had turned to rain, which threatened to spoil the sleighing. On January 21, 1788, Adams decided to go to Exeter, New Hampshire, to hear the debates there on the

[10] *Pennsylvania Journal*, October 20, 1787.
[11] *Ibid.*, December 1, 1787.
[12] John Quincy Adams, "Diary of John Quincy Adams," Massachusetts Historical Society *Proceedings*, 2nd Series, xvi, 335, 349, 355-58, 365-67.
[13] *Pennsylvania Journal*, January 2, 1788.

Constitution. The roads were bad, probably due to the rain, and it took four hours by sleigh to make the trip. The town was well filled because of the convention, the debates were not worth the ride on a cold day, "but the satisfaction of riding with an amiable girl, and the novelty of the town" compensated Adams somewhat for his trip.[14] If Adams could ride to New Hampshire just for the pleasure of seeing the convention the people could surely get to the elections and the delegates should have gotten to the convention without much trouble.

Farther south, December 26, 1787 was noted in Philadelphia mainly for "the uncommon mildness of the weather," which made fuel and provisions cheap at that date.[15] Near Pittsburgh a traveler, Mrs. Mary Dewee, had trouble getting a boat down the Ohio because of the shortage of water. Two or three inches of snow fell on October 29, but on November 6, the day of the election, some of the men went from where the boat was stranded to Pittsburgh for supplies and there was no mention of bad weather.[16] Washington's *Diaries* show that the Virginia climate was about the same then as now, for Washington hunted foxes and rode to his plantations almost every day.[17] And the *Virginia Almanac* predicted weather in 1788 about what it is at the present time.[18]

According to what Beard implied, the Federalists should have been aided most in those states where the election and convention were held in the winter. But again the correlation does not hold. The Antifederalists put up some of their strongest opposition in New Hampshire, Massachusetts, and Virginia, so the insinuation that the weather was part of the conspiracy to put over the Constitution must be ruled out. In agricultural America the conspiracy interpretation would have had some

[14] "Diary of John Quincy Adams," xvi, 370-71, 385-86.

[15] *Pennsylvania Journal*, December 26, 1787.

[16] "Mrs. Mary Dewee's Journal from Philadelphia to Kentucky, 1787-88," *Pennsylvania Magazine of History and Biography*, xxviii (1904), 191.

[17] *The Diaries of George Washington, 1748-1799*, ed. John C. Fitzpatrick, 4 vols. (Boston and New York, 1925), i and ii, passim.

[18] *The Virginia Almanac, for the Year of Our Lord, 1788* . . . (Richmond, 1787?), entry for March, 1788.

real basis if the elections and conventions had been held in the summer and early fall when the farmers were engaged in harvesting.

Using some of the evidence easily available, and not Beard's generalizations, one might well conclude that instead of ratification's having resulted from a conspiracy perpetrated in an undemocratic society during inclement winter weather, the Constitution was adopted with a great show of indifference and most of the elections were held in the fall and spring when the weather was good, when the harvest season was not in full swing, and when most people could go to the polls.

# "THE ECONOMICS OF THE VOTE
# ON THE CONSTITUTION"

CHAPTER X furnishes something of a refinement of the half of the Beard thesis that the Constitution was put over by personalty interests. Throughout the chapter Beard tried to show that the vote for the Constitution came from regions where personalty was strong while the vote against it came almost uniformly from agricultural and debtor regions. But then Beard went further than he had gone in previous chapters. Since so many leaders in the movement for ratification were large security holders and securities constituted such a large portion of personalty, he said, the security holders were a very considerable, if not the chief, element in the dynamic personalty group behind the Constitution.

Again Beard outlined the work that should be done before we can make such an economic interpretation, but again he said he would be forced to rely on secondary writers who had not done the work either. We would have to have economic biographies of the 160,000 who favored and opposed the Constitution, so we can study them as "economic beings." Not having this essential material, Beard said he would rely on "certain general truths" already established by such scholars as Libby, Harding, and Ambler. So again we should thank Beard for pointing the way, but we should realize that he did not go behind the secondary works to the sources to get his interpretation.

Some of the fallacies of the Beard argument are quickly discernible in his treatment of New Hampshire. He used Libby's *Geographical Distribution of the Vote on the Constitution* to show that the two commercial sections of that state, the coast and the Connecticut Valley, favored the Constitution while the agricultural interior opposed it. The catch to this argument is that all New Hampshire, except for Portsmouth proper, was predominantly agricultural, including the Connecticut Valley. A farmer living five miles out of Portsmouth had just as much interest in agriculture as one living fifty miles out. One or both may well have realized that the future prosperity of the farmers depended on commerce, which would be helped by a new government, but this is a different problem. The fact remains that most of the people of New Hampshire were farmers, and the vote on the Constitution must be explained using this fact.

The figures used for New Hampshire, while intended to support the Beard thesis, merely emphasize this preponderance of agriculture in the state. Beard gives figures to show that Rockingham County, which included Portsmouth, possessed two-thirds of the state's stock in trade, £42,512 out of £61,711; two-thirds of the money at interest, £22,770 out of £35,985; but less than half of the realty, £317,970 out of £893,327. These figures for 1793 would have been different in 1787, as Beard admitted in a footnote, because in 1787 Vermont was joined with New Hampshire; and they would also have been different because they were taken after Hamilton's funding and assumption programs, which Beard did not mention. But taken as they are, what do they prove? There is no doubt that two-thirds of the stock and money at interest were in Rockingham County, but the total, £65,282, is still small compared with the £317,970 in realty in the same county. Why did Rockingham County vote Federalist when realty predominated nearly five to one over personalty, and why did so many farmers elsewhere in the state vote for the Constitution, as they had to do if it was to be ratified?

Libby's division of Massachusetts into sections as economic and social units simply does not hold up under analysis. With the exception of a few port towns, eastern interests were agricultural, as the perusal of the tax records shows so clearly. And there was very little difference of interest between the agricultural towns in the eastern and other sections of the state. Support for Shays' Rebellion came from all parts of the state, for the Shaysites dominated the legislature in 1787. Libby's analysis of the "commercial" settlements along the

Connecticut River takes a curious turn at this point. He said the northern part of the valley, farthest from the coast, was Antifederalist, while the southern part was Federalist. Yet in the Connecticut Valley in New Hampshire, which is still farther north and farther from the coast, the Federalists predominated.

Harding's division of the state into classes in his *Massachusetts and the Federal Constitution*, and Beard's interpretation of Harding's views (p. 258), also fail to explain ratification in Massachusetts. Harding said that part of the struggle was a real or fancied conflict of interest between agriculture and commerce, which has an element of truth in it, but that underlying this was a pronounced antagonism between aristocratic and democratic elements in Massachusetts society. Beard interpreted this aristocratic-democratic conflict as just another way of saying a wealthy upper class was pitted against the agrarian element. This division raises the question of whether or not people in this country have ever voted on an economic class basis. If they had done so in 1788, when, according to Beard, the farmers were against ratification, the Constitution would never have had a ghost of a chance, for the farmers outnumbered other elements in the population at least ten to one.

From the evidence I have presented on voting in the Massachusetts towns, it is obvious that we must interpret the vote in the ratifying conventions with a great deal of care. For example, Great Barrington voted 55 to 51 for the Constitution[1] while Sheffield voted 86 to 78 for it.[2] The convention vote of these two towns would appear as 100 per cent in favor of ratification, whereas the popular vote would be only 141 to 129, or 52.22 per cent to 47.78 per cent. So Libby's percentages of the vote in the various sections could be highly misleading as an index of the popular vote. This criticism would hold true for all the states, although we would expect to find a larger popular majority in the states that ratified unanimously than we would in states such as Massachusetts and Virginia, where the vote was close.

[1] Whiting MSS, Mason Library, Great Barrington, November 26, 1787.
[2] Sheffield Town Records, II, 52-53. December 10, 1787.

Figures on page 262 show the fallacy of using the designation creditor and debtor areas and interpreting their actions on that basis. In explaining why Worcester County voted against ratification, Beard pointed out that the county had £31,892 in money at interest. This was not surprising, he said, for Worcester was the center of Shays' Rebellion in behalf of debtors and their creditors were presumably close by. In short, if some of the people of a community were debtors, doubtless others were creditors, and we cannot talk about creditor and debtor areas.

The list of men from Suffolk County who were delegates to the ratifying convention and security holders (pp. 263-64) raises some important questions. If 22 of the 34 who voted for the Constitution were security holders, why did the other 12 vote as they did? And if the 14 men from the small farming towns around Boston had securities, how widespread was the ownership of securities? Did most men possess some? For we must remember that failure to support the government during the Revolution was as unpatriotic as failure to buy war bonds during World War II. And finally, how many securities did these men own and how did their securities compare in value with their realty?

Beard's account of Connecticut and the map opposite page 265 show the difficulty of making sweeping generalizations about the economics of the vote on the Constitution. A few pages before, Beard had the southern part of the Connecticut Valley in Massachusetts as Federalist (p. 257), but here he said there was a group of opposition towns in northern Connecticut connected with opposition towns in southern Massachusetts. Then there was no effort to compare security holders and total population. Hartford, a Federalist town with many security holders, may well have had fewer in proportion to the population than Guilford, an Antifederalist town.

The correlation between the number of security holders in a town and the town's vote on the Constitution (map, p. 265) holds good in some instances but not in others. Towns with many security holders (New Haven, Windsor, Hartford, Wethersfield, Middletown) all voted for the Constitution. But

174

there were twenty towns without any security holders whatever which also voted for the Constitution (Salisbury, Kent, Warren, Washington, Newtown, Southbury, Woodbury, Watertown, Bethlehem, Winchester, Hartland, Stratford, Bozrah, Franklin, Union, Voluntown, Brooklyn, Killingly) and only nine without security holders which voted against the Constitution (Sharon, Barkhamsted, Colebrook, Woodbridge, Hamden, Durham, Enfield, Ellington, Hampton). Of towns with only one to four security holders, twenty voted for the Constitution (Canaan, New Fairfield, Ridgefield, Redding, Derby, Waterbury, Southington, Bristol, Killingworth, Haddam, East Haddam, Tolland, Groton, Montville, Lisbon, Windham, Ashford, Plainfield, Canterbury, Thompson) and seven voted against (Cornwall, North Haven, Branford, Wallingford, Simsbury, Granby, Somers). It would certainly be difficult to explain the vote of these fifty-six towns on the basis of the Beard thesis of personalty vs. realty, especially since most of them were agricultural. Why did Guilford, with sixteen security holders, vote against the Constitution, while adjoining Killingworth, with only three, voted for it?

Contrary to Beard's assumption, a searching study into the vote in the town meetings can and will be made, and it should reveal which towns voted for the Constitution, which against, which elected delegates but did not express a preference, and how large the vote was. And why should Beard assume (footnote 1, p. 266) that towns not represented or not voting in the convention were *against* the Constitution? There is no justification for such an assumption, although it does make the opposition appear larger than it was.

The list of public paper holders who favored the Constitution (p. 267) means nothing without information on how much each man held in relation to his real estate. If he possessed a few dollars in securities, would that outweigh a farm worth £800? The tax records, town records, probate records, and records of deeds would give this information in detail. One could easily concede that a man worth tens of thousands of dollars in securities would be motivated one way by his economic interests, but what about the men with only a few dollars' worth?

Beard's account of John Chester (p. 268) is rather curious considering his statement on page 266—"No documents, no history." He said John Chester did not appear on the books as a holder of securities, but Thomas and Sarah Chester of the same town did, and besides, John was a colonel in the war and "doubtless received the soldiers' certificates or other paper at some time." If so, would not thousands of soldiers and their relatives have had securities and have favored the Constitution?

The account of New York merely raises some unanswerable questions in the light of the evidence given. If personalty was so predominant in New York, as Beard's table on page 36 would seem to indicate, why was New York not among the first states to ratify? If the paper money party was in control in 1786, what had happened to them in 1787? Why did the fourteen delegates who were not security holders vote with the sixteen security holders for the Constitution? And finally, why did the so-called workingmen of New York City vote for the Constitution, as Beard said they did (footnote 1, p. 25)? Did they have large personalty holdings? The Beard explanation of New York simply does not give the answers.

Neither is his account of New Jersey adequate. There is no evidence that the Federalists pushed through ratification without giving the agrarian party time to organize. The agrarian paper money party had control of the legislature, yet the Constitution was adopted unanimously. Why not accept Madison's statement quoted in the footnote (p. 271) that there did not appear to be any opposition in New Jersey, and then try to find out why that was so instead of insinuating underhandedness? It is just possible that most of the people favored the Constitution and that the unanimous vote represented something approximating public opinion. And are we to infer from footnote 1 on page 272 that a farmer worth perhaps several hundred pounds in real estate—an average farm, as my work on Massachusetts shows—would vote against his agricul-

tural interests and for the Constitution if he owned a certificate
worth $10 ( £3)?

Beard passed lightly over ratification in Delaware, an agricultural state with a strong paper money party, which ratified
unanimously. Actually, Delaware should not have accepted
the Constitution if the Beard interpretation were correct.
Defective records did not prevent Beard from reaching conclusions on other states, and the fact that the debates in Delaware had never been published should not have prevented
their use. We would still want to know why the agricultural
states of New Jersey and Delaware ratified unanimously.

Criticisms similar to those for the other states hold for the
discussion of Pennsylvania. The two-to-one vote in that state,
46 to 23, was hardly a "sharp division," and Beard's main
interpretation of the sectional division was taken from Libby.
The truth is that all the counties enumerated by Libby as
Federalist were agricultural counties in 1787 except one—
Philadelphia. We can easily understand if we accept the Beard
thesis why the convention delegates who had securities voted
for ratification, but what about those without securities? For
example, only 5 of the 10 delegates from Philadelphia can be
accounted for, not to mention only 2 out of 6 from Chester.
If only 19 out of the 46 who voted for ratification held
securities, why did not the other 27 join with the 23 who voted
against the Constitution?

When we analyze the short biographies of the members of
the Pennsylvania convention, also taken from a secondary work,
McMaster and Stone's *Pennsylvania and the Federal Constitution,* we cannot explain their actions on the basis of economics. There seems to be a great similarity between the
economic status of the two groups—there were farmers on both
sides and businessmen on both sides. There were substantial
property owners on both sides. Even the farmers in the convention split 10 to 13, which is not a very clear indication of a
sharp division between capital and agriculture, and this does
not account for the many delegates who were elected by the
votes of farmers.

If mercantile interests in Maryland favored the Constitution, what about the "working men" in Baltimore, and just how many "urban centers" were there in a state where by far the largest town, Baltimore, had a population of only 13,000? If the opposition came from rural districts, did this include planters, and if so, why was the vote 63 to 11 for ratification? If the planters were extensive and the small farmers restricted, from what other sources were paper money advocates recruited? And if the urban centers were Federalist, why was Baltimore County Antifederalist? Nothing in Beard's account explains the 63-to-11 vote in favor of the Constitution, for there was certainly no haste in Maryland, and the entire account came from Libby, not the sources.

Again Beard relied solely on Ambler's *Sectionalism in Virginia* and on Libby for his discussion of Virginia, without even checking the sources, and either these two gentlemen are wrong or the sources are wrong. Ambler claimed that Tidewater society resembled that of England with its class divisions, including the "very poor" yeomen, and its system of entail and primogeniture to preserve this stratified society. The sources, as I have already said, stress the difference between English society and American society, especially in the fact that there were few poor in this country, and point out that the ending of entail and primogeniture would preserve the largely middle-class society then existing here.[3] One or the other of these accounts must be erroneous, but until we have better evidence to the contrary, we should follow the sources rather than Ambler.

Then there are inconsistencies in the Virginia story when that story is measured by the Beard thesis. For example, the Piedmont region above the Tidewater was democratic and largely against the Constitution, while the valley beyond the Piedmont was democratic and voted heavily for the Constitution. Beard rightfully said that the valley sentiment for the new government had not yet been traced to its economic reasons, which might at least raise a suspicion that its reasons were not economic. The Kentucky region, which should have resembled

---

[3] *The Records of the Federal Convention of 1787*, ed. Max Farrand, 4 vols. (New Haven, 1937), I, 398-404.

the Piedmont and valley, at least to a degree, was almost solid against ratification. Having said all this, Ambler then contradicted himself by saying that the western regions of the state "were practically indifferent." It should be noted also that, as Ambler stated, the "democratic leaders" of the interior based their opposition on the fact that adoption of the Constitution would sacrifice state sovereignty—a political rather than an economic issue. Ambler did not even mention the class conflict as a factor in his discussion of the West.

The list of names on pages 286-87 does not appear to prove much of anything. Of the 28 men, 13 had securities of their own, 13 had no securities, and 2 were executors of estates with securities. Since only one of those not holding securities voted against the Constitution, this particular economic factor did not make much difference one way or the other. Furthermore, if the securities they held were Virginia paper, securities did not mean anything, for the Convention discussed and rejected federal assumption of state debts. Even if the list signified anything in the first place, we would still have to ascertain whether the securities were funded Confederation paper or assumed state debts. Then we would have to determine the realty holdings of these men to see how realty compared with securities.

North Carolina, being predominantly a small-farmer state, provides the best apparent correlation between economic interests and ratification of the Constitution. In fact, North Carolina is about the only state in which the correlation holds (Tables III and IV, Chapter VIII above). Under the Beard thesis the state theoretically should have opposed the Constitution, and it did until after the new government went into effect. Why it changed Beard did not explain satisfactorily. Perhaps the people actually were motivated by a desire for amendments to the Constitution before they would join the Union. If so, one must remember that three of these amendments were designed in part to protect property. It must be kept in mind, however, that other agricultural states—Delaware, New Jersey, and Georgia, ratified unanimously.

Although Beard said that ratification in South Carolina

could be explained on economic grounds "with the utmost simplicity," the facts do not bear out his general interpretation. He used Libby for his division of the state into the wealthy Federalist coastal area and the small-farmer Antifederalist back country. It is true a great majority of the stock in trade was located in Charleston County and City, £109,800 out of £127,337, but it is also true that most of the real estate was located there too, £549,909 out of £656,272. Furthermore, the real estate was five times as much as the stock in trade; therefore, it is the real estate which must be explained in any economic interpretation.

There are also many other unanswered questions in Beard's discussion of South Carolina. Outside of Charleston, how important were mercantile and commercial interests, even in the area along the coast? If only fourteen of thirty-one delegates held public securities, why did the other seventeen favor the Constitution? We would also want to know which men on Beard's list (p. 289) held how many securities, and how those securities compared with their other economic interests.

Beard dismissed Georgia, an agricultural state which ratified early and unanimously, with the explanation by Libby that the state was motivated by danger from the Indians. This was about the only state in which Beard did not attempt to represent personalty as the dominant factor. He also admitted that neither he nor anyone else had done thorough research in the unprinted sources of Georgia.

Beard's conclusions (pp. 290-91) in this chapter are warranted only if one has a desire to believe the Beard thesis without regard for evidence. There is a refinement here—that personalty was behind the Constitution and that as "securities constituted such a large portion of personalty, this economic interest must have formed a very considerable dynamic element, if not the preponderating element, in bringing about the adoption of the new system." The delegates to the state conventions had "actual economic advantages at stake" and the opposition came from agricultural and debtor areas. But in spite of his generalization, the fact still remains that the country was predominantly agricultural, that some agricultural

180

states ratified unanimously, and that "workers" in the "cities" generally voted for the Constitution. These farmers and workers were neither large holders of personalty in general nor large holders of public securities in particular, at least not from Beard's evidence.

# CHAPTER XI

# "THE ECONOMIC CONFLICT
# OVER RATIFICATION
# AS VIEWED BY CONTEMPORARIES"

HAVING discovered to his own satisfaction the nature of the social conflict over the Constitution—that it was put over undemocratically by personalty interests and especially public security holders—Beard then turned to a final question. Did the leading thinkers of the time realize the nature of the conflict? Were they aware of the issues involved?

The answer to this question is naturally important, not only for the leaders but also for the people at large, for if the people were not aware of the essential issues, these issues are of no significance in explaining their actions. If the people in general did not understand that the controversy was between the small farmer and debtor on one side and personalty on the other, their vote for or against the Constitution cannot be explained on this ground.

The critical reader will be warned at the outset by some of Beard's qualifications. He said that space prohibited a full account, and that therefore he would limit himself to a few illustrative and representative opinions. We would want to examine some of the sources to see whether they were representative or whether Beard merely selected opinions which fitted his thesis. Then he said that no one could read the sources of the years 1787-89 without concluding that there was "a deep-seated conflict between a popular party based on paper money and agrarian interests, and a conservative party centered in the towns and resting on financial, mercantile, and personal property interests generally" (p. 292). Having said that, however, Beard gave the reader his proper clue. He admitted that much of the fulmination in pamphlets was concerned with various features of the Constitution, that is, political controversies over the form of the new government. But, he concluded, the writers who really went to the bottom of matters, such as the authors of *The Federalist* and leading Antifederalists, gave careful attention to basic elements as well as incidental details. In other words, the reader is warned that the people at large may well have considered as important the things that Beard brushed off as unimportant, and that even the leaders took into consideration the "incidental" details as well as the "fundamental" issues.

This difference between Madison's ideas of what was significant in the Constitution and what others considered important in that document is well illustrated by Madison's letter to Jefferson (p. 293). Madison talked about a pamphlet which gave the alterations to the Constitution proposed by the ratifying conventions. These were various and numerous, he said, but they omitted many of the real grounds of opposition, which Madison considered to be sections on treaties, paper money, and contracts. It is obvious that Madison and the pamphleteer differed in their interpretation of the opposition to the Constitution. Perhaps Madison, who thought in economic terms as much as any member of the Convention, believed that the main opposition came from the treaty, paper money, and contract clauses. Or perhaps he believed that these clauses should have caused the most opposition. But the pamphlet he was talking about obviously stressed other objections, and we cannot say that these other objections were less important to the people who held them than Madison's were to Madison.

Beard's quotation from an "Address to the Freemen of America" in the *American Museum* for June, 1787 (Beard, pp. 293-94) is a good example of my contention that the Constitution could have appealed to many groups and interests. The "Address" directed its appeal to public creditors, soldiers, and citizens who had served the country, western settlers who needed protection from the Indians, farmers who suffered from heavy taxes, merchants who were discriminated against in foreign markets, and unemployed manufacturers and mechanics. Why assume that this was just a blind, and that public creditors were the only ones who understood the real situation? It is just conceivable that a man whose wife and children had been scalped by the Indians might actually vote for a strong government which could give him some protection. Even a shoemaker, whose business was poor because of the flood of cheap British goods, could easily feel the same way. Has not organized labor generally favored a protective tariff, or is it just something that the industrialist advocates? Of course the Federalists had to conciliate many groups, just as any political party does; and, as this selection from the "Address" so eloquently demonstrates, the material advantages to be expected from the Constitution would not necessarily accrue to the personalty interests alone.

John Marshall and the acrimonious Federalist-Antifederalist propaganda should be accepted with a great deal of discrimination. Then as now, the aim of the political propagandist was to picture his side as purer than it probably was and to paint the opponent as black as possible. Both sides, however, talked about freedom of the press, freedom of religion, trial by jury, and liberty (pp. 294-95). And of course Marshall was no objective, unbiased historian. He wrote his *Life of Washington* during the bitter Federalist-Jeffersonian controversy, of which he himself, as chief justice, was an integral part. Marshall's account of the closeness of the vote on the Constitution (Beard, p. 299) does not square very well with the facts, for no one knew what the popular vote was. Beard seems to imply that the Constitution needed to be sanctioned by the whole people before it could be said that it came from the people. This, of course, has never been true in a democracy, and probably never could be true as long as people have differences of opinion and interest. All we can do is to abide by the decision of a majority of those who express an opinion, leaving the minority the right to become the majority if they can.

It is easy to be misled into the belief that the parties in 1787 were at opposite extremes from each other in their views. This would be a grave mistake. The differences were more of degree than of kind, as witnessed by the many statements of Antifederalists that the Constitution would be acceptable with a few changes, and that they would abide by the decision of the people if the people adopted the Constitution. Further evidence that the two parties were not widely separated can be seen in the speed with which the Federalists amended the Constitution to remedy the defects pointed out by its critics. The truth is that neither side could have been extreme, or gotten too far out of touch with the people, without facing the prospect of inevitable defeat. Modern political parties in this country have discovered the wisdom of this political axiom.

Beard then turned from general observations to the conflict in the states, and in dealing with New Hampshire he divided the people "sharply" into an "aristocratic" and a "country" party. His evidence from the *New Hampshire Spy*, however, does not support this division. The writer appealed for support from the honest man, the mercantile interest, the mechanical interest, and the honest farmer, showing how each would benefit by the Constitution. This is not just an appeal to personalty, especially to the public security branch of personalty. The alignment of mercantile and mechanical interests would also appear to be an incompatible marriage if the Beard thesis is correct. Since New Hampshire was largely agricultural and a large number of farmers had to vote for the Constitution if it was to be adopted, many a farmer must have considered himself an aristocrat, an honest man, or an honest farmer.

If the contest in Massachusetts had been "a sharp conflict between the personalty interests on the one hand and the small farmers and debtors on the other" as Beard said (p. 301), Massachusetts would have stayed out of the Union. The small farmers could have snowed under the ratifying convention by at least ten to one if they had been united in their views. Just who the debtors were only Beard knew, for, as far as I can tell, no one has ever made a study to determine this. Shaysites and their sympathizers controlled the state legislature and could as easily have controlled the convention. The fact is, however, that the farmers were fairly well divided, as the elections in the agricultural towns of Malden, Andover, Springfield, Hadley, Great Barrington, and Sheffield have indicated. General Knox, whom Beard quoted, was not exactly an objective observer, and was expressing fear rather than actuality. The fact that a few men talked about annihilation of debts did not mean that the attitude was general. Knox would be about as reliable now as the person who says that the colleges are "hotbeds of communism" or that all union workers are communists.

Again Beard quoted evidence to show that the Federalists were appealing to all sorts of interests, not just personalty holders or public security holders. Even the Knox statement said that the people of Maine were basing their support for the Constitution on whether or not it would facilitate their desire for statehood. Then the letter favoring ratification in the *Massachusetts Gazette* (Beard, p. 302) appealed to the interests of merchants, mechanics, farmers, landholders, gentlemen, men of property, soldiers, lawyers, clergy, and all men with a liberal education. Only a clairvoyant could say which of these groups were swayed by these arguments and which saw the Constitution as Beard saw it.

Stephen Higginson was another witness who was not exactly objective. The Higginson statement (p. 303) was made in March, 1787, when Shays' Rebellion was just running its course. Higginson reflects conservative opinion, but there is much evidence on the other side to refute him. By the time the Constitution was up for sanction, the people of the interior parts of the state who had "by far too much political knowledge" had captured control of the government and had not carried out any of the wild schemes that Higginson attributed to them. There is no justification for using Higginson's views on Shays' Rebellion as evidence on the Constitution. And if Beard had read John Adams carefully, he would have found that there was a great difference between a "natural aristocracy" and an "aristocracy of wealth." A natural aristocracy simply meant men with ability, talent, and training, the kind of an aristocracy that Jefferson believed in.

The reader will quickly note Beard's questionable use of Rufus King's statement to fit his thesis (p. 304). Beard had King saying that the opposition to the Constitution was grounded on antagonism to property. What King actually said was that opposition was due to "apprehension that the liberties of the people are in danger," and that "a distrust of men of property or education" had a greater influence than any specific objections to the Constitution. Property was only one of several factors here, but to Beard property was the only item.

Even the quotation from "Cornelius" does not support Beard's thesis, although he apparently thought it did. "Cornelius" divided society vertically into two property groups, the landed and the mercantile. He apparently thought that the merchants and mechanics had interests in common, which is hard to explain with the Beard interpretation, and that this combined mercantile interest was opposed to the landed group, not just to small farmers and debtors. There is some truth in such a division, but the antagonism is obviously not as great as "Cornelius" pictured it, or the merchants would have been driven out of business after Shays' Rebellion. This sort of thing is similar to the propaganda used by Federalists to the effect that Jefferson would bankrupt the merchants, and we know the extent to which Jefferson wiped out commerce simply because he was anticommercial.

There are confusion of ideas, evidence which refutes Beard's generalizations, and contradictions all mixed up together in Beard's discussion of Connecticut. He posed the usual conflict between "agrarianism and personalty," and he used the term "agrarian" several times but did not explain whether he meant agricultural or leveler. The term has both meanings, and it makes a difference whether we use it in one sense or the other. Oliver Ellsworth, whom Beard quoted, was talking about farmers (p. 306), not about levelers. There is little significance in the fact that Ellsworth, who was not a farmer, posed as one in his propaganda. Both sides used this technique to put forth ideas that would appeal to different interest groups.

Ellsworth's later classification of the opponents of the Constitution (pp. 307-08) certainly does not support an exclusively economic interpretation. Ellsworth said the leading opponents of the Constitution were Tories who thought the adoption of a stronger government would embarrass Great Britain. This, of course, is not the Beard thesis. Ellsworth's second category of opponents, the debtors, does support Beard's view, but the third group, the politicians, does not help his interpretation any. We cannot discard the Tories and officeholders, as Beard would have us do, and accept the "agrarian party" as the weightiest in the opposition. If Beard meant farmers when he said agrarian, then the farmers did not even enter into this later classification by Ellsworth.

Arguments used in the Connecticut legislature against sending delegates to Philadelphia (pp. 308-09) do not show that "resistance came from the smaller agrarian interests" as Beard said. Granger opposed the sending of delegates to Philadelphia because he thought "the liberties of the people would be endangered by it," and he feared that such things "would have a tendency to produce a regal government in this country." We do not know why Humphrey sanctioned Rhode Island's refusal to send delegates, while Perkins (p. 309) brought in the affluent against the people. Beard should have used only Perkins, but even Perkins did not make the division one of personalty against small farmers.

As in other states, small farmers in Connecticut had to vote for the Constitution or it would not have been adopted. The map opposite page 265 eloquently testifies to this statement.

As Hamilton pointed out in New York, the issues were not all class or even economic determinist in nature. In addition to economic elements behind the Constitution, there was the prestige of the framers, especially the universal popularity of Washington, and a strong belief among the people in general that the Articles of Confederation could not preserve the Union. Opposed were state officials who stood to lose power and the fear among the democratic elements of raising a few men to positions of great power. Most of these factors, it seems to me, were either political or personal in nature, not economic and especially not personalty-realty as Beard would have us believe. In addition, we have already seen that *The Federalist* appealed to every interest imaginable. The Fathers of the Constitution were far too experienced as politicians to believe that a document appealing primarily to special class interests could ever be adopted in a democratic society.

Pennsylvania was another state where the Constitution would not have been adopted if the conflict had been between town and country, personalty and realty, as Beard said it was. There is no justification for inserting the word "agrarians" to signify "Western people," or "radical party" to substitute for "Constitutional," as Beard did (pp. 310-11), except that Harding did this in his "Party Struggles over the First Pennsylvania Constitution" and Beard followed Harding's interpretation. Gouverneur Morris's statement that he dreaded the action of the back counties and still more the opposition of politicians who would lose power could be interpreted to mean that sectional interests and political ambitions were more important than class divisions in Pennsylvania. Here Beard has Franklin in tandem with Washington as one of the "great names" in support of the Constitution, while on page 197 he said Franklin was considered as a doubtful supporter of the Constitution. In spite of Antifederalist propaganda soliciting the agricultural vote, the incontrovertible fact remains that Pennsylvania ratified by a vote of 46 to 23, with Philadelphia having only 28,000 people out of a population of 350,000. At least some of the "country people" must have voted for ratification.

There are a few other points to be noted or repeated about ratification in Pennsylvania. Beard finally had a quotation which gave an accurate view of John Adams' philosophy of government—that a balanced government would produce an equilibrium of interests and thus promote the happiness of the whole community. However, the Adams-Madison theory was not one of "balanced economic interests and innocuous legislatures," as Beard stated, but balanced economic interests so that no one could control the legislature for its own particular benefit. This idea is strange coming from Beard, for previously he had talked as though a balanced government would aid the upper classes. The assumption from his interpretation is that the Federalists wanted a legislature that would pass protective tariffs, funding and assumption laws, commercial legislation, and land laws to help the personalty group. This does not imply an "innocuous" legislature. The quotation about single governments—that is, governments without checks and balances—being tyrannies was almost exactly Jefferson's view, so obviously conservatives were not the only ones who advocated checks and balances. And finally, we need to remember

Franklin's statement that the Constitution had been argued in the newspapers so long that the people were tired of the issue, and to note that only 13,000 out of more than 70,000 qualified voters took the trouble to vote in Pennsylvania.

If the contest in Maryland "was keen and spirited and every side of the question was threshed out in newspaper articles and pamphlets," and if it was a "struggle between debtors and creditors, between people of substance and the agrarians," and if Maryland ratified 63 to 11 after months of debate, we have the following alternatives: most of the people in Maryland must have been wealthy creditors or Beard's analysis must have been wrong. Actually, Beard quoted only an infinitesimal part of the evidence on both sides, evidence which would show that there were many arguments and many issues at stake. These, and not the ones cited by Beard, explain why Maryland ratified 63 to 11, for I am quite sure that the people in Maryland were not wealthy creditors at the ratio of nearly six to one.

Beard's explanation of Virginia is simply not consistent with his own thesis. On page 235 he said both sides were ably led, that it was a magnificent battle of talents. Madison supported this view by saying that "men of intelligence, patriotism, property, and independent circumstances" divided over the issue of ratification. Beard, however, discounted both of these views and tended to accept Marshall, who was not a leading figure in the move for the Constitution and who wrote some twenty years after its adoption and under circumstances that would make his interpretation suspect. Madison's statement that the "superiority of abilities" favored the Constitution and Charles Lee's claim that the men with the most knowledge, ability, and personal influence were for the Constitution do not mean economic determinism. When Patrick Henry said most of the small farmers were opposed, he was merely expressing an opinion—and I think a hope—rather than a fact. If that had been true, their representatives would have voted against ratification.

North Carolina was one of the few states that fitted the Beard thesis. It was agricultural, it had little in the way of personalty, and it refused to ratify the Constitution until there was a good prospect that the amendments it demanded would be adopted. The only question is whether North Carolina opposed the Constitution for the reasons attributed by Beard.

If the conflict in North Carolina was between a paper money–debtor party and men of substance, as Beard said, he failed to pick the right evidence to illustrate his generalization. For instance, William R. Davie appealed to "the merchant or farmer" in defending restrictions on paper money, installment laws, and pine-barren acts. Governor Johnston did the same when he said that every man of property, whether merchant, planter, mechanic, or other, must have felt the evil effects of paper money. In other words, a farmer who was not in debt might not have the same views as a farmer who was in debt. In the letter of one Maclaine to James Iredell, cited by Beard, the issue was political, not economic. Maclaine said that if the people of New Hanover County were left to themselves, they would favor the Constitution, but that the demagogues, a *few* persons in debt, and almost every public officer were in the opposition. Presumably these people were using their influence on the others. When Maclaine said that his and Iredell's friend Huske and Colonel Read had joined "all the low scoundrels in the County," he was not saying, as Beard interpreted, that this meant "the country party." Maclaine did not even mention a "country party." Even the secondary account by McRee, *Life and Correspondence of James Iredell* (Beard, pp. 320-21), injected political issues into the economic conflict between merchants of Wilmington and the farmers of New Hanover County. The antagonism of the country people, he said, was based on the fact that some of the leading men of Wilmington either were Tories or were lukewarm in their support for the Revolution.

Maclaine spoke of the "common people" twice in his letter in ways both to bolster and to refute the Beard thesis. At one point he said he expected to receive a copy of *The Federalist*, whose writings were judicious and ingenious but not calculated to win the support of the common people. Beard might well have used this as evidence that the authors of *The Federalist* appealed to the interests of the upper rather than the lower classes. On the other hand, why were Huske and Colonel Read using underhanded means to prejudice the "common people" against the Constitution unless the common people had the right to vote? Furthermore, if Maclaine's and Iredell's friend Huske had joined Colonel Read in the opposition, this should be evidence of a split in the ranks of the so-called upper classes.

When we get to South Carolina we find some very odd reasoning being used by Beard. That source materials for that state are not available to the northern student is no excuse if the sources are available in South Carolina. We assume that a scholar will go where the sources are available. So in lieu of the sources, Beard said "it may easily be imagined" that the leaders of the state observed the essential nature of the conflict, agrarian back country against commercial seaboard. Beard then substituted arguments over the South Carolina constitution of 1790 as evidence for the conflict over the federal Constitution. But this evidence furnishes an insight into social conditions in the state which Beard failed to emphasize. The contemporary writer "Appius" divided the state into sections, upper and lower counties, pointing out that the two differed in almost every respect. One was accustomed to expense, large salaries, and commerce; the other demanded frugality, low salaries, and manufacturing. "Appius" made two points of special interest. One was that the people of the upper counties were men of "moderate fortunes," not propertyless or debtor farmers. The other was that while the seaboard favored commerce as a means of exporting its surplus and importing articles of consumption, the back country favored manufacturing. Here were two personalty interests in conflict with each other.

Beard's explanation simply does not account for what happened in South Carolina. The people had all winter to weigh the arguments for and against the Constitution, and as the evidence in the footnote shows (p. 323), the Antifederalists had been particularly active in the back country. Except for Charleston, the state was predominantly agricultural, yet South Carolina ratified by a vote of 149 to 73.

Georgia should never have ratified the Constitution if we were to accept the Beard interpretation. The state was strictly agricultural, it had very little in personalty—and it ratified unanimously. Maybe defense against the Indians was really an issue in Georgia, not just a blind which would prevent an expression of discord between realty and personalty. Perhaps realty and personalty actually had something in common in wanting a strong federal government that could shoulder the Indian problem, and perhaps this even explains why Georgia ratified in such a hurry and by a unanimous vote.

As in the other chapters, Beard's evidence does not prove what he said it proved. Contemporaries thought there were many issues involved besides the conflict of personalty, especially securities, against small farmers and debtors. Personalty and debts were included, but these were only a few of the items mentioned by the people of the time. Sometimes there were farmers against merchants; sections against sections; or political controversies including loyalty to leaders, hatred of Tories, opposition of state officeholders to a stronger government, and fear that the Constitution would eliminate freedom of the press, freedom of religion, or just plain liberty itself. These various factors are apparent from Beard's own evidence, not to mention the evidence which he omitted.

AT THE END of Chapter XI Beard summarized his findings in fourteen paragraphs under the heading of "Conclusions" (pp. 324-25). Actually, these fourteen conclusions merely add up to the two halves of the Beard thesis. One half, that the Constitution originated with and was carried through by personalty interests—money, public securities, manufactures, and commerce—is to be found in paragraphs two, three, six, seven, eight, twelve, thirteen, and fourteen. The other half—that the Constitution was put over undemocratically in an undemocratic society—is expressed in paragraphs four, five, nine, ten, eleven, and fourteen. The lumping of these conclusions under two general headings makes it easier for the reader to see the broad outlines of the Beard thesis.

Before we examine these two major divisions of the thesis, however, some comment is relevant on the implications contained in the first paragraph. In it Beard characterized his book as a long and arid survey, something in the nature of a catalogue. Whether this characterization was designed to give his book the appearance of a coldly objective study based on the facts we do not know. If so, nothing could be further from reality. As reviewers pointed out in 1913, and as subsequent developments have demonstrated, the book is anything but an arid catalogue of facts. Its pages are replete with interpretation, sometimes stated, sometimes implied. Our task has been to examine Beard's evidence to see whether it justifies the interpretation which Beard gave it. We have tried to discover whether he used the historical method properly in arriving at his thesis.

If historical method means the gathering of data from primary sources, the critical evaluation of the evidence thus gathered, and the drawing of conclusions consistent with this evidence, then we must conclude that Beard has done great violation to such method in this book. He admitted that the evidence had not been collected which, given the proper use of historical method, should have precluded the writing of the book. Yet he nevertheless proceeded on the assumption that a valid interpretation could be built on secondary writings whose authors had likewise failed to collect the evidence. If we accept Beard's own maxim, "no evidence, no history," and his own admission that the data had never been collected, the answer to whether he used historical method properly is self-evident.

Neither was Beard critical of the evidence which he did use. He was accused in 1913, and one might still suspect him, of using only that evidence which appeared to support his thesis. The amount of realty in the country compared with the personalty, the vote in New York, and the omission of the part of *The Federalist* No. 10 which did not fit his thesis are only a few examples of the uncritical use of evidence to be found in the book. Sometimes he accepted secondary accounts at face value without checking them with the sources; at other times he allowed unfounded rumors and traditions to color his work.

Finally, the conclusions which he drew were not justified even by the kind of evidence which he used. If we accepted his evidence strictly at face value, it would still not add up to the fact that the Constitution was put over undemocratically in an undemocratic society by personalty. The citing of property qualifications does not prove that a mass of men were disfranchised. And if we accept his figures on property holdings, either we do not know what most of the delegates had in realty and personalty, or we know that realty outnumbered personalty three to one (eighteen to six). Simply showing that a man held public securities is not sufficient to prove that he acted only in terms of his public securities. If we ignore Beard's own generalizations and accept only his evidence, we would have to conclude that most of the property in the country in 1787 was real estate, that real property was widely distributed in rural areas, which included most of the country, and that even the men who were directly concerned with the Constitution, and especially Washington, were large holders of realty.

Perhaps we can never be completely objective in history, but certainly we can be more objective than Beard was in this book. Naturally the historian must always be aware of the biases, the subjectivity, the pitfalls that confront him, but this does not mean that he should not make an effort to overcome these obstacles. Whether Beard had his thesis before he had his evidence, as some have said, is a question that each reader must answer for himself. Certain it is that the evidence does not justify the thesis.

So instead of the Beard interpretation that the Constitution was put over undemocratically in an undemocratic society by personal property, the following fourteen paragraphs are offered as a possible interpretation of the Constitution and as suggestions for future research on that document.

1. The movement for the Constitution was originated and carried through by men who had long been important in both economic and political affairs in their respective states. Some of them owned personalty, more of them owned realty, and if their property was adversely affected by conditions under the Articles of Confederation, so also was the property of the bulk of the people in the country, middle-class farmers as well as town artisans.

2. The movement for the Constitution, like most important movements, was undoubtedly started by a small group of men. They were probably interested personally in the outcome of their labors, but the benefits which they expected were not confined to personal property or, for that matter, strictly to things economic. And if their own interests would be enhanced by a new government, similar interests of other men, whether agricultural or commercial, would also be enhanced.

3. Naturally there was no popular vote on the calling of the convention which drafted the Constitution. Election of delegates by state legislatures was the constitutional method under the Articles of Confederation, and had been the method long established in this country. Delegates to the Albany Congress, the Stamp Act Congress, the First Continental Congress, the Second Continental Congress, and subsequent congresses under the Articles were all elected by state legislatures, not by the people. Even the Articles of Confederation had been sanctioned by state legislatures, not by popular vote. This is not to say that the Constitutional Convention should not have been elected directly by the people, but only that such a procedure would have been unusual at the time. Some of the

opponents of the Constitution later stressed, without avail, the fact that the Convention had not been directly elected. But at the time the Convention met, the people in general seemed to be about as much concerned over the fact that they had not elected the delegates as the people of this country are now concerned over the fact that they do not elect our delegates to the United Nations.

4. Present evidence seems to indicate that there were no "propertyless masses" who were excluded from the suffrage at the time. Most men were middle-class farmers who owned realty and were qualified voters, and, as the men in the Convention said, mechanics had always voted in the cities. Until credible evidence proves otherwise, we can assume that state legislatures were fairly representative at the time. We cannot condone the fact that a few men were probably disfranchised by prevailing property qualifications, but it makes a great deal of difference to an interpretation of the Constitution whether the disfranchised comprised ninety-five per cent of the adult men or only five per cent. Figures which give percentages of voters in terms of the entire population are misleading, since less than twenty per cent of the people were adult men. And finally, the voting qualifications favored realty, not personalty.

5. If the members of the Convention were directly interested in the outcome of their work and expected to derive benefits from the establishment of the new system, so also did most of the people of the country. We have many statements to the effect that the people in general expected substantial benefits from the labors of the Convention.

6. The Constitution was not just an economic document, although economic factors were undoubtedly important. Since most of the people were middle-class and had private property, practically everybody was interested in the protection of property. A constitution which did not protect property would have been rejected without any question, for the American people had fought the Revolution for the preservation of life, liberty, and property. Many people believed that the Constitution did not go far enough to protect property, and they wrote these views into the amendments to the Constitution. But property

was not the only concern of those who wrote and ratified the Constitution, and we would be doing a grave injustice to the political sagacity of the Founding Fathers if we assumed that property or personal gain was their only motive.

7. Naturally the delegates recognized that the protection of property was important under government, but they also recognized that personal rights were equally important. In fact, persons and property were usually bracketed together as the chief objects of government protection.

8. If three-fourths of the adult males failed to vote on the election of delegates to ratifying conventions, this fact signified indifference, not disfranchisement. We must not confuse those who could *not* vote with those who *could* vote but failed to exercise their right. Many men at the time bewailed the fact that only a small portion of the voters ever exercised their prerogative. But this in itself should stand as evidence that the conflict over the Constitution was not very bitter, for if these people had felt strongly one way or the other, more of them would have voted.

Even if we deny the evidence which I have presented and insist that American society was undemocratic in 1787, we must still accept the fact that the men who wrote the Constitution believed that they were writing it for a democratic society. They did not hide behind an iron curtain of secrecy and devise the kind of conservative government that they wanted without regard to the views and interests of "the people." More than anything else, they were aware that "the people" would have to ratify what they proposed, and that therefore any government which would be acceptable to the people must of necessity incorporate much of what was customary at the time. The men at Philadelphia were practical politicians, not political theorists. They recognized the multitude of different ideas and interests that had to be reconciled and compromised before a constitution would be acceptable. They were far too practical, and represented far too many clashing interests themselves, to fashion a government weighted in favor of personalty or to believe that the people would adopt such a government.

9. If the Constitution was ratified by a vote of only one-sixth

of the adult men, that again demonstrates indifference and not disfranchisement. Of the one-fourth of the adult males who voted, nearly two-thirds favored the Constitution. Present evidence does not permit us to say what the popular vote was except as it was measured by the votes of the ratifying conventions.

10. Until we know what the popular vote was, we cannot say that it is questionable whether a majority of the voters in several states favored the Constitution. Too many delegates were sent uninstructed. Neither can we count the towns which did not send delegates on the side of those opposed to the Constitution. Both items would signify indifference rather than sharp conflict over ratification.

11. The ratifying conventions were elected for the specific purpose of adopting or rejecting the Constitution. The people in general had anywhere from several weeks to several months to decide the question. If they did not like the new government, or if they did not know whether they liked it, they could have voted *no* and there would have been no Constitution. Naturally the leaders in the ratifying conventions represented the same interests as the members of the Constitutional Convention—mainly realty and some personalty. But they also represented their constituents in these same interests, especially realty.

12. If the conflict over ratification had been between substantial personalty interests on the one hand and small farmers and debtors on the other, there would not have been a constitution. The small farmers comprised such an overwhelming percentage of the voters that they could have rejected the new government without any trouble. Farmers and debtors are not synonymous terms and should not be confused as such. A town-by-town or county-by-county record of the vote would show clearly how the farmers voted.

13. The Constitution was created about as much by the whole people as any government could be which embraced a large area and depended on representation rather than on direct participation. It was also created in part by the states, for as the *Records* show, there was strong state sentiment at

the time which had to be appeased by compromise. And it was created by compromising a whole host of interests throughout the country, without which compromises it could never have been adopted.

14. If the intellectual historians are correct, we cannot explain the Constitution without considering the psychological factors also. Men are motivated by what they believe as well as by what they have. Sometimes their actions can be explained on the basis of what they hope to have or hope that their children will have. Madison understood this fact when he said that the universal hope of acquiring property tended to dispose people to look favorably upon property. It is even possible that some men support a given economic system when they themselves have nothing to gain by it. So we would want to know what the people in 1787 thought of their class status. Did workers and small farmers believe that they were lower-class, or did they, as many workers do now, consider themselves middle-class? Were the common people trying to eliminate the Washingtons, Adamses, Hamiltons, and Pinckneys, or were they trying to join them?

As did Beard's fourteen conclusions, these fourteen suggestions really add up to two major propositions: the Constitution was adopted in a society which was fundamentally democratic, not undemocratic; and it was adopted by a people who were primarily middle-class property owners, especially farmers who owned realty, not just by the owners of personalty. At present these points seem to be justified by the evidence, but if better evidence in the future disproves or modifies them, we must accept that evidence and change our interpretation accordingly.

After this critical analysis, we should at least not begin future research on this period of American history with the illusion that the Beard thesis of the Constitution is valid. If historians insist on accepting the Beard thesis in spite of this analysis, however, they must do so with the full knowledge that their acceptance is founded on "an act of faith," not an analysis of historical method, and that they are indulging in a "noble dream," not history.

"act of faith," history as an, 10

Adams, James Truslow, work cited, 70n

Adams, John, 200; political philosophy of, 116, 123, 189; on aristocracy, 186

Adams, John Quincy, views on ratification, 155; views on weather, 1787, 168-69

adult men, percentage of in population, 64, 197

agricultural areas, opposed the Constitution, 180

agricultural interest, failure to account for influence of, 54; importance of underestimated by Beard, 90; and vote on Constitution, 171, 176-77; preponderance of in New Hampshire, 172, *See also* landed interest

agricultural towns, in Massachusetts support stronger union, 59; and vote on Constitution, 175

agricultural states, favored the Constitution, 156; ratification in, 177. *See also* agricultural interest, landed interest

"agrarian," Madison on, 108; meaning of, 187; in Pennsylvania, 189; use of term, 190

Albany Congress, delegates to, elected by legislatures, 196

Alexandria, Virginia, 87

Ambler, C. H., use of by Beard, 45-46; work cited, 59, 171, 178-79

amendments to Constitution, demands for, 179; protected property, 197

American Historical Association, Beard elected president of, 9; 1934 meeting, 11

*American Museum*, cited, 183

American Revolution, 48, 86, 174, 191; interpretation of, 19-21, 98, 130; as a social movement, 70-71; aims of, 197. *See also* "dual revolution"

Andover, Massachusetts, vote on the Constitution in, 150, 166, 185

Antifederalists, 83, 149, 150, 153, 155, 162, 163, 167, 173, 174, 178, 183; and weather, 1787, 169; believed in protection of property, 108; differences between, and Federalists, 184; activities in South Carolina, 180, 192; propaganda by, 189; solicit farmer vote, 189

"Appius," cited, 192

aristocracy, 173; Hudson River, position of, 47; defined, 186

Armstrong, John, letter of, 60

Articles of Confederation, 57, 59, 60, 114, 135, 140; effect of on personalty, 56; elections under, 62; interpretation of, 130; amendment of, 138; plans to abolish, 138; overthrow of a *coup d'état*, 138; and ratification of the Constitution, 141; overthrow of, 154; and popular vote on Constitution, 157; inadequacy of, 188; effect on property, 196; and the Constitutional Convention, 196; adopted by state legislatures, 196

artisans, as manufacturers, 52-53; reason of for supporting the Constitution, 94; importance of, 196. *See also* mechanics, workingmen

Ashford, Connecticut, security holders in, 175

Ashley, John, Jr., 150, 160

assumption of state debts, 141, 179; rejected by Constitutional Convention, 51. *See also* Hamilton

Athenians, 41

Austin, Anthony, 160-61

"backwoods," voters on Constitution in, 166

balanced government, 126, 189. *See also* checks and balances

Baldwin, Abraham, 40n, 89; property of, 74; political philosophy of, 114

Baltimore, voters in, 163; vote of workingmen in, 178; population of, 178

Baltimore County, votes Antifederalist, 178

Bancroft, George, interpretation by, 26

Bank of the United States, 57

Barkhamsted, Connecticut, security holders in, 175

Bassett, Richard, 89; property of, 74; political philosophy of, 134

Beard, Charles A., 3; analysis of economic interests, 1787, 54; and objectivity, 195-96; as an economic determinist, 30; conclusions by, 194ff; elected president of American Historical Association, 9; historical method of gains stature, 18-19; influence of Founding Fathers on, 14; influence of Madison's *Federalist* No. 10 on, 14, 17; influence of Marx on, 13, 14, 16; interpretation of the Constitution, *see* Beard thesis; interpretation of history, 9-11, 14; modification of views, 1935, 1943, 1944, 18; neglects agricultural interest, 54; on *An Economic Interpretation,* 1935, 16; on economic determinism, 16, 26; on economic interpretation, 13, 15; on historical method, 12-14; on Madison as an economic determinist, 29; on objective historians, 12-13; on social structure, 29-30; order of discussing ratification, 143; outlines research to be done, 33, 56-57; predicted trend toward collective democracy, 10; presidential address before American Historical Association, 1933, 9;

purpose in writing *An Economic Interpretation,* 4; resignation from Columbia University, 5, 16; underestimates importance of agricultural interest, 90; use of evidence by, 29, 34-37, 49, 51, 52, 57-60, 63-64, 72, 84, 102, 103, 111, 123, 136, 148, 151, 153, 161, 164, 166, 176, 180, 186, 187, 190-92, 194, 195; use of *Federalist* No. 10, 27-32, 195; use of historical method, 6-9, 17, 22, 24, 27, 33-37, 49, 54, 57-58, 60, 63-64, 66-68, 82, 84, 89-90, 102, 104-05, 111, 123, 136, 141, 148, 164, 192, 194-95, 200; use of implication, 57; use of innuendo, 148, 153; use of primary sources, 22; use of secondary works by, 34, 57, 90, 149, 151, 152, 171, 177, 178, 180, 189, 195; writings of, 1910-1915, 24

Beard's preface, reason for analysis of, 23

Beard thesis, 3, 83, 85, 90, 97, 115, 116, 117, 119, 120, 125, 127, 128, 132-34, 136, 139-40, 144, 146, 157, 165, 171-72, 175, 177-78, 180, 182, 185-87, 190, 193-96; accepted by current writers, 18n, 18-19, 23; and democracy, 34-35; based on Chapter V, 73; contradictions in, 35, 67, 73, 187; criticisms of, 107; influence of on other writings, 9; influence of personalty on, 31; method of analyzing, 22-23; modified, 1935-44, 18; need for critical analysis of, 21; not supported by *The Federalist,* 93-94; statement of, 34, 54, 61; validity of questioned, 34, 35, 44, 48-49, 54, 200

Bedford, Gunning, 42n, 89; property of, 74; on checks and balances, 100; political philosophy of, 114

Bethlehem, Connecticut, security holders in, 175

bills of credit, restrictions of in Constitution, 110
Bishop, Cortlandt Field, work cited, 68
Blackstone, cited, 109
Blair, John, 89; property of, 75; political philosophy of, 134
Blaney, Captain Benjamin, 150
Blinkoff, Maurice, work on Beard cited, 3n, 4n, 8, 9, 15
Blount, William, 89; property of, 75
"Books That Changed Our Minds," 15
Boston, 168; merchants and mechanics as voters in, 39; voters in, 104; vote on Constitution in, 161, 166; and ratification, 174
Boudinot, Elias, 57, 58
Bowdoin, James, advocated stronger union, 59
Bozrah, Connecticut, security holders in, 175
Branford, Connecticut, security holders in, 175
Brearley, David, 89; property of, 75; political philosophy of, 135
Bristol, Connecticut, security holders in, 175
British, *see* England, Great Britain
Brooklyn, Connecticut, security holders in, 175
Broom, Jacob 89; property of, 75; political philosophy of, 115
Butler, Nicholas Murray, on Beard's work, 8
Butler, Pierce, 42n, 84, 89; shows influence of the people, 41; property of, 75-76; on suffrage, 103; political philosophy of, 115

Caesar, 138
Canaan, Connecticut, security holders in, 175
Canterbury, Connecticut, security holders in, 175
capital, farmers depended on towns for, 46
capitalist classes, support Constitution, 32

Carroll, Daniel, 42n, 89; property of, 76; political philosophy of, 115
census of 1790, 64
Chamberlain, John, on Beard's work, 8
Chandler, Julian Alvin Carroll, work cited, 68
Channing, Edward, on Beard's work, 8
Chapter V, importance of, 5, 6, 17, 18, 23
Charleston, South Carolina, 192; property in, 180
checks and balances, 130; purpose of, 97, 98, 189; Convention delegates on, 99ff
Chester, John, 176
Cincinnati, Society of the, 88
Civil War, and Madison's division of society, 1787, 97
classes, 112; Madison on, 101; in the United States, 37, 44; in Virginia, 178
class conflict, 8, 59, 112, 121, 125, 182; and the Constitution, 11; absence of, 1787, 20; and Shays' Rebellion, 60; and ratification, 179
class interests, 124, 128
class structure, Madison on, 95
Cleveland, Frederick Albert, work cited, 70n
Clymer, George, 89; property of, 76; political philosophy of, 115
Colebrook, Connecticut, security holders in, 175
collective democracy, Beard on, 10-11
college textbooks, influence of Beard on, 9
colonial legislatures, composition of, 90. *See also* state legislatures
colonial society, interpreted as undemocratic, 19
Columbia University, 7, 8; Beard's resignation from, 5, 16
Commager, Henry Steele, on Beard's work, 8
commerce, importance of in foreign

and domestic controversies, 111
commercial interests, and manufacturing, 53; and voting franchise, 101-02; and the Beard
interpretation, *see* Beard thesis,
merchants
common people, 118; as voters,
38-39; possessed the franchise,
106; and ratification, 163; and
voting rights, 191-92
communism, 186
compromise, in the Constitutional
Convention, 107, 124, 126, 198;
importance of, 200
Confederation Congress, delegates
to elected by state legislatures,
62; cultural status of delegates,
90; and amendment of Articles
of Confederation, 138
Confederation period, 19, 93, 124;
insufficiency of and *Federalist
Papers*, 27; inadequacies of, 139;
and legality of the Constitutional
Convention, 141
Congress, 104
Connecticut, 38, 39, 77, 80, 85,
109, 118, 131, 135, 142; tax
figures for, 49; voting qualifications in, 63; correlations on
ratification of Constitution in,
145ff; interpretation of ratification in, 150-51; and vote on the
Constitution, 174ff; security holders in, 174-75; class divisions in,
187; farmers in, favor Constitution, 188; opposition in to Constitutional Convention, 188
Connecticut ratifying convention,
167
Connecticut River, 172
Connecticut Valley, and the Constitution, 150, 171, 173, 174
conservative party, 182
conspiracy theory of the Constitution, *see* Constitution conspiracy
theory of
Constitution, as an economic document, 3, 92-111; and democracy,
4, 34-35, 37; and the Progressive
movement, 7; as a conservative

counterrevolution, 19; juristic interpretation of, 26; purpose of,
26; nature of, explained by 85
*Federalist Papers*, 30; designed
to benefit class interests, 31; influence of the people on, 41;
influence of manufacturing and
shipping on, 52-53; interests
favoring, 56; movement for, 56-
60, 196; conspiracy theory of,
56, 61, 138, 141, 143, 169, 176;
importance of farmers in adoption of, 50-51, 90-91; voting
qualifications in, 103; restrictions
on paper money in, 110; as a
conservative *coup d'état*, 138,
141, 153; lack of opposition to,
144; support for, 156, 186; ille-
gality of, 157; appeal of, to
various groups, 183-85; conflicts
over, 184, 193; amendments to,
protected property, 185, 197;
opposition to, 188-89, 191;
Franklin on, 190; and protection
of property, 197; suggested interpretation of, 196-200; as the
work of the whole people, 199.
*See also* ratification of Constitution

Constitutional Convention, dominated by personality interests, 3;
aim of members, 14; economic
interests of delegates to, 17; debates in, 21; debates reveal extent of economic democracy,
1787, 43; rejects assumption of
state debts, 51; lack of democracy in election of, 62; economic
interests of delegates, 73-91;
compromises in, 107, 124; political doctrines of delegates to,
112-37; purposes of, 154; no
popular vote for, 157; attitude
of the people toward election of
delegates to, 157, 197; opposition in Connecticut to, 188;
popular vote and, 196. *See also*
Constitutional Convention delegates
Constitutional Convention dele-

gates, on democracy, 38-44, 67; influence of the people on, 41; property safeguards in election of, 61-72; purposes of, 73; having personalty in excess of realty, 89; having realty in excess of personalty, 89; list of, 89; fear of innovation, 106; political doctrines of, 112-37; purposes of, 138, 196; not democratically elected, 139; property holdings of, 73-91, 195-96

constitutional history, defined, 27

Constitutional Party in Pennsylvania, 189

contract clause of the Constitution, 108-09, 116, 122; restrictions on future contracts, 109; and opposition to the Constitution, 183

Continental Congress, *see* Articles of Confederation, First Continental Congress, Second Continental Congress

Continental debt, 49

contradictions, in Beard thesis, 35-36, 67, 73

"Cornelius," cited, 187

Cornwall, Connecticut, security holders in, 175

Corwin, Edward S., review by, 8

counterrevolution, Constitution as a, *see* Constitution as a counterrevolution

country party, in North Carolina, 191

*coup d'état*, Constitution as a, 16, 138, 141, 153; defined, 138

Craven, Avery Odelle, work cited, 70n

creditor areas, 174

creditors, and the Constitution, 7; location of, 46; in Maryland, 190

custom, importance of, 198

Davidson, Henry P., 7

Davie, William R., 89; property of, 76; on paper money, 110; political philosophy of, 116; on ratification, 191

Dayton, Jonathan, 42n, 89; property of, 76

debt, Continental, 49

debt, domestic, 51

debtor areas, 174; opposed the Constitution, 180

debtor classes, attitude of, 61

debtor farmers, 47; political activities of, 54

debtors, 97, 125, 185; opposed Constitution, 3, 31; and the Constitution, 7; as voters, 38, 67; farmers as, 46; location of, 46; importance of, in ratification, 166; and vote on Constitution, 171; in Maryland, 190; and ratification in North Carolina, 191; importance of, 199

debts, state, 49

Declaration of Independence, and popular vote, 157

Delaware, 38, 41, 74, 76, 85, 114, 115, 130, 134; voting qualifications in, 65; vote on ratification, 142, 177; correlations on ratification, 145ff; interpretation of ratification in, 151; and ratification, 179

Delaware ratifying convention, 167

delegates to Constitutional Convention, *see* Constitutional Convention, delegates to

democracy, 117, 119, 120, 121, 124, 126, 127, 128, 130, 133, 136, 139, 173; absence of in formation of Constitution, 4; lack of in colonial times, 19; rise of under Andrew Jackson, 19-20; in Massachusetts constitutions, 20; and the Beard thesis, 34-35; and adoption of the Constitution, 34-35; extent of, 37-44, 136, 198; Sherman on, 38; Franklin on, 38-39; Charles Pinckney on, 43-44, 84; and Convention debates, 44; and the Constitution, 54; lack of in election of Constitutional Convention, 61; lack of, 1787, 61-62;

Gouverneur Morris on, 65; wide distribution of realty promoted, 67; problem of, neglected by historians, 68; work of McKinley on, 68-69; in Massachusetts, 69, 72; current writers on, 70-71; in Virginia, 71, 178; threat of to personalty, 92; checks on, 100; and Articles of Confederation, 138-39; and ratification of the Constitution, 148ff, 170; and Shays' Rebellion, 150, 160; and popular vote on Constitution, 157ff; and state ratifying conventions, 158; in New England, 159; and indifference of voters, 160; meaning of, 165; lack of, 194, 195; as a basis for the Constitution, 200; extent of, 1787, 200. *See also* disfranchisement, representation, suffrage, voting, voting qualifications

democracy, economic, *see* economic democracy

Derby, Connecticut, security holders in, 175

Dickinson, John, 40n, 42n, 89; on number of voters, 38; property of, 76-77; on suffrage, 103, 104, 105; on ex post facto laws, 109; political philosophy of, 117; on monarchy, 117

Dinwiddie, Governor, proclamation of, 1754, 86

disfranchisement, 112, 165, 195, 198, 199; groups affected, 34-35; extent of not determinable, 35; not extensive, 1787, 38; extent of, 44, 197; of Shaysites, 60; not extensive in New Hampshire, 62; disproved by Beard, 113; and ratifying conventions, 158-59; defined, 159; in Boston, 162; of the masses, 165

Dodd, William E., review by, 4; on Beard's work, 8

domestic debt, 51

Douglass, Elisha P., work cited, 71

"dual revolution," interpretation of,

19; lack of, 20-21. *See also* American Revolution

Durham, Connecticut, security holders in, 175

Dwight, Elijah, 150

East Haddam, Connecticut, security holders in, 175

economic conflict over ratification, 182-93

economic democracy, 75; as revealed by Convention debates, 43

economic determinism, 8, 26, 32, 93; Beard as advocate of, 16; Marxian influence on Beard's, 16; Madison on, 29; Beard on, 30

economic factors, importance of, 197

economic interests, 1787, 21, 30, 33, 34; analysis of erroneous, 54; of members of the Convention, 73-91

economic interpretation of history, 4, 11, 26, 92, 93; Beard on, 13; Beard on in 1935, 15; ingredients for, 31; ingredients for, lacking, 54-55

*Economic Interpretation of the Constitution of the United States, An,* importance of, 3, 5, 16-18; thesis of, 3; Beard's purpose in writing, 4; reviews of, 4-8; importance of Introduction to 1935 edition, 13-14, 16, 19; Beard's views of, 1935, 16; thesis now generally accepted by historians, 17; importance of "Conclusions," 19; based on Madison's *Federalist* No. 10, 29; interpretation of, 194

"Economic Man," 6-7

economics, and vote on Constitution, 171-81

elections, under Articles of Confederation, 62. *See also* disfranchisement, suffrage, voting, voting qualifications

Ellington, Connecticut, security holders in, 175

Elliot's *Debates*, 7

Ellsworth, Oliver, 40n, 42n, 57, 58, 89, 133, 187; on extent of democracy, 39; property of, 77; views on suffrage, 103, 105, 106; political philosophy of, 117; on popular ratification, 158

Enfield, Connecticut, security holders in, 175

England, 119; independence from, 19; voters in, 38; suffrage in, 119; contrasted with America, 178. *See also* Great Britain

entail, of slaves in Virginia, 48; docking of, 48

entail and primogeniture, 178; elimination of, 44

equality, in United States, 1787, 43-44

evidence, use of by Beard, *see* Beard, use of evidence

ex post facto laws, 109

executive, views of the people on, 41

executive council, 41

Exeter, New Hampshire, ratification of Constitution in, 168

factories, paucity of in 1787, 52-53

farmers, 193; number of, 7, 20; opposed Constitution, 3, 31; small, as voters, 38, 67; social position of in back country, 45; as debtors, 46; depended on towns for capital, 46; debtor, as voters, 47; debtor, controlled state legislatures, 47; unity of interests of, 48; economic interests of, 50-51; supported Constitution, 50-51, 56; possible gains by adoption of Constitution, 52; and Shays' Rebellion, 60; dominated state legislatures, 1787, 61; prosperity of, 1787, 90; importance of, in adoption of Constitution, 90-91; reasons of, for supporting the Constitution, 94; holdings of in North Carolina, 107; as voters, 166; and ratification, 166; vote of divided on Constitution, 166, 185; importance of, 171-72, 173, 185, 188, 196, 199; vote of in Pennsylvania, 177; predominance of, 1787, 185; support Constitution in Connecticut, 188; on Constitution, 190; and ratification in North Carolina, 191; class status of, 200. *See also* "agrarian," landed interest, realty interest

farms, size of, 62

Farrand, Max, on Beard's work, 8

Faulkner, Harold U., on Beard's work, 8; work cited, 70n

federal government, idea of, 98. *See also* national government

*Federalist* No. 6, 111

*Federalist* No. 10, 56, 94, 95, 97, 124, 136, 137; influence on Beard, 14, 17; use of by Beard, 27, 195; contents of, 28; omission of part of by Beard, 29; questionable use of by Beard, 32, 92

*Federalist* No. 35, 48

Federalist Party, 95, 115, 148-49, 162, 163, 172; weather as aid to, 169

*Federalist, The*, 92, 96, 99, 116, 136, 183; content of 85 papers, 27; importance of all 85 numbers, 30; importance of in the Beard interpretation, 92-93; expressed political views of delegates, 112; appeal of to all classes and interests, 188; and the "common people," 191

Federalists, 150, 153, 173, 177, 178, 184, 187; victory in New York, 151; in Pennsylvania, 151; in Connecticut, 174; in New Jersey, 176; in South Carolina, 180; and amendments to Constitution, 185; appealed to many interests, 185; aims of, 189

Fellows, John, 160

Few, William, 89; property of, 77

First Continental Congress, and popular vote, 157; delegates elected by legislatures, 196

Fitzsimons, Thomas, 57, 58, 89; property of, 77; on suffrage, 103, political philosophy of, 118

Founding Fathers, 5; influence of writings of on Beard, 14; stage a *coup d'état*, 16; motives of, 16, 21, 31, 32, 92, 166, 198; economic holdings of, 18; speculations of, 58; on democracy, 72; characteristics of, 90; and contract clause, 109; inconsistencies of views of, 113; prestige of, 188; as experienced politicians, 188; and democracy, 198. *See also* Constitutional Convention delegates

foreign debt, 51

France, 130

franchise, 113, 126, 131-32, 133; widely held, 20; extended to small farmers and debtors, 38. *See also* democracy, voting, voting qualifications

Franklin, Benjamin, 40n, 42n, 89, 124, 129; on extent of democracy, 38-39; on public securities, 52; property of, 77; on suffrage, 106; political philosophy of, 118; on ratification, 151, 154; supports the Constitution, 189; on popular views of the Constitution, 190

Franklin, Connecticut, security holders in, 175

freeholders, 38, 127; number who were voters, 38; as voters, 67, 117; influence of, 101; numbers of, 102, 127; and ratification, 140. *See also* agricultural interest, farmers, landed interest, realty, suffrage

freemen, in New York City, 64

French and Indian War, 86

French Revolution, 117

funding program, 141; Gilman and Lansing on, 51. *See also* Hamilton, public securities

Georgia, 74, 77, 79, 83, 88, 114, 120, 128; voters in, 35, 44; voting qualifications in, 66; constitution of, 122; vote on ratification, 142; correlation on ratification in, 145ff; and ratification, 152, 179, 180, 193

Georgia ratifying convention, 167

Gerry, Elbridge, 40n, 42n, 89; on democracy, 38, 40; on influence of the people, 42; objected to assumption of state debts, 51; property of, 78; on checks and balances, 99; on suffrage, 104; political philosophy of, 119-20; on ratification, 154; objections to Constitution, 154; and popular ratification, 158

Gilman, Nicholas, 89; on funding program, 51; urged New Hampshire to buy public securities, 52; property of, 77; political philosophy of, 120

Gorham, Nathaniel, 40n, 42n, 57, 58, 89, 118, 133, 139, 141; on extent of democracy, 39; property of, 78; on suffrage, 103-04, 106; political philosophy of, 120

government, function of, 27

Granby, Connecticut, security holders in, 175

Great Barrington, Massachusetts, vote on Constitution, 150, 166, 167, 173, 185

Great Britain, 98, 99, 108, 187; British imperialism, 93; British constitution could not be used as model, 44, 121, 134. *See also* England

Groton, Connecticut, security holders in, 175

Guilford, Connecticut, security holders in, 174

Haddam, Connecticut, security holders in, 175

Hadley, Massachusetts, vote on Constitution in, 150, 185

Halifax, Nova Scotia, weather in, 1787, 168

Hall, Arnold B., review by, 5n
Hamden, Connecticut, security holders in, 175
Hamilton, 40n, 42n, 51, 84, 85, 89, 93, 107, 135, 136, 141, 200; author of *The Federalist*, 27; report on manufactures, 36, 53; on democracy, 40, 42-43; on Randolph plan, 43; on class structure, 48; assumption and funding programs, 49, 51, 172; vote against stronger government, 59; property of, 79; purpose of government, 100; on commercial antagonisms, 111; political philosophy of, 121; not supported in Constitutional Convention, 121-22; on divisions in New York, 188
Hamilton's plan of union, 128
Hampton, Connecticut, security holders in, 175
Harbison, Winfred A., work cited, 70n
Harding, Samuel Bannister, cited, 149, 171, 189; interpretation by, 173
Harrison, Richard, election of, 64
Hart, Albert Bushnell, on Beard's work, 8
Hartford, Connecticut, security holders in, 174
Hartland, Connecticut, security holders in, 175
Henry, Patrick, views of ratification in Virginia, 190
Higginson, Stephen, 57, 58; on Shays' Rebellion, 186
historian, frame of reference of, 11
historical interpretation, 26
historical method, Beard on, 12-13, 14; Beard's praised by Lerner, 17; Beard's praised by Hofstadter, 18; Beard's gains stature, 19; and voting, 160. *See also* Beard, use of historical method
historical objectivity, 11, 12-13, 195; Leopold von Ranke on, 9
historical profession, conflicts in

over writing of history, 12-13
historical relativism, Beard on, 10
historical subjectivity, Beard on, 9
history as actuality, Beard on, 9
Hockett, Homer Carey, work cited, 70n
Hofstadter, Richard, views on Beard, 17-18
Holmes, Oliver Wendell, 108
Hoover, Herbert, 79
House of Burgesses, 48
House of Representatives, election of, 97, 128; to protect human rights, 114; purpose of, 116, 121. *See also individual delegates, political philosophy of*
Houston, William C., 89, 135; property of, 79
Houstoun, William, 89; property of, 79; political philosophy of, 122
Hubbard, John, 150, 160
Hudson Valley, landowners in, 47

implication, use of, 57
indentured servants, and voting, 34
independence, 19, 145-46
Indians, 183; and ratification in Georgia, 193
indifference of voters, 149, 160, 165, 170, 198, 199
industry, extent of in 1787, 7, 52-53
Ingersoll, Jared, 89; property of, 79; political philosophy of, 122
initiative and referendum, 158
Insurance Company of North America, 88
intellectual historians, 200
interest, value of, disbursed, 50; disbursed on public debt, 145; per capita value of, disbursed, 147
interpretation of history, Beard on, 10, 11, 14
interpretation of the Constitution, *see* Beard thesis
Iredell, James, 191
Izard, Ralph, 57, 58

Jackson, Andrew, and rise of democracy, 20; democracy before, 68

Jameson, J. Franklin, work of, misinterpreted, 69-71; work cited, 70n; on social revolution, 70-71

Jay, John, 93; author of *The Federalist*, 27

Jefferson, Thomas, 115, 187; views on checks and balances, 98, 124, 189; letter to, 183; on aristocracy, 186

Jenifer, Daniel of St. Thomas, 89; property of, 80; political philosophy of, 135

Jensen, Merrill, work cited, 70n

Johnson, William Samuel, 57, 58, 89; property of, 80; on Hamilton, 122; political philosophy of, 135

Johnston, Henry P., work cited, 63

Johnston, Governor, of North Carolina, views on ratification, 191

judiciary, as a check on democracy, 98; appointment of, 98

juristic interpretation of the Constitution, 26

Kelly, Alfred Hinsey, work cited, 70n

Kent, Connecticut, security holders in, 175

Kentucky, 50; opposed the Constitution, 178

Killingly, Connecticut, security holders in, 175

Killingworth, Connecticut, security holders in, 175

King, Rufus, 40n, 42n, 57, 58, 89; property of, 80; on purpose of government, 100; on obligation of contracts, 108; political philosophy, 122; cited, 186

Knox, Henry, 40n; on Shays' Rebellion, 60; cited, 185

Labaree, Leonard Woods, work cited, 70n

labor, organized, 184

labor unions, 93

laborers, 93

laboring class, *see* working class

land, influence of cheap, 44, 99; price of in Virginia, 45-46; value of, 50, 145; speculation in, 58; per capita values in states, 147

land grants, in Virginia, 45-46

land speculation, and sectional conflicts, 45. *See also* personalty

land speculators, 79

landed interest, importance of, 95-96; influence of in state legislatures, 100; controlled ratification, 106; controlled state legislatures, 106, 134; opposed to mercantile interest, 187. *See also* agricultural interest, Constitution, ratification

Langdon, John, 42n, 89; property of, 80; political philosophy of, 135

Lansing, John, 42n, 89; on funding program, 51; property of, 80; political philosophy of, 135

Latané, John H., review by, 7

Latimer, George, 162

law, nature of, 27

Lee, Charles, on ratification in Virginia, 190

Lee, Richard Henry, on middle class, 46; on debtors, 166

Lerner, Max, 19; on Beard, 15-17, 30

Libby, Orin G., review by, 8; cited by Beard, 171, 177, 178, 180; criticism of, 172, 173

liberty, 193; in United States, 132

Lippmann, Walter, on Beard's work, 8

Lisbon, Connecticut, security holders in, 175

Livingston, William, 89; property of, 80; political philosophy of, 123

lower class, 45, 112, 200. *See also* class conflict, classes

Madison, James, 40n, 42n, 44, 89, 92, 93, 94, 122, 127, 129, 136, 137; influence on Beard, 14, 17,

27; and *Federalist* No. 10, 28-29; as an "economic determinist," 29; on social structure, 1787, 30; on suffrage, 36, 102, 103; and Beard thesis, 37; on government, 37; favored freeholders as voters, 38; on number of voters, 38; on influence of the people, 42; on voters, 67; property of, 81; views of in Constitutional Convention, 95; not an economic determinist, 95; on slavery conflict, 96; on checks and balances, 99, 100; on voting franchise, 101; on agrarianism, 108; on contracts, 108; on Bedford, 114; political philosophy of, 124, 189; on Articles of Confederation, 139; on New Jersey, 176; on conflict over the Constitution, 183; on ratification in Virginia, 190; on men's motives, 200

Madisonian division of society, 31

Main, Jackson Turner, work cited, 71

Maine, 163; reasons for supporting the Constitution, 186

Malden, Massachusetts, vote on the Constitution, 150, 185

manufacturers, on commerce, 53; and voting franchise, 102

manufacturing, extent of, 1787, 7, 53; benefits to, from Constitution, 52; in South Carolina, 192. *See also* personalty

Marblehead, Massachusetts, vote on Constitution in, 166; weather in 1787, 168

Marshall, John, on contract clause, 109; views of, 184; on ratification in Virginia, 190

Maryland, 76, 80, 81, 82, 109, 115, 124, 125, 126, 135, 163; voting qualifications in, 65; vote on ratification, 142, 177-78; correlations on ratification, 145ff; interpretation of ratification in, 152; social divisions in, 190; ratification in, 190

Maryland ratifying convention, 124, 167

Marx, Karl, 8; influence on Beard, 13, 14, 16

Marxian division of society, not Madisonian, 31

Marxian theory of history, 11

Massachusetts, 19, 38, 46, 58, 78, 80, 85, 96, 122, 132, 166; rejected constitution of 1778, 20; constitution of 1780, 20, 114; voting qualifications in, 39, 62, 65, 69; government controlled by Shaysites, 1787, 47; tax figures for, 49; legislature of, advocates stronger union, 59; legislature of and Shaysites, 60; democracy in, 69, 72; vote on ratification, 142; correlations on ratification, 145ff; interpretation of ratification in, 149-50; voters in, 161; weather in 1787, 168; and opposition to the Constitution, 169; vote in, 173; and ratification, 173-74; class conflicts in, 185

*Massachusetts Gazette*, cited, 186

Massachusetts ratifying convention, 167-68; debates in, 154

masses, disfranchised by property qualifications, 4, 165; and the Constitution, 5; right to vote, 21; apathy and indifference of, 61

Mason, George, 40n, 42n, 89; on extent of democracy, 39-41; shows influence of the people, 41; property of, 81; on checks and balances, 100, 124; on suffrage, 103, 104, 106; political philosophy of, 125; and abolition of Articles of Confederation, 138; on ratification by nine states, 158; on popular ratification, 158

Martin, Alexander, 89; property of, 81; political philosophy of, 125

Martin Luther, 42n, 89, 115; property of, 81, 82; political philosophy of, 125; opposed Constitution, 152

McClurg, James, 89, 124; property

of, 82; political philosophy of, 123

McCormick, Richard P., work cited, 70n

McHenry, James, 40n, 42n, 89; property of, 82; political philosophy of, 124; election to ratifying convention, 163

McKinley, Albert Edward, work on democracy, 68-69; value of work, 68-70

McMaster and Stone, cited, 177

mechanics, as voters, 35, 39, 117, 162; as manufacturers, 52-53; and merchants, 187

mercantile interests, in South Carolina, 180; opposed to landed interest, 187

merchants, 193. *See also* northern merchants

Mercer, John Francis, 40n, 84, 89; property of, 82; political philosophy of, 126

middle class, 85, 93, 178, 200; importance of, 20, 156, 196; predominated, 1787, 43-44, 197, 200; Charles Pinckney on, 43-44; R. H. Lee's views on, 46; and the Constitution, 54; in South Carolina, 192

Mifflin, Jonathan, 82-83

Mifflin, Thomas, 89, 127; property of, 82

military power, and economic interpretation, 107

monarchy, advocates of, 117

Montville, Connecticut, security holders in, 175

Morgan, J. P., 7

Morison, Samuel Eliot, on Beard's work, 8

Morris, Gouverneur, 40n, 42n, 89; on number of freeholders who were voters, 38; on democracy, 65; property of, 83; on suffrage, 102, 104, 105; on contracts, 108; political philosophy of, 127; on legality of Constitutional Convention, 141; on divisions in Pennsylvania, 189

Morris, Robert, 89; and speculation, 58, 78, 83; property of, 83; political philosophy of, 128

Munroe, John A., work cited, 70n

Napoleon, 138

national debt, 51

national government, 121; idea of, 98

national legislature, to elect executive, 123

nationalism, 59; in *The Federalist*, 93; and economic interpretation, 107

Negroes, free in New York City, 1790, 64. *See also* slavery

New England, 107; suffrage in, 69; voters in, 159

New Fairfield, Connecticut, security holders in, 175

New Hampshire, 77, 80, 120, 135, 173; tax figures for, 49; and public securities, 52; voting qualifications in, 62; vote on ratification, 142, 171; correlations on ratification, 145ff; interpretation of ratification in, 148; weather in 1787, 168-69; opposition to the Constitution in, 169; and agriculture, 171; class divisions in, 185

New Hampshire ratifying convention, 167-69

*New Hampshire Spy*, cited, 185

New Hanover County, North Carolina, views of people in, 191

New Haven, Connecticut, security holders in, 174

"new history," 13

New Jersey, 40, 75, 76, 79, 80, 83, 123, 128, 135, 177; voting qualifications in, 64-65; vote on ratification, 142, 176; correlations on ratification, 145ff; interpretation of ratification in, 151; and ratification, 179

New Jersey ratifying convention, 167

*New Republic*, symposium by, 1938, 15

New York, 57, 59, 79, 80, 89, 135; ratifying convention elected by manhood suffrage, 64; checks and balances in constitution of, 99; vote on ratification, 142, 162-63; correlations on ratification in, 145ff; interpretation of ratification in, 151; inequitable representation in, 163; ratification in, 176; divisions in, 188

New York City, workingmen in favored the Constitution, 37, 53; merchants and mechanics as voters in, 39; voting qualifications in, 63; voters in, 63-64, 104; vote of workingmen in, 176; vote in, 195

New York ratifying convention, 167

*New York Times*, review in, 5; letters in on *An Economic Interpretation*, 7; Taft's views of *An Economic Interpretation* in, 7n; on Beard, 16

Newbury, Massachusetts, support for the Constitution in, 155

Newburyport, Massachusetts, support for Constitution in, 155; weather in 1787, 168

Newcomer, Lee Nathaniel, work cited, 70n

Newtown, Connecticut, security holders in, 175

nonfreeholders, as voters, 38, 39

North Dakota, 90

North Carolina, 75, 76, 81, 85, 88, 116, 125, 132, 133; voting qualifications in, 65; delegates' views on checks and balances, 99; interests of protected by the Constitution, 107; ratification of Constitution, 142, 152, 190-91; correlations on ratification in, 145ff; interpretation of ratification in, 152; freeholders in, 159; vote on Constitution in, 179

North Carolina ratifying convention, 110, 167

North Haven, Connecticut, security holders in, 175

Norfolk, Virginia, voters in, 65

northern merchants, alliance with southern planters, 47

objectivity, *see* historical objectivity

officeholders, 193; and adoption of the Constitution, 187

Ohio River, 87

Paine, Thomas, on voting, 163

paper money, 47, 125, 191; restrictions on, 109-10; and opposition to the Constitution, 183

paper money party, control by, in Delaware, 177; in Maryland, 178; in New Jersey, 176; in North Carolina, 191

Paterson plan, 123

Paterson, William, 40n, 42n, 89; views on democracy, 40; shows the influence of the people, 42; property of, 83; political philosophy of, 128

patriotic history, 12

Paullin, Charles Oscar, cited, 164

Pennsylvania, 41, 76, 77, 79, 82, 83, 88, 96, 115, 122, 127, 128, 134; society in, 7; voters in, 35, 44, 69, 163, 190; petition from, 59; voting qualifications in, 65, 69; vote on ratification in, 142, 177; correlations on ratification in, 145ff; interpretation of ratification in, 151; divisions in, 188; Constitutional Party in, 189; ratification of Constitution in, 189; population of, 189

Pennsylvania ratifying convention, 167, 177

people, the, influence of on the Constitutional Convention, 41, 113, 121-22, 127-28, 130-32, 134-35, 185, 198; as property owners, 136; and ratification, 140, 141; favored property, 1787, 200

personal property, held by Convention delegates, 74-89. *See also* personalty

personal rights, importance of, 198

personalty, importance of in formation of Constitution, 3, 48, 54, 89, 90, 136, 165, 171, 194, 199; influence of as half of Beard thesis, 31; defined, 31; as dynamic element behind move for Constitution, 33; predominance of realty over, 50; effect of Articles of Confederation on, 56; importance of in election of Convention delegates, 68; Constitution to protect, 92; and voting qualifications in the Constitution, 101; influence of on suffrage qualifications, 104; and ratification, 140; correlation of and vote on Constitution 144; and the Constitution as a conservative *coup d'état*, 153; influence of in Georgia, 180; compared with realty, 195

personalty interests, conflict of, 192

Phelps, Oliver, speculation of, 58

Philadelphia, 118, 138; merchants and mechanics as voters in, 39; price of securities in, 52; voters in, 104; population of, 162, 189; weather in 1787, 169; and vote on the Constitution, 177

Philadelphia County, 177

philosophy of history, Beard on, 11

Piedmont, vote on Constitution, 178

Pierce, William, 42n, 89, 120; property of, 83; political philosophy of, 128

Pinckney, Charles, 40n, 48, 89, 200; view that Constitution must fit the people, 39; on middle-class society, 1787, 43-44; property of, 84; on checks and balances, 99; political philosophy of, 129

Pinckney, Charles Cotesworth, 42n, 48, 89, 200; property of, 84; political philosophy of, 129

Pittsburgh, weather in 1787, 169

Plainfield, Connecticut, security holders in, 175

poor, extent of the, 178. *See also* economic democracy, middle class

popular party, 182

popular vote, on the Constitution, 152ff, 157-70, 184; and Constitutional Convention, 196; on Constitution not known, 199. *See also* Constitutional Convention, ratification of Constitution

population, extent of rural, 67; of Baltimore, 178; of Philadelphia, 189; of Pennsylvania, 189. *See also* urban population

Porter, Elisha, 150

Porter, Kirk Harold, work cited, 70n

Portsmouth, New Hampshire, 171; property in, 172

Preface, aims of Beard stated in, 4

president, choice of, 97; to be elected by national legislature, 123

press, freedom of the, 193

private property, safeguarded by Constitution, 3; extent of ownership of, 197. *See also* landed interest, personalty, realty

Proclamation of 1763, 86

Progressive movement, 8; and the Constitution, 5; influence on Beard, 14

Progressive Party, and *An Economic Interpretation*, 7; and Constitution, 7

proletariat, 127

propaganda, and Federalists, 165, 187; use of, 184; and Antifederalists, 189

property, ownership widespread, 20; and *Federalist* No. 10, 28-29; weight of in politics, 54; safeguarded by voting qualifications, 61-72; widespread ownership of in 1787, 102, 108; protected by Constitution, 108; favored by the people, 200

property owners, extent of in 1787, 200

propertyless masses, absence of in 1787, 197

property qualifications for office holding, 4, 61; reasons for omission from Constitution, 100-01

property qualifications for representation, favored realty over personalty, 61-72

property qualifications for voting, see voting qualifications

property safeguards in election of delegates, 61-72. See also voting qualifications

protective tariff, 79; demanded by artisans and mechanics, 53; favored by organized labor, 184

psychological factors, and the Constitution, 200

public debt, 49. See also public securities

public securities, 119; depreciation of, 49; importance of for the Constitution, 51-52, 171, 180, 195; price of, 52; speculation in, 57-58; held by delegates, 74-89; importance of in Beard thesis, 90; and ratification, 174, 177, 179; influence of compared with that of realty, 175; importance of in South Carolina, 180. See also security holders

Randolph, Edmund, 40n, 42n, 89; on democracy, 40; shows influence of the people, 41; property of, 84; political philosophy of, 130

Randolph, Sir John, 84

Randolph plan, too democratic, 43

Ranke, Leopold von, historical method of, 9

ratification of Constitution, 3, 4, 138-56; by Shaysites, 47, 60; controlled by landed interests, 106; by freeholders, 140; order and vote on, 142; order in which Beard discussed, 143; vote on, 144, 149, 152-53, 157-60, 171-81, 184, 189-92, 199; correlation of vote on, 144; correlation of land and interest with, 145; correlation of realty and personalty with, 146-48; interpretation of in the states, 148; indifference of voters toward, 149, 160, 165, 170, 199; fraud in, 149; contemporary views on, 154ff; by the people, 158; effect of winter weather on, 163-64, 167-70; ignorance and apathy as factors in, 165; conventions for, 167; correlation of security holders and vote on, 174-75; economic conflict over, 182-93. See also Beard thesis, checks and balances, farmers, personalty, property qualifications, suffrage, voting, Shays' Rebellion

ratifying conventions, 138, 139

Read, Colonel, 191

Read, George, 42n, 89; shows influence of the people, 41, property of, 85; political philosophy of, 130

real estate, slaves as in Virginia, 48. See also realty

realty opposed Constitution, 31; predominance of over personalty, 49-50, 172, 195; valuation of houses omitted by Beard, 50; wide distribution promoted democracy, 67; held by Convention delegates, 74-89; correlation with vote on Constitution, 144; and ratification, 144-48; influence of compared with that of personalty, 175; control by, in New Jersey, 176; in Charleston, South Carolina, 180; importance of in 1787, 195

Redding, Connecticut, security holders in, 175

religion, freedom of, 193

representation, property qualifications for, 61-72; under Constitution, 121; inequitable in New York, 163; in state legislatures, 197

Republican Party, 95

reviews, *see Economic Interpretation, An,* reviews of

Rhode Island, 139; vote against strong government, 59; ratification of Constitution, 142, 152; correlations on ratification, 145ff; interpretation of ratification in, 152; refusal of to send delegates to Constitutional Convention, 188

Ridgefield, Connecticut, security holders in, 175

Rockingham County, New Hampshire, 172

Rutledge, John, 40n, 42n, 89, 129; property of, 85; on suffrage, 106; political philosophy of, 131

Salisbury, Connecticut, security holders in, 175

Scharf and Westcott, work cited, 119

Schlesinger, Arthur Meier, Sr., work cited, 70n

Schuyler, Philip, as a security holder, 57

scientific historians, 11, 26

scientific method, importance of to Beard, 10; in history, 10; and democracy, 10-11

secondary works, *see* Beard, use of secondary works

Second Continental Congress, popular vote for, 157; delegates elected by legislatures, 196

sectional conflicts, 126; validity of concept of, 45; Madison's views on, 96

sectionalism, 116, 193; and vote on Constitution, 177; in South Carolina, 180, 192; and the Constitution, 189

securities, and the Constitution, *see* public securities

security holders, importance of for adoption of the Constitution, 51-52, 171, 179; gain to resulting from adoption of the Constitution, 52; correlation of and vote on the Constitution, 174-75; in

Connecticut, 174-75. *See also* public securities

Senate, 98; election of, 97, 100, 128; to represent property, 114; purpose of, 116

Sharon, Connecticut, security holders in, 175

Shays' Rebellion, 47, 61, 90, 155, 174, 186, 187; Knox on, 60; and democracy, 150; and popular vote, 160; support for, 172

Shaysites, ratified Constitution, 47, 60; controlled Massachusetts government, 1787, 47, 60, 185; dominated Massachusetts legislature in 1787, 149-50, 172; and vote on Constitution, 160

Sheffield, Massachusetts, vote on the Constitution in, 150, 160, 166, 185

Sherman, Roger, 40n, 42n, 89, 132; on democracy, 38; shows influence of the people on Constitution, 41; property of, 85; on checks and balances, 100; political philosophy of, 131

shipping and the Constitution, 52-53. *See also* commercial interests

Simsbury, Connecticut, security holders in, 175

slavery, 75, 133-34; importance of, 96, 130; and checks and balances, 100; protection of, 115; as major conflict in the United States, 122, 125, 135; importance of in Constitutional Convention, 131

slaves, and voting, 34; considered real estate in Virginia, 48; as personalty or realty, 48, 114; of Convention delegates, 73ff

Smith, Theodore Clark, criticizes Beard, 11

socialism, influence on historical writing, 8, 11

society, divisions in, 187. *See also* class conflict, lower classes, middle class, slavery, upper class

soldiers' certificates, 176

Solon, 41, 114

Somers, Connecticut, security holders in, 175

sources, use of by Beard, 90. *See also* Beard, use of historical method

South Carolina, 41, 75, 84, 85, 115, 129, 131; ratifying convention in, 39, 167; voting qualifications in, 65-66; vote on ratification, 142, 164, 179, 192; correlations on ratification in, 145ff; ratification in, 152; constitution of 1790, 192; sectionalism in, 192

South Dakota, 90

Southbury, Connecticut, security holders in, 175

southern planters, position of on Constitution, 47. *See also* landed interest, realty

Southington, Connecticut, security holders in, 175

Spaight, Richard Dobbs, 89; property of, 85; political philosophy of, 132

Spaulding, E. W., on Beard's work, 8

speculation, in public securities, 57, 58; land, 58, 76, 78; by Convention delegates, 74. *See also* personalty

Springfield, Massachusetts, 150; vote on Constitution in, 185

Stamp Act Congress, delegates elected by legislature, 196

state banks, 110

state debts, 51; assumption of rejected in Constitutional Convention, 51. *See also* assumption, Hamilton

state legislatures, 97; controlled by debtor farmers, 47; controlled by landed interests, 100, 134; right to impair future contracts, 109; and ratification, 138-40; election of delegates by, 196; representation in, 197. *See also* Shaysites, *states by name*

state ratifying conventions, influence of personalty in, 3; considered democratic, 1787, 158; and the disfranchised, 159; dates of meetings, 167; interests of delegates, 180; interests represented by, 199. *See also* Constitution, ratification, *states by name*

state sovereignty, and vote on the Constitution, 179

states, large vs. small, 96; interests of, 100; order of ratification of Constitution, 143; interpretation of ratification in, 149ff

states' rights, 131, 135, 199. *See also delegates by name*

Stratford, Connecticut, security holders in, 175

Strong, Caleb, 89; property of, 85; political philosophy of, 132

subjectivity, *see* historical subjectivity

Suffolk County, Massachusetts, 174

suffrage, 8, 97, 118, 127, 159, 197; discussion of in Constitutional Convention, 36; extent of, 39; widely extended in New Hampshire, 62; in Virginia, 69; in New England, 69; delegates' views on, 102-06. *See also* democracy, voting qualifications

suffrage qualifications, *see* voting qualifications

Supreme Court, 98; and contract clause, 109

Sydnor, Charles S., work cited, 71

Taft, William Howard, criticizes *An Economic Interpretation*, 7; on Beard's work, 8

tax returns, show predominance of realty over personalty, 49

taxation, 49, 107

taxes, in New Hampshire, 49; assessed valuation, 50

tenants, favored the Constitution, 56; as voters in Virginia, 71

Tennessee, 50, 75

Teutonic school, interpretation by, 26

"That Noble Dream," 12

Thompson, Connecticut, security holders in, 175

tidewater, society in, 178

Tolland, Connecticut, security holders in, 175

Tolles, Frederick B., work cited, 70, 71n

Taylor, Robert J., work cited, 70n

Thayer, Theodore, work cited, 70n

Tories, 57, 187, 193; and ratification in North Carolina, 191

towns, number in Virginia, 71; vote of in Massachusetts, 149; importance of, 165; vote of in Connecticut, 174-75; vote on Constitution, 173-75; views on Constitution, 199

Treasury records, 90

treaties, and opposition to the Constitution, 183

Turner, Frederick Jackson, importance of, 17

Union, Connecticut, security holders in, 175

United States, class structure in, 37; equality in, 44; distribution of property in, 102. *See also* Bank of the United States

upper classes, 173; and the Constitution, 5; Constitution to protect, 19; divided in North Carolina, 192

"urban centers," extent of, 178

urban population, extent of, 67

Vermont, 50, 172

Virginia, 39, 40, 48, 75, 81, 82, 84, 88, 96, 109, 123, 124, 125, 130, 134; sectionalism in, 45; favored small landowners, 45-46; attitude of merchants in, 59; voting qualifications in, 65, 69, 71; towns in, 71; vote on ratification in, 142, 173, 178, 190; correlations on ratification, 145ff; interpretation of ratification in, 152; weather in 1787, 169; and opposition to the Constitution, 169

*Virginia Almanac,* 169

Virginia Constitution, checks and balances in, 98

Virginia ratifying convention, 167

Voluntown, Connecticut, security holders in, 175

vote, on ratification, 142, 154, 160-61, 173, 184, 199; percentage of on Constitution, 144; on Constitution in Pennsylvania, 151; popular, on Constitution, 153, 157-70; on Constitution in Philadelphia, 162; total on Constitution, 164; economic factors in, 171. *See also* ratification of Constitution

voters, number of in ratification of Constitution, 4; number of, 20, 38, 159, 161; in Georgia, 35, 44; in Pennsylvania, 35, 69, 163, 190; in New York, 37; in England, 38; the poor were, 38; small farmers and debtors were, 38, 47, 67; nonfreeholders were, 38, 39; common people were, 38-39; merchants and mechanics in cities were, 39; in New York City, 63-64; in Norfolk, Virginia, 65; in Williamsburg, Virginia, 65; in Massachusetts, 69, 161; in Virginia, 71; tenants as in Virginia, 71; in cities, 104; indifference of, 160, 161, 162, 198; indifference of in Pennsylvania, 163; indifference of in Baltimore, 163; in "backwoods," 166; middle-class farmers as, 166, 197. *See also* suffrage, voting qualifications

voting, 120; numbers disqualified from, 35; delegates to Constitutional Convention favored restriction to freeholders, 67; Thomas Paine on, 163; on Constitution in Connecticut, 174ff; of workingmen in New York City, 176; rights of common people, 192; indifference to, 198. *See also* democracy, suffrage, voting qualifications

voting qualifications, 4, 21, 61-72,

99-106, 139, 150, 165, 195; numbers disfranchised by, 35; under the Constitution, 38; disfranchised the "mass," 47; favored realty over personalty, 61-72, 197; in Massachusetts, 62; in Connecticut, 63; in New York, 63; in New Jersey, 64-65; reasons for omission of from Constitution, 92, 100, 104-05; influence of personalty on, 104; and election of ratifying conventions, 159. *See also* democracy, suffrage, voters

Walker, J. B., cited, 148
Wallingford, Connecticut, security holders in, 175
war, causes of, 111
Warren, Connecticut, security holders in, 175
Washington, Connecticut, security holders in, 175
Washington, D.C., 76, 87
Washington, George, 48, 89, 90, 169, 200; comment on citation from, 59; interests of, 60; property of, 85-88; as a debtor, 88; on representation, 121; political philosophy of, 133; prestige of, 188; supports the Constitution, 189; as realty holder, 195
Watertown, Connecticut, security holders in, 175
weather, influence of winter on ratification, 163-64; importance of, 165, 167-70
West, the, 116
Wethersfield, Connecticut, security holders in, 174

Whiting, William, Esq., 150
Williamsburg, Virginia, voters in, 65
Williamson, Hugh, 42n, 57, 58, 89; property of, 88; political philosophy of, 133
Wilmington, North Carolina, 191
Wilson, James, 40n, 42n, 89; shows influence of the people, 41; property of, 88; on checks and balances, 100; on suffrage, 103, 106; on contracts, 108; political philosophy of, 134
Winchester, Connecticut, security holders in, 175
Winchester, Virginia, 87
Windsor, Connecticut, security holders in, 174-75
women, and voting, 34
Woodbury, Connecticut, security holders in, 175
Worcester County, Massachusetts, debtors and creditors in, 174
working class, absence of in 1787, 36; numbers of, 36; disfranchisement of, 36; favored the Constitution in New York, 37
workingmen, favored the Constitution, 53; vote of in New York City, 176; vote of in Baltimore, 178; vote of on Constitution, 181; class status of, 200
World War II, 174
"Written History as an Act of Faith," 9
Wythe, George, 89; property of, 88; political philosophy of, 134

Yates, Robert, 135; property of, 89